The
FLAGSTAD
Manuscript

LOUIS BIANCOLLI

G. P. Putnam's Sons   New York

COPYRIGHT, 1952, BY LOUIS BIANCOLLI

ALL RIGHTS RESERVED. THIS BOOK, OR PARTS THEREOF, MUST
NOT BE REPRODUCED IN ANY FORM WITHOUT PERMISSION.
PUBLISHED ON THE SAME DAY IN THE DOMINION OF CANADA
BY THOMAS ALLEN, LTD., TORONTO.

In Part Three of this book there are excerpts from many reviews of Madame
Flagstad's appearances both in this country and in England. The material
quoted is in copyright and is used by permission:

The Chicago Tribune, copyright, 1947
The London *Times,* copyright, 1951
The New York Daily News, copyright, 1935
The New York Herald Tribune, copyright, 1935, '36, '37, '47, '51
The New York Journal-American, copyright, 1935, '36, '52
The New York Post, copyright, 1935, '36
The New York Times, copyright, 1935, '36, '37, '47, '51, '52
The New York World-Telegram & Sun, copyright, 1935, '36, '37
The San Francisco Chronicle, copyright, 1949

Library of Congress Catalog Card Number: 52-9828

Second Impression

MANUFACTURED IN THE UNITED STATES OF AMERICA

Van Rees Press • New York

Kirsten Flagstad in her garden

Preface

I have never really wanted to write a book. I don't think my life concerns anybody but myself. I don't care one bit what my reputation will be when I stop singing. I might just as well be dead when I finally retire from opera and concert work. That is all that should interest the world. I want no one to intrude on the privacy that will be mine after that. Immortality as an artist means nothing to me. Fame, glory—they are empty, meaningless words. One does what one can. For me all of the fuss will end the day I give up singing.

And then, no matter what I or anyone else puts down in a book, there will still be so much nobody will ever know about me. I am really quite different even from what you may think, you Biancolli, who are writing this all down as I talk. I know pretty well what I am. And this much I will admit in all frankness: I am extremely simple, the complete opposite of complicated. I am not a bit difficult. I am just the average person who walks the earth, not at all the sort of person that anyone could possibly think capable of doing the queer things good, ordinary people refrain from doing.

It still astonishes me to think that I, who have never been loose or immoral in my private life, should ever have been suspected of being loose or immoral in my politics. I have never quite understood how anybody could believe such a transforma-

PREFACE

tion possible. I am bewildered that so simple a person as myself should be accused of strange and intricate matters that never could possibly have entered my mind at any time.

Let me make this very clear again: I am not an artist except when I am dealing with art, and when I am not dealing with art, I am the most commonplace person in the world. I am not a bit mysterious or unusual or complex. I am an absolutely average Norwegian, and we Norwegians in general are neither sophisticated nor complicated. I think we are pretty decent people. To look for sinister motives or dark secrets in my character or life is to look for something that is not there. I am and have been what I say I am. That may be a disappointment to some people who would have preferred to find a woman of glamour and mystery in a singer of my standing. I cannot help it. Apart from my work, I am just an average woman.

Before all else I wanted a simple and tranquil home life, and a husband to love and respect me. I had both and I lost them. I want the rest of my life to be restful and uneventful, a life of books, a few friends, a tidy home, a little private music—and my good memories. I want to be left alone. I don't think that is asking too much. I believe I have earned it.

—Kirsten Flagstad

Contents

PREFACE BY KIRSTEN FLAGSTAD   v

INTRODUCTION BY LOUIS BIANCOLLI   xi

Part One:
    THE EARLY MANUSCRIPT   3

Part Two:
    THE LATER MANUSCRIPT   89

Part Three:
    THE REVIEWING STAND   241
ROLES SUNG BY KIRSTEN FLAGSTAD   282

INDEX   285

List of Illustrations

Kirsten Flagstad in her garden.	Frontispiece
	Facing page
Dressed for her first dance, at nine years of age.	10
Confirmation (1911).	10
Debut in opera, as Nuri in *Tiefland* (Dec. 12, 1913).	11
Ganymed in *Die Schöne Galathee* (1919).	11
In musical comedy *Her Excellency* (1927).	44
With Karen-Marie Flagstad in The Cousin from Batavia (1927).	44
Two costumes from *Der Orloff* (1928).	45
Tosca in Göteborg (1929).	76
Desdemona in *Otello* (1929).	76
Aida (Göteborg, 1930).	77
Elisabeth in *Tannhäuser*. (Göteborg, 1934).	77
Sieglinde in *Die Walküre*. (Metropolitan debut, 1935).	108
Isolde (1935).	109
Brünnhilde in *Die Walküre* (1935).	140
Leonore in *Fidelio*.	141
Kirsten Flagstad and her husband on vacation (1938).	172
Kundry in *Parsifal* (London, 1951).	173
With Maggie Teyte, in *Dido and Aeneas* (London, 1951).	204
Alcestis (Metropolitan, 1952).	205

Introduction

FROM what I have to say, I hope it will be clear why I decided to call this book *The Flagstad Manuscript,* rather than *The Flagstad Story* or some such title. It is a story that goes back twelve years, to a spring day when material was first gathered for a book projected by the late Pitts Sanborn, with my collaboration.

Now the original plan had been to do a biography. For inclusion in this volume, there was assembled a substantial cross section of the New York reviews of each of Mme. Flagstad's roles as she performed them for the first time at the Metropolitan. This material, to be used as an appendix, was to constitute an important part of the book as a critical survey.

An appendix of this sort would have been out of the question in a book bearing an autobiographical title such as *The Story of My Life.* Much of this supplementary matter consists of praise of the highest order from the critics. It could scarcely have been reprinted by Mme. Flagstad as titular author of the book. There is no false modesty about Kirsten Flagstad—but neither is she an exhibitionist. Pride rather than conceit is her quality. I should add that the decision to do the book this way was mine alone. Mme. Flagstad left it to my discretion, as she did so many other matters, and I persuaded the publishers that under the circumstances this was the only solution.

INTRODUCTION

There is this too to be said in favor of the plan I have adopted: it made possible the use of material pertaining to the last phase of Mme. Flagstad's career that would inevitably have been excluded from a book carrying her name as author or even co-author. Moreover, there was her reluctance to do the book at all. This was at all times sincere, a matter of temperament, rather than of circumstance. Her dread of violated privacy, combined with an ingrained reticence, all but defeated me. It was this same refusal to speak up that displeased and disappointed her friends after the war, when the time came for making her position clear.

"Those who believe in me," she said once when I urged her to give a full account of herself to the press, "must take me on trust. The others will never believe me no matter what I say. When it is all over, I shall have something to say. But only for the book."

When she finally spoke up, as she did in the many meetings we had in 1950 and later, I am convinced she held back nothing —nothing, that is, that came within her direct knowledge. By this time she was almost eager to speak of herself, and to do so through the medium of a permanent and irrevocable record. That record she had long assumed would be a biography, as originally planned. But when, after Pitts Sanborn's death in 1941, I took on the assignment alone, I found that as often as she could see me and as fast as I was able to take down her narration in shorthand, I was gathering up additional material for an *autobiography* rather than raw material for a biography.

In her last year in America before the war, Mme. Flagstad's schedule became abnormally crowded. After making several efforts to see her at this time, I received an anguished plea for mercy, dated January 26th, which I reproduce exactly as she wrote it, abbreviations and all, because it gives such an extraordinary cross section of a primadonna's supposedly glamorous life.

xii

INTRODUCTION

Dear Mr. Biancolli:—
I have tried to find a time for us to have a chat even if very short. It is no use calling me on Saturday as I would not have found any in the near future. That you may see for yourself what I have to do, I give you the following list of my activities. Have mercy!!

Jan. 27 Trenton—concert
    28 orchestra rehearsal Götterdämmerung
    29 Götterd.
    30 orch. reh. Lohengrin
    31 Lohengrin
Feb. 1 Hairdresser, Fidelio reh. leaving 5 o'clock
    2 Boston
    3 Northampton
    4 Tristan Philadelphia, leaving about 4
    5 reh. Fidelio
    6 Tannhäuser
    7 reh. Fidelio
    8 Tristan
    9 reh. Fidelio
Feb. 11 Washington
    12 Walküre
    13 Dress rehearsal Fidelio
    17 Tristan
Feb. 18 Buffalo
    20 Siegfried
    22 Fidelio
    24 Binghamton

Well, here you have my schedule. The spare time I have in between I need for a rest, or at least to be alone. Feb. 27th or 28th are the first days I might see you if nothing else turns up. I *might* sing Feb. 26th. I sing Tristan March 1st and then I am leaving on tour until April 6th. I sing then April 9-11-12 and leave again next morning and I hope to go home Apr. 19th so that Apr. 8th is the last free day I have.

If you add to this all I have to do for myself in arranging my life outside my work (as a man you would not know about dress-

xiii

INTRODUCTION

makers, or any of the numerous things) all mail to answer, packing. I never see my friends any more, no time to spare. I use my free time to rest.

The worst is that I am sleepless since November or late October, using all kinds of sleeping medicine and following the numerous advices I get. I have been in bed from 11 last night to 4:30, went up and started to write you as I cannot sleep anyway. Do you understand my situation?

I naturally felt extremely guilty. I knew about her protracted insomnia, the inhuman drain of overwork, the haunting anxiety and uncertainty about her family in Norway; I had seen it in the burning tension and nervous mobility of her face. For months before she left for Norway Kirsten Flagstad was under a ghastly strain. Knowing that, I hesitated to impose my inquisitiveness any further. But my reporter's persistence finally won over all scruples of gallantry. I wanted one more working session before she left America—who could tell, perhaps for good. That last session she granted me.

At this meeting I asked Mme. Flagstad for permission to do the book on my own and in my own way. This permission she gave me without reservation.

I believe our meeting occurred on the April 8th that she had referred to in her letter "as the last free day I have." I did not keep her long. After working for perhaps two hours, I put away my notebook.

"It is still a rather small book," I said.

"Well, then, wait till I come back—and I shall give you more."

"When will that be?"

"Maybe next season—who can say? I've purchased a return trip ticket, you know."

I need hardly point out that along with scores of others, including Herbert Hoover, I had been strongly urging her not to go back. That she was looking forward to returning to America and that in the relatively near future, I never for a moment doubted. The craving for husband, home, and home-

INTRODUCTION

land had obviously become an obsession. Yet behind it I suspected a professional restlessness that would always reassert itself. An artistic compulsion was in her blood to stay, all avowals to the contrary.

After she departed for home in April, 1941, I had no further contact with Kirsten Flagstad till I wrote to her early in April of 1946. I had a feeling she might be concerned about the manuscript. I wrote assuring her it was safely tucked away in my closet. From Kristiansand came a reply dated April 29th:

> Dear Mr. Biancolli,
>
> Thank you very much for your kind letter. I have been thinking of you quite often wondering if you would keep your promise, not to publish anything of the manuscript for the book before I had read and sanctioned it. I am happy to know that I could trust you.
>
> I believe the best thing would be to wait until I come back to America, which I hope will be in the near future, and we could then continue our conversations to finish the book according to the original plan:—*A true story of my life.*
>
> As soon as I arrive I will contact you to talk things over.
>
> I am very well and am looking forward to meeting you again. With kindest greetings
>
> Yours very sincerely
(signed) Kirsten Flagstad

There was nothing to do but wait. Almost a year went by before we were again reading of Mme. Flagstad in the press. News of her triumphs in Paris, London, and Milan reached America. It was evident that she had begun the long journey back. Agitation began to stir again in several newspaper columns. Speculation was rife concerning the mood of the Metropolitan, though Mr. Edward Johnson had made it quite clear that, because of some known opposition among his subscribers, he was not thinking, at the moment, of inviting Mme. Flagstad back.

Several reputable critics had already taken a strong stand

INTRODUCTION

against the singer's return. Opinion was sharply divided, those in favor of welcoming her back using the thesis that art was above politics, and that, in any case, no one had proved anything against Mme. Flagstad except that she had gone back to her country when it was in the hands of the enemy. Feeling ran high and continued high for a considerable time; until, in fact, the fourth and fifth seasons of her return to America, when it suddenly declined and then completely subsided.

Each of the various charges made against her is taken up at some length in Mme. Flagstad's own narrative. I am presenting her, not defending or analyzing her. Since she never felt there was a "Flagstad case," there is no need of an attorney, and I have no desire to be one. I am merely offering a few observations out of fairness to a woman whose name and honor were caught for a time in an apparently hopeless muddle of suspicion, distrust and unrelenting hatred.

That she came through the ordeal without ill-will or vindictiveness is to Mme. Flagstad's lasting credit. Perhaps I ought to say this much about my own attitude. I did not like the idea of her going back to Nazi-occupied Norway. I would have been the first to rejoice over the news that Kirsten Flagstad, at the risk of her life, had joined the Underground. I knew, however, that such a thought was quixotic, that there was not the remotest chance of political activity of any sort on her part. This was not her quality, nor her function, perhaps. Moreover, the man she loved and had married was scarcely the type to encourage any such heroic proclivities had she possessed them. Without ever having met Mr. Johansen, I believe they were basically of the same passive temperament, preferring to sit out a situation rather than attempt to influence it one way or the other. Hero and heroine worship dies hard. It was difficult for many people to reconcile this attitude with the fearless readiness of Brünnhilde to risk incalculable punishment by protecting Sieglinde. They expected, if only subconsciously, nothing short of the heroic from their favorite Wagnerian soprano.

xvi

INTRODUCTION

When at last, twelve years after I first took pencil in hand to take down what she had to say, the material for this book was all transcribed, assembled and pieced together in a more or less orderly narrative, I made a rather obvious discovery. There were really *two* books; or, rather, the autobiography of Kirsten Flagstad fell into two distinct and separate parts. There was the first section, which was given to me in the months preceding her departure for Norway in April, 1941. That manuscript was complete almost up to the day of her flight by clipper to Lisbon on her way home, and that manuscript remained in my closet throughout the war, a buried memorial of an abruptly truncated career. It was not retrieved from its hiding place till 1950, when I resumed work with Mme. Flagstad on the book. When she finally returned to the book, she picked up from where she had left off, retracing her steps only where subsequent happenings made it necessary to enlarge on matters that might otherwise have proved of little or no consequence in a career of such scope. From that first reunion up to the week of her final departure for Europe, in the spring of 1952, we met from time to time, whenever her taxing schedule permitted, till we had brought the chronicle down to the immediate present.

It was when this second section of the book was completed, that I saw I had two autobiographies—the autobiography of the woman who went home to Norway in 1941, and the autobiography of the woman who came back. The gap made a psychological difference of a marked emotional character. I knew then that neither I nor Mme. Flagstad had any right to tamper with the early manuscript as it stood. That belonged to another period and if not quite to another person, certainly to a different and less vehement personality. Although this first section differed in pace and mood and idiom from the second, we felt it had to remain as it was. I suspected, too, that what value it possessed as a document might be forfeited by any subsequent editing.

I realized also that if and when the book was published, it

xvii

INTRODUCTION

would have to contain an explanation of the manuscript, of its genesis and form. I was dealing equally with a book and a woman's life. The woman's life was in the first person in a narrative that I had recorded in shorthand. It had been given no more than those few elementary touches of style that are deemed necessary to prepare a story of this kind for publication. Such as it is, Mme. Flagstad has a style of her own in a language that is not her own. That language she has been sedulously studying since her childhood. After the war, her command of English improved enormously. She scarcely ever gropes long for the correct word or idiom nowadays. I have done my best, with the aid of both my shorthand and what I have been told is an ear for individual speaking rhythm, to preserve the quality of her style in both parts of the book. It was considerations of this nature that brought home the necessity of breaking away, at least in this instance, from the usual formulas of "ghosted" or "as told to" autobiographies. This autobiography is Mme. Flagstad's, but the manuscript is mine, and it has been my job to introduce the manuscript, and in introducing the manuscript, to introduce the woman and singer whose life-story it tells.

It has not been easy to obtain what I did have from her, and I know it was far from easy for Mme. Flagstad to give all that she did. I have preserved among my notes a statement made late one night in her hotel suite. I remember her face and neck were flushed and tense.

"I always try to push this away from me," she said. "These talks with you are so hard on me. You see, I don't want ever to think about what has happened, and telling you all this brings everything back. You force me to live it over again, and it is painful. I get tight in my throat when I talk of these things, and then I can never fall asleep after you've gone."

When she was that way, I was tempted to tear up my notes and drop the whole idea of the book. I even proposed this to her time and again during her last season here. I assured her that if at the last moment she recoiled from the prospect of publication,

xviii

INTRODUCTION

it would be all right with me. We would simply destroy the manuscript. I told her repeatedly she was under no compulsion to do the book, that I had no thought of holding her to her letters assigning all rights to me. I am afraid I suggested abandoning the project once too often.

"Don't say that again," she rebuked me. "I'll come to believe you have lost interest or have found a more interesting subject for a book. I told you once I would go through with it, and you know I have tried never to break my word. Now where were we. . . ?"

Such is the story of *The Flagstad Manuscript*. That was her part of the book, her contribution, her life. I was her amanuensis, and, in view of the unique and generous arrangement, her legatee too. The rest has been my choice. I alone am responsible for whatever merits or demerits of selection and proportion it may exhibit. This surrounding material constitutes the other side of the compromise. To a small extent the original idea of a biography has survived in these appended sections, and perhaps in this introduction too. I would be the first to admit that this material is little more than a frame for the picture that is the central and determining portion of this book. It is what Kirsten Flagstad has to reveal of her personal life and career, and of the way she has reacted to both, that will inevitably determine the value of this book. The rest is an informative supplement, but still a supplement to what is the living core of the book.

I honestly believe that by the time she said good-by to America, Kirsten Flagstad had routed any lingering suspicions and doubts about her. Even the rancor that had been flaring up regularly in certain quarters of the press seemed to have vanished completely. That she had done, alone and unaided, through her simple integrity as an artist and a woman.

It was an extraordinary personal victory, and I hope that this book conveys something of the quality of the woman who won it.

—LOUIS BIANCOLLI

PART ONE: *The Early Manuscript*

Chapter One

MY FATHER was a violinist from Hamar and my mother a piano player in Christiania, which is now Oslo, the capital of Norway. When they were still very young they met in the small orchestra of what was then the Christiania Theater, fell in love, and were married.

On both sides of the family we are of old Norwegian farmer stock that goes back many generations. As far as we have been able to discover, Father had no musical background whatsoever. It was quite different in Mother's family, however. Although her father was a farmer by trade, he cultivated music as a hobby and played violin at weddings and other social gatherings. One of his brothers was a professional cellist of some standing who later died in Paris. Grandfather had eight children, only three of whom survived—Mother and her two brothers.

Both of my uncles on Mother's side were musicians, one of them a violinist and conductor of serious repute. The other remained more of the amateur type of musician. Most of his time was spent in farming, but when his work permitted he played the organ in church. In fact, he was organist for over sixty years in the two churches of his community. He demanded two things of all his children—that they master the rudiments of farming and learn how to play the organ. An active and tireless man, he also organized and directed boys' orchestras. With

3

all his other duties, he even found time to lead a military band. All six of his children became musicians, two of them professional ones.

Mother started to play the organ at nine in church, and by then she could also play the piano with great skill. At twelve the State appointed her official organist in church and paid her a regular salary. Mother used to tell us how, because she was so small, she had to stand on the pedals. When she was fifteen she went to Oslo to continue her musical studies. On the day of her departure Grandfather said to her, "You are so ugly you had better learn how to make your own living. No one will ever marry you." She had wonderful red hair. Mother came to Oslo, studied hard, and soon got a job at the Christiania Theater, where she met Father. In 1892, at the age of twenty, she married him.

Their first child, Olav, was born late in 1893, and died fourteen months later in Hamar. It was a bad time for musicians and most of the younger ones were dismissed from their jobs. Father was one. He found himself with a wife, a son, and no job. So he went back to Hamar with Mother and little Olav and moved in with his parents. Olav's death occurred shortly after they arrived.

For a time Father had to give up music. He worked in a factory that canned condensed milk. Mother took in pupils and was able to continue her music that way. Soon she announced to Father that she was expecting another child. That was me. Father then decided to return to Oslo and take up shorthand and prepare himself for a stenographic appointment in the Storting, the Norwegian parliament. He studied intensively for some months, passed the examinations, and then got a position. Meanwhile I was born in Hamar, where Mother had remained while Father was studying in Olso. The date was July 12, 1895.

It came as a great disappointment to Father's parents that I was a girl. Grandfather wouldn't so much as look at me, he was so disappointed. Mother and Father had lost their first boy and

The Early Manuscript

I, a girl, had come a year later to replace him. Grandfather felt cheated.

Some time in 1895 we all moved to Oslo. Musical activity had started again and musicians flocked back to their places. Father's training and experience once more found outlet. He never gave up his job as Storting stenographer though. For a good part of his life he kept two jobs. He worked like nobody else I have ever known, with the possible exception of my mother. When he had too much to do at the theater, he was allowed to hire a deputy for his Storting duties. There were twenty Storting stenographers like Father, and the State permitted them to take over each other's assignments in an emergency. Father worked day and night for years and years.

After working for some years at the Central Theater as violinist, Father rose to be conductor. He led many performances of light operas by Johann Strauss and Franz von Suppé. *Boccaccio* was one of his favorites. He gave grand opera there too. He was a good conductor but never a really good violinist, though he loved to scrape away at it, to the horror of my mother, who was fanatical about musical accuracy. When I was older I used to accompany Father in Beethoven's sonatas for violin and piano.

Mother then played the piano in the orchestra, besides coaching the chorus for opera and operetta. She was awfully good at that. Both my parents remained in active service there for seventeen or eighteen years—that is, until the world war. Then Father's work at the Storting became more important. He was made editor of the Storting's official newspaper and had to give up more and more of his musical activities. Finally he restricted himself to occasional appearances at the theater. After the war these became even fewer. One of the last things he did as a musician was to compose two or three musical comedies which were produced in several theaters and were very well received.

Father was a remarkable scholar in many ways. To the last he remained an eager student. Among his hobbies were languages and philology. He enjoyed translating opera texts into Norwegian, and did many of the official versions. His translation of Saint-Saëns' *Samson et Dalila* is still regarded as a model of its kind in Norwegian. Later when I was singing opera I appeared in Father's Norwegian version of Beethoven's *Fidelio*, given in concert form. He also translated Bizet's *Carmen* as well as many Italian operas. Languages were a passion with him, French being a particular favorite of his. Father was mostly self-taught in this respect. He used to read scientific works till four o'clock in the morning. Mother was often terribly annoyed. She used to complain, "If only he would read something I understood!"

You could ask Father anything. He loved helping us with our lessons. When he didn't know the answer he would drop whatever he was doing and study up on it until he could give us an adequate reply. Nothing pleased my father more than to be asked questions about the arts and sciences. He was pensioned by the Storting in 1925 and died in 1930. It was a terrible blow, losing Father.

One result of my father's work at the Storting was that I learned to write very fast longhand. As a young girl I often wrote down what he dictated from his shorthand notes. (Father had never learned to use a typewriter.) We all managed to cooperate somehow. Our family was like a business concern. Everybody worked. Mother took in pupils for piano study and coached singers for the theater. Often her work took her away from home, on opera and operetta tours, for instance. My very first appearance in public was turning pages for Mother at a concert of chamber music. I was about ten then and the concert was given in a small musical club called the Kvartettforeningen. Mother frequently played piano in ensembles.

At home we often played theater, either indoors or out in the little garden that Mother kept. My oldest brother was very clever at it, and intensely musical in his settings. His favorite piece for opening a new play was the first movement from Beethoven's first trio. I would play the prima donna. I wore long white dresses and veils. I loved veils. My brother always cast me

The Early Manuscript

as some mysterious woman out of a legend. He wrote out everything and always arranged the music. At that time I did not even know the name of Richard Wagner. Neither did my brother. So he never cast me as Brünnhilde or Elisabeth. Perhaps it was just as well.

I should mention the other members of our growing family. My brother Ole, three years younger than I, was born in 1898. He was named after my grandfather. That was the custom. Father, who was christened Michael, was named after his grandfather. Ole is a very good cellist, and still makes his living at it. He studied in Norway and Italy, and for a great many years played in a band in the Grand Hotel at Oslo. Besides the cello, he is quite handy with the saxophone and accordion. Ole's son Michael has organized bands of his own and his specialty is popular music, yet like the rest of the family he can't resist taking part in performances of classical music when the occasion arises. Whenever there was a chance Ole even conducted several operas in Oslo. He is married and has two children, both named after their grandparents. That's how we were all named.

Lasse was born in 1903. He became a concert pianist and made his debut with the Oslo Philharmonic at the age of eighteen. Lasse is decidedly the sportsman of the family. He is the best skier, an excellent swimmer, and used to play a fine game of football. His wife is an actress. Like Ole, he has two children. Lasse was frequently my accompanist in Norway and Sweden, and he once played accompaniments for me in London and Paris.

Karen Marie, who bears the names of our grandfather and mother both, arrived in 1904. Like myself, she was perhaps a little unwanted. A tiny little thing, she looked awfully frail and sickly, and surprised us all by growing into a remarkably pretty and healthy woman, though small, like my mother. Karen Marie has sung in opera and operetta. In 1940, we were supposed to sing in *Fidelio* together but the plan fell through. Norway was occupied. Operettas by Lehár and Offenbach are more her specialty.

THE FLAGSTAD MANUSCRIPT

There was no room for poor little Karen Marie at the piano when she was a child, with so many others taking turns at it. As a consequence she never really got the musical education I had, which was a pity, though she made a thorough study of singing later. Karen is married and has two children. I think I should emphasize here that Mother never really taught any of us. She had other pupils, who brought her the money that helped pay the expenses of running a large family. And besides, she was kept too busy with household duties.

As for my own musical education, I don't think it is surprising that in such a family I should have started to play the piano at six. That was in 1901. Martin Ursin, my mother's teacher, gave me my first lessons. He was the strictest kind of martinet. Like Father, Ursin made a hobby of languages, and his favorite was also French. It was a mania with him. When we did exercises he would follow the fingering by calling out irregular French verbs and their tenses. I had to practice an hour a day. That was the worst thing you could ask me to do. I hated it. But I couldn't escape it. Mother would sit by with her embroidery and see to it that I did my lessons properly. My one consolation was starting new pieces. Somehow I learned to read very easily at the beginning, and I have always been good at it since.

I soon began learning songs. That had a special appeal for me. We had a Schubert album for alto in the house. I learned to sing many of the *Lieder* to my own accompaniment. Of course I did it solely for my own pleasure. The idea of becoming a singer never once entered my head. I wasn't conscious of singing yet as a special activity. When I started to give it serious thought Father insisted I was not a soprano but a contralto, since he was used to hearing me sing these songs, which were mostly for the deep registers.

Then we went to school. The place was a short distance from the city, about a half-hour away, and it was called the Slemdal School, a private institution for boys and girls. Music was not part of the routine. I stayed there for three years and left when

The Early Manuscript

I was nine. I studied next at Ragna Nielsen's school in Oslo. Mme. Nielsen was a leader of the Norwegian feminist movement. I started to study French there, though German turned out to be my best subject. I didn't take to English at all. For some reason I couldn't stand it. One English story, though, fascinated me strangely. That was "Dick Whittington and His Cat." I finished my studies, which did not include music, in July, 1911, after nine years in school.

That year I entered what would probably be called high school here, remaining till 1913, as preparation for university school. The intention was to become a doctor. That had always been Mother's ambition. Nobody ever thought of making a pianist out of me, let alone a singer. Mother believed music was something to cultivate on the side, a way to earn a little extra money, perhaps, but not as a career. Anyway, not for a woman. I decided to complete the preparatory work in two years instead of three, with the result that I overdid it and got very sick. You see, I was the youngest of the children in class and didn't want to be left behind when the others had graduated. I had to stop before I finished. I went back for more later, after I had recovered, but never completed my preparatory studies. Actually I didn't feel so badly that I had sacrificed all chances of having a career. What I wanted most of all was to get married. Home life looked like a big enough career to me. As for ambition, I had none whatsoever. My brother Ole and my sister did go through to graduation. Mother wanted Ole to become a doctor, too. But Ole wanted to play the cello, and that settled it.

Even without school and music my home life was active enough. I was taught to help with the housework at a very early age. Mother always kept me around her. I learned to wash and mend and iron. Whatever was required in a household became part of my job. Conditions being what they were, I had to relieve my mother of many duties around the house. She was an excellent housekeeper. Neither of us ever had any distaste for housework. Both of us made a great virtue of orderliness. We

THE FLAGSTAD MANUSCRIPT

enjoyed the routine and I still do. I like to attend to things myself. Cooking was the one household art Mother never taught me, though Mother was an excellent cook herself. Her cuisine was famous among the artists and professionals who visited our home. We used to have big parties. Musicians and actors came frequently. Though there wasn't much money it was regarded as a very hospitable home. Father was the one who always worried about money. Socially my mother was the center of activities, thanks largely to her good-humor and food.

With Mother attending to so many other things I was given the care of the two youngest children. Karen Marie was just a baby then. Mother often took those tours with the Central Theater company, playing the piano and conducting. Father of course had his work at home in Oslo and stayed behind. When Mother was away I took complete charge of the house. How proud I was! I would go up to Father and ask him gravely what he wanted for dinner. Then I would do the necessary shopping. This happened again and again from the time I was ten to when I was about fifteen. Often in the evenings my brother would get out his cello and Father his violin. I would sit at the piano, and we would play trios by Beethoven.

Our piano was a large upright—a Schmidt, with large old-fashioned lamps on each side of it. It was placed so that my father could sit behind it and smoke one of his many pipes. He loved doing that. But how it annoyed me! I had to scold Father repeatedly about ashes and things, and he was always complaining that I placed his pipes in the pipe racks where they belonged, which was never where he would leave them. Still, Father always treated me with respect for the way I took charge in Mother's absence. But tobacco ashes have always been a source of irritation with me. Perhaps that's why I myself don't smoke. I happen to be very fussy about tidiness. I have tried to relax and become less so in the past few years after noticing how it embarrasses people.

Dressed for her first dance, at nine years of age.

FINNE.

FINNE.

Confirmation (1911).

Debut in opera, as Nuri in *Tiefland* (Dec. 12, 1913).

Ganymed in *Die Schöne Galathee* (1919).

Chapter Two

WHEN I was ten I had my first contact with Wagner. As a birthday gift I received a score of *Lohengrin*. I went right ahead and studied it from start to finish. That was my first opera score. I studied it without cuts. By then I knew German pretty well. I memorized the whole role of Elsa and sang and played it by myself. Mother and Father were highly pleased to see me putting the gift to such good use and continued to give me scores as presents.

The next one I received was a German score of *Aïda*. I was crazy about it and fell instantly in love with Verdi's music. Sometimes at parties I would be asked to sing. That's how I started to get some real practice, never with the idea of training to become a singer. Neither had Father any such idea. He did like me to sing to him, though. Mother had put a chaise longue in his favorite spot behind the upright piano. He would often take an after-dinner nap there. Sometimes he would ask me to come and sing for him. I loved singing for Father and of course I always accompanied myself on the piano.

Mother had many singers dropping in to coach with her. At times she would call me into the music room, not to show me off but to have me help in a duet. She would say, "Kirsten, please sing this duet from Puccini with the gentleman here." I would drop whatever housework or homework I was doing at the moment. It always made me feel grownup. When I was eleven Mother once called me in to sing Senta for a man who was studying Wagner's *Fliegende Holländer*. I sang it from the score. That was the way I slowly came to work with opera. It came as naturally as breathing, with no conscious effort on my part.

My confirmation as a member of my church occurred when I was sixteen. It meant so much to me. Perhaps I should explain why. After six months of study in catechism and the Bible there was an examination. After that came the party. A large family party has always been the practice in Norway on such occasions. The party meant my first long dress. What was equally exciting, my hair went up. At sixteen I was as tall as I am now, having grown tremendously in a few years. The party took place on the evening of my confirmation. Among those whom Mother had invited were two sisters, friends of the family. One was an actress, an unusually good one and a fine singer besides. She had often sung under Father's direction at the theater. The other was a voice teacher.

As always happens at such affairs, when the party was in full swing Mother called out to me, "Kirsten, come and sing for us."

I had always been a little shy. But with my hair up, my long dress, my confirmation, my party, I felt grown up and sure of myself. I sang Elsa's Dream from Wagner's *Lohengrin*. What a noise I made! My voice was completely beyond my control. I was in the habit of singing these things with full voice.

"No," said the voice teacher to Mother later, "you should not let her do that! What little voice she has she's wrecking for good."

She offered to give me vocal lessons. And that's how it started. One day, after I had been studying two or three months with her, she said to me, "Well, Kirsten, within three years you will be ready to make your debut."

I laughed, and so did my parents when I told them about it. We all knew, of course, how singing teachers often encourage

12

The Early Manuscript

their pupils excessively. But I mastered all the fundamentals with her. I was never forced to relearn anything. None of us put much stock in her prediction, I least of all. But I discovered I loved singing and learning what there was to know about it. I thought it great fun. So I started to learn more and more roles by myself.

My teacher's name was Ellen Schytte Jacobsen. She is still alive and very well known in Scandinavia. I studied three full years with her and actually made my debut in two years, one year earlier than she had predicted. You see, she was right after all.

Mme. Jacobsen was especially good in breathing and relaxing the throat. She had a lovely voice herself. The lessons were all free and she would never take anything when I offered it. She was never tired of repeating how gifted I was, though frankly we never took her word for it.

By the time I was twenty I had studied thirty roles without anyone's assistance. I did only exercises with Mme. Jacobsen. Mother would often accompany me through the roles, but nothing more. She was a good operatic coach, but strange as it may seem, she never coached me before Isolde, which didn't come till 1932.

Among these roles I studied by myself were Elsa, Aïda, Senta, Marguerite, Mimi, Tosca, Nedda, Violetta, Pamina, Cherubino, Susanna and the Countess; Zerlina, Martha, and the Goose Girl in *Königskinder*. Since we had only a French translation of *Pagliacci* I was obliged to learn Nedda in that language. *Faust* I learned both in French and German—and then sang it in Norwegian many years later. *Aïda* and *Tosca* I had learned in German because the scores we had at home were in German.

Violetta in *La Traviata* I first learned in Italian—and what Italian! Strictly self-taught. Still, it wasn't so bad, considering.

I enjoyed doing Violetta even though it was by myself. I regret that I have never sung it on the stage. It was my one coloratura role. As for the scores themselves, Father either bought them for

THE FLAGSTAD MANUSCRIPT

me or borrowed them from other people. I also enjoyed singing Zerlina, though I never sang in *Don Giovanni* on the stage. All these roles I studied for my own pleasure. That some day I might actually appear in many of these operas never even crossed my mind. Dalila was another role I worked on, studying it first in French and then in Father's Norwegian translation. I have never had a chance to do Dalila on the stage, also to my regret.

Naturally that covers only the singing part of my musical studies of the time. There was the piano besides. I had learned to play it very well, not so well that I seriously considered a concert career, but I felt I might be able to earn my own living at it in time. One day when I was fifteen or so a man called up Father and said he needed a pianist urgently to play dance music at a ball he was managing. Father was then vice-chairman of the local music guild and such appeals were not unusual. The man asked Father if he knew of someone who could come within a half-hour.

"Why don't *you* do it?" Father said, turning to me.

"Oh, I can't really, Father!" I said.

"Come on, be brave, my child!" he said. "Act like a true Flagstad! You know you read notes as easily as you breathe."

The fact is I had been playing waltzes, polonaises and marches for my own and the family's amusement for ever so long. Well, I went to the ball and played the piano. I played till two in the morning. And that wasn't the only time, believe me! In fact, it became quite a habit. Whenever they were in need of a pianist for such occasions, they remembered young Kirsten Flagstad. This went on for a year at least. The work was simple enough, but the physical strain was sometimes awful. Knowing the music well and being able to read without any difficulty made it possible.

I really didn't mind it. In fact, I enjoyed the feeling of doing something professional and getting paid for it. But there was one sour note. Some of my friends in school heard about my playing

The Early Manuscript

this popular music and said in horror, "You play dance music —*you?*"

When I told Father about it he comforted me by saying, "Don't let it worry you. You should feel proud that you can do such a thing, and they would too if they could."

My classmates thought it was beneath my dignity to play for dancing. Father didn't and I didn't and that's all that counted.

Before I go on I should like to narrate an experience I had on Christmas morning of 1913, right after my debut, because it was perhaps the greatest compliment ever paid me. I had been asked to sing in jail. It was the strictest jail in Oslo, solitary confinement and all that. The chaplain had asked me to sing some songs after the services.

I was very nervous. It was an awful experience for a young girl. From where I was singing in the pulpit I could see the prisoners, each in a seat with high screens on either side, so they couldn't see each other. Their eyes could rest only on the pulpit, where I was standing.

Instead of singing strictly religious songs I thought a little gaiety would go better, some *Lieder*, say. I was dressed in a bright color, not in black. They could see me and I could see them, which was worse. It was horrible. Some of them were not interested at all, but frankly bored. Somehow I managed to sing some songs by Grieg and Kjerulf. A few of the prisoners listened attentively. That was enough to inspire me. At first I didn't think I could ever start. Then before I knew it, it was all over. The chaplain showed me around the jail and invited me to return at Easter for some more singing.

When I came back at Easter they made a little change in the arrangement. I was not to stand in the pulpit as before. The way I now stood I couldn't see the prisoners. It made it a great deal easier for me. When my little recital was over, the warden of the jail called me to his office.

"I want to tell you a story," he said. "You should always treasure it. You will never get a greater compliment as long as

15

you live. Eight days ago a man was released from jail. He had been here for some years. He came to me to say good-by and asked me, 'Is that girl coming back to sing at Easter?' I said yes. 'Can I stay here till Easter, so I can hear her sing?' he asked me." The warden told me that in opening the outgoing mail he was amazed to discover how the singing had affected some of the prisoners. He said to me, "You ought to be proud of what you have done, young lady."

I regard that Christmas as one of the important days of my life. It helped mature me and make me conscious of the effect of singing on the minds and feelings of people.

Another important event was my debut as a serious pianist. There was a lady who went around reciting poems. Two of the pieces called for piano accompaniment. She would recite Ase's death from Ibsen's *Peer Gynt* and I would play Grieg's music. Then there was *Bergljot* by Björnson, also with musical accompaniment. To open the program I played Beethoven's "Pathétique" sonata. I went on tour with the lady and town papers often carried reviews of the event. The critics were very nice to me. This also helped me earn some pocket money.

My chief outdoor sport at that time was skiing, as it is for almost every Norwegian. Every Sunday sixty to seventy thousand people leave Oslo alone to go skiing. There is a wonderful ski terrain around Oslo. I took part in many contests, and even won one of them. Later when I started singing professionally I had to give it up. My contract prohibited me from skiing for fear of accidents. I was always a very good swimmer, too, and still love the feel of cold water around me.

On December 12, 1913, I made my debut in Eugen d'Albert's *Tiefland,* at the Oslo National Theater. I had no coach for the part of Nuri. This is how it all came about. Early that spring Mother had gone as accompanist with a singer for an audition at the opera house. There was to be a performance of *Tiefland* in the fall and they were casting for it. This singer wanted to do the chief female role of Marta. "I'm afraid you won't do as

The Early Manuscript

Marta," said the director. "There is one other role available in the opera, but you're too old for it. That's Nuri, and she's supposed to be twelve or thirteen years old in the story. We'll have to find someone else."

Of course a thought quickly flashed in Mother's brain. She immediately ordered a score of *Tiefland* from Germany. Some time passed before it finally arrived. Mother then took me aside and showed it to me. "Learn this as fast as you can!" she said. I already knew what she had in mind. I thought it a grand idea! I went ahead and learned it as I learned everything else. In August I had an audition at the opera. I sang the whole part in German. I was the thirteenth candidate to apply for the role and the successful one. They engaged me immediately at a staggering rate—fifty kroner, about twelve dollars and half! This was really a tremendous sum to me. I had never dreamed it. I saw myself becoming rich on it. I signed up for twenty performances. This was to be the Norwegian premiere of *Tiefland*, the only opera given at the National Theater that year. Of course I had to relearn it in a Norwegian translation after having studied it in German. The following June it was given again five or six times. I was Nuri in all the performances.

I shall never forget my first orchestral rehearsal. When it was over, the conductor tapped on the desk with his baton and said to the musicians, "Gentlemen, I think we should all feel honored. This is truly a musician's daughter. Miss Flagstad is the only one who has not made a single mistake in the whole rehearsal."

I was so proud! My, how proud I felt. His words gave me the courage I needed for the debut.

I wasn't a bit nervous at the performance. We had a very well-known Danish tenor in the cast by the name of Wilhelm Herold, then at the end of his career. He was a brilliant actor and a magnificent singer and his Pedro was famous. Herold was also stage manager in this production. Though it was my debut, Herold apparently had such confidence in me that he

THE FLAGSTAD MANUSCRIPT

left me to my own devices on the stage and never gave me instructions of any kind. As for myself, I felt completely at home. This was very surprising, really, because I had never had a wish to go on the stage and had not so much as thought of it.

Well, I got beautiful notices, and that's how my career really began. I continued studying with Mme. Jacobsen. My debut had made me realize that I could do something professional here and I decided definitely to become a singer.

I must mention what followed my debut. On the day of the performance I made myself an evening dress to wear that night after the performance. Because of the importance of the occasion I was being taken to a restaurant for the first time in my life! My parents were giving me a debut party. I was flushed with success. Everybody came over and congratulated me. And I had on the very grown-up evening dress that I had made earlier that day. It was one of the biggest days of my whole life. As long as I live I shall never forget it.

Then came the first check. How thrilled I was! I bought new window curtains with it for the living room at home. My having become a singer did not affect my home atmosphere much. I was still treated as a girl and I remained a most obedient daughter.

The critics seemed to agree that I had a small voice of nice quality and that I was very musical. Of course the family was so well known. The name Flagstad, because of Mother and Father and other members of the family, was already established in Norway. Another Flagstad just had to be good. Everyone was extremely nice to me, even the critic who was regarded as the severest of all, Hjalmar Borgström.

King Haakon had been to my debut. Later when I came back to Norway from America and had the occasion to thank him for an honor he had conferred upon me, he reminded me of my debut. You can imagine how thrilled I was that he should remember me. "I have followed your career all along," he remarked. He told me how proud he was of me. "You have been

The Early Manuscript

my ambassador of art to America," he said. King Haakon came often to concerts and opera performances in which I took part. I saw him last in 1939 when I again went to his castle to thank him for a third distinction he had bestowed upon me.

The season at the Oslo National Theater combined drama and opera. When the first world war broke out, the managers decided to give something light. They thought operetta would cheer the people up more than grand opera. Through this change of policy I got my second role. The operetta was Planquette's *Chimes of Normandy*. It was an important role—Germaine, a countess or marchioness. Besides singing, I had to speak some lines in the part. With this I had some trouble!

I have a deep speaking voice. To do the countess right I tried hard in the spoken lines to raise my voice. It sounded awfully unnatural, to say the least. Finally, the conductor composed a special waltz for me so I could sing what I was supposed to tell the hero. Sometime later, in 1915, the theater presented two operas by the Norwegian composer Schjelderup. They were called *Holy Night* and *Spring Night*, both short. Eidé Norena, whom Americans have heard at the Metropolitan, had the principal parts in both. Both my own roles were small. But doing them added to my confidence and knowledge of the stage.

About this time I wanted very much to go to Germany to continue studying. Like everybody else I recognized it as a center for singing. But of course the war was on and I had to give up my hopes. Then some people offered me the money to study in Sweden for one year. They had heard me sing and felt it was worth while financing my further studies. I accepted after consulting my parents. It was a private donation and I was free to use it as I wished.

Chapter Three

IN the meantime I had changed teachers. The new one's name was Albert Westwang, a well-known Norwegian basso and singing teacher. I spent a year studying with him. I remember how we struggled for long breath in Elisabeth's Prayer in *Tannhäuser*. Westwang laid emphasis on breathing. He had a very deep basso voice himself. His low tones were tremendous. He sang a beautiful Sarastro in *Zauberflöte*. Of course Westwang, as well as everyone else, encouraged me to take the money and go to Stockholm. I had decided on Stockholm myself. The money amounted to three thousand kroner, about $750.

Well, I stayed two and a half years in Stockholm, all spent in study. I made no concert or opera appearances. I went back to Oslo for a single concert in March, 1918. When the $750 was gone and I was getting prepared to return, I had another stroke of good luck. Someone else interested in my career donated an additional 10,000 kroner, about $2500. This was to cover the remaining year and a half. I didn't return to Oslo until Christmastime in 1918.

Now I must introduce you to Dr. Gillis Bratt. He was a widely known throat specialist in Stockholm, as well as a famous singing teacher. He was also prominent in Germany. He is dead now. Opinions varied about him. You won't find many people

The Early Manuscript

to praise him now. How I happened to come to him is a story in itself. Mother and Father went with me to Stockholm. Halfdan Christensen, the director of the National Theater of Oslo, had given me a letter of introduction to Count von Stedink, the director of the Stockholm Royal Theater. You know, for free tickets and that sort of courtesy often exchanged by opera companies. Count von Stedink asked me where I was going to study. I told him I had no idea. He advised me to go to hear *Faust* that night and to listen carefully to three singers, the tenor, the soprano, and the baritone.

"They are pupils of the same teacher," he said. "His name is Dr. Bratt. I would advise you to go to him. But go and hear for yourself tonight."

The tenor was Joseph Hislop, from Edinburgh. He had a very beautiful voice and knew how to use it. I decided on the spot to go to Dr. Bratt. He gave me an audition and I sang *Madama Butterfly* for him. He looked at me curiously.

"Have you ever sung in public?" he asked.

I replied that I had.

"No, you haven't! Because if you had, nobody could have heard you!" I saw at once that Dr. Bratt was a very positive man.

"Oh, yes, they did!" I insisted angrily.

"Well," he went on, "that was only a child's voice they heard. Your voice, young lady, is much too small, and I know why. I think we can fix it, however. You seem to be very musical. Anyway we will try you out."

Dr. Bratt was a very busy man. Besides his extensive medical practice he taught singing, as a sideline, you might say. His rates were surprisingly low. I drilled with him twice a week, a half-hour each time. He was very severe. He shouted. He was known to scare his pupils out of their wits. They would come out crying from their lessons. I broke down only once in his presence. He had shouted at me, "You don't even try to do as I say!"

And tears streamed down my face. Suddenly he felt sorry.

21

THE FLAGSTAD MANUSCRIPT

He gave me some candy and said, "Of course, I didn't mean it that way."

Dr. Bratt told me that my vocal cords did not close and that was the reason for my small voice. Air went through between the vocal chords. What he did was to close my vocal chords. By this means my voice grew in three months to three times its size. Dr. Bratt soon discovered that I learned fast. During those two lessons a week we would do four or five songs and several pages from opera. I went on coaching myself in opera parts, but Dr. Bratt really controlled everything I did in the way of actual singing. Meanwhile, I tried to go back to the piano. I experimented for four weeks, but I found I wasn't getting anywhere because of lack of time. There were more important things to do.

I had enrolled in the Swedish branch of the Dalcroze School of Dancing. I took four dance lessons a week. I studied classical dancing, of course just for the stage—*plastique,* dramatic, and so forth. I remember we had the "Valse Triste" of Sibelius to do once.

The study of *plastique* is responsible for every movement I make on the stage. Every time I raise my arms it is there. Every single gesture comes from it. I have never been obliged to study any role's gestures or movements because of my training in *plastique.* It taught me to co-ordinate movements with music. Anybody who has learned to dance finds it easier to get around on the stage. There are ways of moving hands, feet, the whole body. Otherwise you run the risk of looking like a wooden doll.

While in Stockholm I went to four or five operas every week. I heard thirty-five different operas in one year. Stockholm had practically a whole-year season, with only a six- or seven-week recess when the theater was closed. I attended recitals and concerts and the theater a good deal. And I worked. How hard I worked! I lived alone. I had seen an ad in the papers. A room with piano and breakfast. It was just what I wanted. They were a simple little family, plain people, but nice

The Early Manuscript

and quiet. That was my first year in Stockholm. The next year Grace Grung came to live in the house where I was boarding. She was a well-known actress from Bergen, best known for her Ibsen roles. She had been given one year's leave of absence to study voice, that is, speaking voice, with Dr. Bratt. We became very good friends. She used to read aloud for me, and I was thus introduced to many literary classics, chiefly of Ibsen and Björnson. Grace Grung was a few years older than I and much more mature in every way. She had lots and lots of brains. I was an innocent little thing beside her. She had an excellent influence over me. She taught me a great deal that proved very useful. We both worked hard and we loved it.

About that time I also studied Swedish with a Swedish actress. We went over the works of Selma Lagerlöf, and I have remained a devotee of hers ever since. She writes the most beautiful prose. Once Dr. Bratt got me to sing at the weekly meeting of the Artists' Guild. By then I had acquired great fluency in Swedish and I was complimented on the way I sang some Swedish songs.

I interrupted my studies to return to Oslo in March, 1918, to make my recital debut as a singer. The event took place in the auditorium of the University of Oslo. A man named Piero Coppola was my accompanist, and later became my conductor. On the same program with me was the baritone of the three singers whom Count von Stedink of the Stockholm opera had advised me to pay attention to in that performance of *Faust*. He was Carl Richter, a Swede. I opened with "Ritorna vincitor" from *Aïda*. It went well. Then I sang some songs by Hugo Wolf and Richard Strauss, as well as Grieg, and we finished up with two duets from Mozart's *Nozze di Figaro* and *Don Giovanni*. As an encore we did a third duet, from *Zauberflöte*. I remember the flowers covered the whole stage.

I had wonderful notices, especially from Borgström. Who could have suspected at my debut, he said, that with my tiny voice, I would develop into something important? I must be an excellent worker, he speculated. Nothing could have pleased

23

THE FLAGSTAD MANUSCRIPT

me more! Borgström did say that I didn't know very much what Richard Strauss's *Cäcilie* was about, and I suppose I didn't. But he was very nice and encouraging.

After my recital I went back immediately to Stockholm for my last half-year there. I was now preparing for a debut at the Stockholm Opera. That had been Dr. Bratt's goal all along. He had said to me, "I don't want you to go through the opera school, because you already know what they have to teach you, but I'm not going to let you have an audition until I think you're absolutely ready. When the time comes I'll say so." Then he told me he thought I might be prepared in the spring of 1919. I proceeded to learn several operas in Swedish. And then, suddenly, someone got the idea to give grand opera again in Oslo.

An enterprising Englishman named Singer came up for a fair in Norway. He put on musical shows in an amusement park, and apparently earned lots of money. He had a small theater where they gave vaudeville. One day Mr. Singer decided to give Oslo a permanent opera house. Everybody thought it ridiculous. But they got started on it, and naturally, Mother was promptly connected with it. She began preparing the chorus. They approached me in April, 1918. I just smiled and said no. I didn't take it seriously. Well, they went on without me. Calling themselves the Opéra-Comique, they engaged every available singer in Norway and started with Saint-Saëns' *Samson et Dalila*. When I came home at Christmas they asked me again to join up with them and suggested that I do Nedda in *Pagliacci*. I again refused, explaining that I was going back to Stockholm to study. This was Christmas, 1918. In the spring of 1919 Dr. Bratt was sure I would be making my debut at the Stockholm Opera. Perhaps I should have gone back. But I didn't. I signed up with the Oslo outfit. You see, I had met my first husband.

His name was Sigurd Hall. I had been to school with his brother and I suppose the two of them had talked about me.

24

The Early Manuscript

Later he told me he felt he had known me all along through his brother. At the time I barely knew him. When I came back to Oslo that Christmas he phoned me one evening and asked me to go to the theater with him. I thought it was his brother calling me and accepted. It turned out to be Sigurd instead. We had a good laugh over it. Well, we fell in love and after a short romance were married on May 14, 1919. This was very much against my mother's wishes. She made some fuss about it when I began bringing him to my house and introducing him as my sweetheart. She wanted me to have a career. She had ambition. I hadn't. And that was that.

My husband was not especially interested in music. He was a businessman. His father had a large wholesale ironware and kitchenware business and he helped manage it. He was tall, quite good-looking, and a wonderful dancer, and I was very much in love. He was two years older than I. Because I loved him, Mother soon became reconciled to our marrying. We had a small wedding. We took a little house in the suburb of Drobak outside Oslo. I had joined the Opéra-Comique in Oslo and I had still to work. So we had no honeymoon. Later when the company went to Copenhagen my husband came along. Perhaps that might be considered our honeymoon. We stayed fourteen days in Denmark and then came back through Sweden.

I had become a member of the company on January 16th. Meeting my husband decided me against going back to Stockholm. I signed up for Nedda and a role in Johann Strauss's *Zigeunerbaron*. The season had started on November 18th while I was still in Stockholm. I also sang Martha in an opera called *Der Evangelimann* by Kienzl. And in-between I sang operetta.

Incidentally something happened in Copenhagen that might have altered the whole direction of my career. I had come to feel like an opera singer and didn't regard operetta as anything to be taken seriously. I felt great pride in my work. Well, we played a light work of Von Suppé, *Die Schöne Galathee*. I was cast as the young boy who falls in love with the beautiful

25

Galathea. I had to wear tights. I was terribly shy about having so little on, but I had quite a triumph, everyone said I had a great talent for comic roles. The next day an impresario called me up. He said he had something important to talk over with me. Could he see me? He came up to my hotel. He said he was producing a very well-known musical comedy, with beautiful sets and dresses. But his prima donna had left him and they needed someone like me badly.

"You'll be leading lady from now on," he said invitingly.

"Oh, no!" I replied with great dignity. "I'm sorry. I'm an opera singer."

I felt sure that was a turning point in my life. Everything would have been completely different if I had accepted that offer.

We went back to Oslo in August, 1919. At the theater my next role was Orestes in Offenbach's *La Belle Hélène*. Then came an operetta by Lehár called *The Little Lark,* and again I sang Nedda. But something was happening to me. I was rapidly losing my voice. My long breath was going. The fact is my child was coming.

I sang up to Christmas. Then I settled down at home and just waited for her to come. She was born in 1920, on the seventeenth of May, the day we celebrate our Constitution. We called her Else-Marie. I did no singing for four months. The baby occupied all my thought. I wasn't interested in anything else. I was absolutely crazy about her and couldn't think of opera or singing or anything. I did sing some lullabies to her, though.

Well, the summer went by and no singing. Mother was becoming frantic over my lack of interest. She tried repeatedly to get me to go back to the Opéra-Comique. I said, "No, no, I'm not at all interested, Mother!"

One day she came to me and said, "Here's a role absolutely made for you, Kirsten. You ought to consider it at least. It's really for you and nobody else."

It was Lehár's *Zigeunerliebe.* Mother had brought the score home with her. We went over it together. I started to sing and

The Early Manuscript

suddenly stopped. Mother and I looked at each other. My voice was at least twice as large as it had been! That gave me such a thrill. Before I knew what I was doing, I had accepted the role. And so it started all over again.

Then they asked me to study Pamina in Mozart's *Zauberflöte*. They wanted it ready in a hurry. One evening the management called me urgently on the telephone to ask if I would sing the First Lady the following night. Having made it a rule never to say no to requests of this kind, I said, "I'll try. I'll let you know tomorrow morning." The role was completely new to me and I had less than twenty-four hours in which to learn it! I sat up all night. I studied the role just by reading it. It was a difficult thing to learn alone. For one thing, the First Lady has to sing all the time in trios. Just before the performance they gave me a short rehearsal with the other two ladies. And then I sang it and somehow everything went smoothly.

The director of the Opéra-Comique had engaged a Hungarian named Alexander Varnay as stage manager. Varnay had been a famous tenor. He virtually ran the company. He had great artistic authority and he knew a great deal. I have never met anyone like him. He taught me a lot and I became a kind of pet child of his. His favorite remark about me was, *"Die Kirsten kann alles*—Kirsten can do anything."

His wife was our coloratura soprano Maria Javor, who now teaches singing in New York. Varnay died while he was still a young man.

After I sang that last-minute First Lady, Varnay said to me, "The lady who should have sung it was a certain dramatic soprano. She was too proud to sing it, so she refused," he said sarcastically. To punish her for refusing to do the part Varnay took Desdemona in Verdi's *Otello* away from her and gave it to me. I had eight days in which to learn the new role, stage rehearsals and everything.

Leo Slezak came to Oslo as guest for that *Otello*. That was an experience in itself. He came to the dress rehearsal. He didn't sing. He did nothing but joke. He overflowed with fun. His Othello was something unbelievable. It was beautiful and grand and frightening. He was terribly tall and terribly bulky. I was so very frail and shrinking beside him. We repeated *Otello* many times that season. At one performance Slezak said to me, "I want to take you around the world to sing *Otello* with me."

I'm sure he said that to all his Desdemonas. He behaved very badly at one of the performances. I shall not tell just how. The next day I refused to sing with him. His wife came to me in his behalf and asked forgiveness. I gave in. That night I was again Slezak's Desdemona. Later he met Father and Mother, and both were deeply impressed by him.

Some time in 1921 I did Amelia in Verdi's *Un Ballo in Maschera*. Again I learned the role in eight days. It was too much for me. I wasn't cut out for the part at that time. It was too dramatic. Then came a big thrill: Puccini's *Fanciulla del West*. I so loved doing that exciting drama! It gave me my first romantic taste of America.

I didn't come back to the Opéra-Comique that summer. I did freelancing mostly. I sang in concerts and did other small jobs. After three years of existence the Opéra-Comique suddenly folded up in September. Mr. Singer had lost all his money.

He still had the house and stage, though, and he wanted to make an operetta and revue theater out of them. He sent for me and asked me if I would continue as prima donna in the new company and on the new policy. I repeated what I had said to the impresario in Copenhagen, "I'm sorry, Mr. Singer, but I'm an opera singer."

Then I went on tour. I sang in Rossini's *Stabat Mater* and was soloist with the Oslo Philharmonic. In the spring an offer came along from the Danish conductor Biering-Petersen, who directed light operetta in Copenhagen. He was then in Oslo, conducting operetta in a small theater called the Majol. He

The Early Manuscript

stipulated such a good salary, besides offering my mother a job as coach and positions to several of my friends, that I accepted. I had to forget my pride in being exclusively an opera singer, as I was in the habit of calling myself. I needed the money badly and anyway I wanted to go back to the theater. We started with Offenbach's *Orphée aux Enfers* in the summer of 1922.

We did operetta there for two years. While I was still at the Majol, Singer reopened the Casino, formerly the Opéra-Comique. He too was doing operetta, but lighter stuff. On the promise that he would soon give opera, I went back to the Casino and during the fall of 1924 I sang in musical comedies. I didn't like to do it, but I had to have the money. You know the sort of entertainment it was. I would come in singing my number with the chorus girls behind me. Once I wore an elaborate costume with lots and lots of feathers on my head. Usually I sang two songs an evening. It was more to give the theater my name on the bills than anything else.

During this Casino period they were giving Beethoven's Ninth Symphony at the Philharmonic concerts. There were something like eight performances in one year, all on Sunday evenings. Of course, before my operetta and musical comedy work I had often sung with them. Now they said they wanted me back to sing the solo part as before. I approached the director of the Casino about it. He felt as highly flattered by the invitation as I was. After all, we were doing revues and this was a request to sing Beethoven. It was quite a leap! He said, "All right. We can switch your numbers around so you can have time to sing in the Ninth Symphony and then come back here and sing musical comedy for us."

So, after singing a song, "I Love You So" in a very showy dress and with the chorus gaily joining in, I would change quickly to a respectable concert dress and rush over to sing the soprano solo in Beethoven's Ninth Symphony. After the concert, I would come back to the Casino, throw off the eve-

THE FLAGSTAD MANUSCRIPT

ning dress and get into another elaborate costume for my next number in the revue.

That year we started to give opera again. The first one must have been *Faust*. I sang with a very well-known Swedish opera singer who came to do Mephistopheles with us. This was about April, 1925. Then I received a letter from John Forsell, the director of the Stockholm Opera. He wrote that he had heard so much about me and was anxious to hear me. I wrote back accepting the invitation. I had a great dread of meeting him, because I knew how opposed he was to Dr. Bratt. Well, I went to Stockholm. I had a vacation coming anyway, and decided I might just as well spend it there.

I came to Forsell's office and began immediately speaking Swedish. I had become quite fluent during my stay in Stockholm. He seemed surprised and asked me, "Where have you learned to speak Swedish so well?"

Well, what was I to say? I replied sheepishly that I had once studied in Sweden. When I proudly told him that I had studied with Gillis Bratt, his face changed. He said something I can't remember and then remarked that after all, I had come for an audition.

"It's quite all right," he said. "We need you very much for certain roles; Juliette in Gounod's opera, for instance. But you have to change your way of singing entirely."

That was the end of that.

"I'm sorry, but I have things to do in Norway and I'm going back," I said.

"Well, return to us when you've changed your mind," he snapped back. Since that talk I have sung at the Stockholm Opera. Forsell was still director. I did not change my way of singing.

Back at the Casino in Oslo in the summer of 1926, I sang in a performance of Johann Strauss's *Fledermaus*, which I love so much. We also did a Norwegian opera, *The Seaman's Bride*, by Aspestrand, and then came *Carmen*. I sang Micaela. We

30

The Early Manuscript

gave that *Carmen* fifty-three times within a half-year! The Carmen was a lady who made quite a sensation in New York and Cincinnati some years ago. I mean Erika Darbo. We were colleagues for years at the Casino. I thought her Carmen was splendid.

Wagner meant hardly anything at all to me apart from my own study of scores. I had heard *Götterdämmerung* in Berlin in 1913 just before my debut in *Tiefland*. I had hoped to hear *Tiefland* there to help me in my study of that opera, but they didn't give it. We heard *Götterdämmerung* instead, and three other operas. We also took in an operetta. I was too tired that evening to remember much about the Wagner opera. Mother, who was also tired, slept through half of it. Wagner meant nothing much to her then.

The first performance of Wagner I ever heard was *Lohengrin* in Oslo in 1916. Then the Oslo Opéra-Comique gave *Tannhäuser* in 1919. I heard that performance and remember it vividly. Lauritz Melchior was guest in that one, and Leo Slezak sang in other performances. They both did a beautiful job. I realized then that I did not have voice enough for Wagner. In fact, I didn't think much about Wagner as it concerned me. I knew next to nothing about the Brünnhilde operas. Wagner meant *Tannhäuser, Lohengrin* and *Der Fliegende Holländer* to me. Father seldom talked about Wagner, if ever. So I might truthfully say that the magic of Wagner up to that time had not reached me. In 1921 I heard *Die Walküre*. And that was all. Brünnhilde, Siegfried, Wotan and the rest of them played no part in my imaginative life.

Chapter Four

DURING the season of 1927–28 we went on an operetta tour. Mother was with us as conductor. We covered a great number of small Norwegian towns. Only part of the Casino company went along. It was our own undertaking and had nothing to do with the Casino management. We were all free to do as we pleased, since we had given up our membership in the company. We carried around our own scenery and used a large hired bus to travel in. It was hard and rough going, especially in the wintertime. We gave four German operettas: *Kinokönigin, Zirkusprinzessin, Der Orloff,* and *Die Bajadere.* Mother was a very strict conductor and by no means indulgent with me because I was her daughter. It was nothing unusual for me. In fact, it was quite a natural thing to have Mother in the pit and myself on the stage. It was a successful tour.

In the spring of 1928 I was called for an audition in Göteborg, Sweden. Some of my former colleagues were there: a Norwegian tenor and a Norwegian conductor. My colleagues had said they wanted me very much to join them there and had put in a good word for me. I was offered a contract for the whole season. They were going to open with *Der Freischütz.* It sounded tempting.

On the train back from the audition a man in our car had some passport difficulty at the border. It was all straightened

The Early Manuscript

out and we all got to talking. He spoke Swedish, but a funny kind of Swedish. He told us he was Finnish.

"You look like an artist," he said to me. I told him that I was.

"What have you been doing?" he asked. I told him.

"Successful?" Yes.

"Have you ever been in Finland?" he asked. I said no.

"Would you like to sing there?" I said I might.

"Are you free this summer?" Yes.

"Why don't you come? We give light operas in the summertime in the open air, and we usually have a Swedish company visiting us." I told him, "What's the use. They have never heard of me in Finland. I don't stand the ghost of a chance being invited."

"Well," he said, "I happen to be the director. I'll cable them at once that I have a prima donna. If they've already hired one, it's just too bad. She'll have to go."

That's how I came to sing in Finland.

In May my husband had to go to Canada for business purposes. By then we had decided to separate and took out the papers. We did not intend to be divorced at the time. After he left, my daughter and I went to Finland. I was quite a success there. We spent one of our most beautiful summers together, Else and I. When the Finnish season ended I went direct to Göteborg to sing opera. It seems strange now when I sing only opera to look on the many years when I went back and forth, from opera to operetta, from Beethoven to musical comedy without thinking anything about it. It was always a job to be done and I did it.

I went on to Göteborg in September and enrolled with the company. Our first opera was Weber's *Der Freischütz*. At that time the opera house in Göteborg was called the Storatheater, that is the "large theatre." They gave four operas a season, as a rule, with light entertainment in-between, that is operettas or musical comedies. I was engaged to do both. The troupe was

33

often jokingly called the Norwegian Opera Company. The reason was obvious. The conductor was Norwegian. The chief tenor was Norwegian. The prima donna who preceded me was Norwegian. And then there was myself. All the principals were Norwegian. So I had no hesitation in going. Besides, the tenor, Conrad Arnesen, had been one of my colleagues years before. The performances were quite good. Three or four weeks were spent in rehearsals, held every day. Everything was done to make the performances as artistic as possible.

We gave *Der Freischütz* twenty-eight times in succession. Think of it! In a comparatively small city like Göteborg. Four times a week, Monday, Tuesday, Thursday and Friday. Those were my opera nights. I was very happy to have my daughter with me, though I'm afraid she didn't like the routine at all. I had her registered in school there, but she didn't seem to get along with the other children. So I had to send her home to my brother and sister-in-law. This was hard on me, for I was quite alone again. Well, anyway, they liked me in Göteborg, if I may say so, right from the start. I got a lot of smaller jobs, singing in church and at local club affairs. I started to earn money on the side, money I didn't expect. It was very convenient for me because I had to pay off debts I owed in Norway. I really needed money badly and I did quite a good job of saving and being sensible about it.

At the same time people had been asking me to teach them singing. I had always said "No," because I felt and still feel that I am not a pedagogue. I'm sure I couldn't teach singing—that is, actually show someone how to go about it. I know pretty well what I do myself, but I have no idea how to get others to do it. But people in Göteborg insisted and said they wanted so very much to study with me. I told them frankly again and again I couldn't. I admitted I might show them some tricks. Well, after a good deal of persuasion, I tried it a little. I think I was able to give them a few good hints anyway. Those extra jobs brought me quite a lot of money when combined with my opera earn-

The Early Manuscript

ings. I paid off the debts in full and with the remainder I decided to take a trip to Central Europe with a friend, which I did in May, 1929.

While at Göteborg I was given a role that gave me a real chance to show what dramatic stuff there was in me. I had always sung roles like Agathe and Micaela, sweet, blameless misses, all of them. That was all very well. But in Göteborg the critics said after *Freischütz* that while it was all to my credit, they would like to see me act a little, instead of keeping my eyes turned forever to heaven.

Then I had an experience I don't think I shall ever forget— the most satisfactory work I have ever done, barring my years here in America. We gave an opera by the Danish composer Carl Nielsen. It was called *Saul and David*. Nielsen was the greatest composer Denmark had ever had. He was still considered quite modern at the time, though this opera was already about twenty-five years old and had been a failure when it was first produced. It was still modern in 1928. Our stage manager was a Dane. He was just wonderful. He and the conductor, the Norwegian Olav Kjelland, who is now head of the Oslo Philharmonic and was conductor at the New York World's Fair in the Norwegian pavilion, decided to give that opera. But Nielsen himself objected flatly. "That's one of those mistakes I made as a young man," he said. "Everybody's forgotten it by now." But Kjelland and the Danish manager insisted. Finally he weakened and gave his consent.

Then we started to rehearse *Saul and David* after being given our roles. Everything went like church. Musicians, chorus, soloists—all concerned put everything into it. It became our religion to make it go. I think it is a wonderful opera, so dramatic and vivid.

I played the role of Mikal. I remember the dramatic scene in which David uses the slingshot. I also had a beautiful scene together with my maids. And when David comes back from his victory over Goliath, that was another dramatic scene, perfectly

35

THE FLAGSTAD MANUSCRIPT

thrilling to act. Saul gets angry, grasps his spear, and hurls it at David. In Göteborg the actor used a real spear and managed the throwing so well that it drove into the planks and shivered there. There I was right in its path, trying to cover David. Each time, at rehearsals and performances, the spear would pass me by a few inches. But Saul never missed. When I think of it, how that spear stuck in the floor and quivered, you can be sure I'm thankful nothing like that happens in Wagner's operas!

The fact is I had played dramatic roles before without making them very dramatic. Now I felt I was really acting on the stage. I was always very shy, but now I was away from my own people. They knew me too well. I had always been afraid, childishly perhaps, that they would take me for whatever bad character I was impersonating. Here in Göteborg I felt freer and bolder as an actress. To my own country people I couldn't be anything but myself. I didn't dare exhibit myself as something I was not. It was a curious difficulty. But when I came to Sweden that timidness left me completely. Mikal was the first role in which I really felt I had done something dramatic and real. The opera was a great success in Göteborg. It was given eighteen times. Nielsen himself conducted it once. Later Copenhagen and Stockholm took it up with great success.

My next job was Aïda. How I loved it! Who wouldn't love to sing Aïda, with her great dramatic conflicts and passionate outpourings? I had long known the role in German. Aïda had been one of those thirty roles I studied by myself before I was twenty. Göteborg staged it beautifully. I wish you could have seen the costumes. I hadn't seen many Aïda's in my life, so I used my judgment in handling the role, with the stage manager coaching a little. Now that I had broken the ice with Mikal, I felt bolder with Aïda. I could dare to show-off something that had long been latent in me, struggling for expression. By then the stage manager had great confidence in me. Shortly after the *Aïda* performance he remarked to me, "I see now what you are really capable of."

36

The Early Manuscript

But that was only true of actual performances. I felt free there, eager to act and sway audiences. But I've never been any good in rehearsal. I still can't rehearse, believe it or not. I'm shy, terribly shy. But when the audience is out there and nobody can interrupt me, then I cut loose, then I feel completely on my own. I felt it then in Göteborg for the first time. That something in me loosened up. I felt I couldn't afford to be shy and goody-goody any more. I suddenly realized why I was on the stage—to give everything that was in me, not only musical notes. My development as an actress began then. I stopped just looking innocent. And with *Aïda* I grew still freer as a dramatic interpreter.

They hadn't yet decided which was to be the fourth opera. Their choice finally fell on Puccini's *La Bohème*. I was asked to sing Mimi. I was a little tall for the role, but I was very slender. There was only time for a single rehearsal. Everybody had done the opera before except me. Of course I had studied it in Norwegian. Actually I knew it better than any other role, though I had never sung it publicly. But how I worshiped Puccini! I used the Norwegian translation, but changed words into Swedish when necessary. I knew both Swedish and Norwegian and made my own translation. Acting Mimi is a fairly simple matter. The power of the role comes through the singing, the gorgeous music. I had one orchestral rehearsal, that was all. I mastered the role in four days and sang it six times in all. It thrilled me so! The critics said I looked much too healthy for the consumptive Mimi, but they liked my singing.

Then I went on tour in the spring. We gave *Tosca*. I had studied this role first in German and Swedish. Tosca was the very first role I prepared with my teacher in Sweden, Dr. Bratt. From the very beginning it had always been the one role I wished to do above all others. But I had decided not to do it until I was thirty because I thought I would not be mature enough for it before then.

I had seen the opera often and knew it perfectly, even in

Swedish. The others had all sung it repeatedly. Again we had only one rehearsal, with orchestra. I made a single request. "If I may just stand beside the orchestra and sing my part to get used to the accompaniment, I am willing to take it on my own to act it at the performance."

I was quite sure of myself, you see. I really knew everything about *Tosca* that was to be known. It interested me more than any other role, and they trusted me.

"All right," they said. "If you say you can do it, we'll take the chance."

We performed it in a small city, Varberg. We gave eleven more performances after that. I've never been so astonished at myself in my life. I believe I acted Tosca the way she should be done. I let myself go completely. I still rejoiced in my new freedom on the stage, and in *Tosca* it broke down whatever resistance still remained in me. The baritone was a superb actor and proved very inspiring to me. He did a remarkable Scarpia, and my own dramatic confidence gained from it. I also played the organ backstage in the second act for the cantata.

I spoke of a trip to Europe. After we had completed our season in Göteborg I took it. I had made a very good friend in Göteborg and we went to Germany together. She was a bacteriologist in a large Swedish hospital. She was not Swedish herself, but came from the Tirol. We bought round-trip tickets. My scientific friend was really the first one to so much as hint that I was destined for the Metropolitan Opera House.

She had it in her mind that I should go to Germany and become a great Wagnerian singer. Of course I attached no importance to her words. I thought she was being nice and friendly, one of those fans who believed in me more than I believed in myself. "No, I'm afraid I'm going to remain in Göteborg," I said to her. "Anyway, I'll stay on there one year more and then, well, who knows, maybe I will try out in Germany." I made it a tentative, half-serious plan. But I was very tired after that Göteborg season. The twenty-eight performances of *Der*

38

The Early Manuscript

Freischütz and the other operas called for relaxation, and all I could think of that summer was rest. But I had underestimated my bacteriologist friend.

We went to Berlin. My companion was more used to traveling than I was, so the trip went very smoothly. She spoke all the languages. We had a little minor trouble at first. For instance, she had planned to stop at a particular hotel she knew. We discovered that the hotel had been closed for three years. So we hunted for another. We hadn't too much money to spend, and what there was we spent on music. Of course, the first thing she thought of, being a very practical person, was to arrange for an audition at the Kroll Opera in Berlin.

"I'm not going to an audition," I insisted. "I'm here on a vacation. Going to hear operas is one thing, but an audition is not on my schedule."

All she said was, "Oh yes it is, my dear Kirsten!"

Well, she took the lead and I followed like a lamb. I protested that I didn't have a piano to work with. And what do you suppose she did? She went straight to a music store and arranged it so I could come and use the store piano to limber up my voice.

Then we went to the Krolloper. The audition was all arranged, thanks to the bacteriologist. I sang *Freischütz* and *Aïda* in Swedish for them, and do you know who was listening to me? Otto Klemperer. He patted me on the head and said, "*Sehr talentvoll!* Can you sing in German as well?"

I said "yes."

And the director interrupted to say that if I could really sing in German I should come the following day and give another audition. That night I went through the same arias again until I felt sure I knew them as well in German as in Swedish. The director asked me if I had any repertory in German. I shook my head.

"We should like very much to have you," he said encouragingly.

39

THE FLAGSTAD MANUSCRIPT

I replied, "Thank you very much, but I plan to stay in Göteborg another year. I have a contract with them. When it expires I'd like very much to come back to Germany to sing for you."

"You will be very welcome," he answered. I wanted to join the regular personnel and do repertory, as most of the Norwegians did who came down there, that is, to learn the trade of the German opera houses.

In May we were in Dresden. En route I was obliged to go over my *Lohengrin* again since I had been engaged to do Elsa in June in Oslo. So while my friend pondered over the mysteries of bacteriology and read scientific books, I went over Wagner's beautiful score. I already knew it in German and was obliged to relearn it in Norwegian, and I did. The change from language to language was becoming an old story and I didn't mind it at all, so long as the translations were singable and I knew the language. I have hesitated to sing operas in Italian because I have not felt completely sure of myself in the language. Of course I knew *Lohengrin* backward, so I did little more than read my score and learn new words for it.

In Dresden we had another audition at the opera house, also arranged by my friend. Fritz Busch refused to listen to me. After all, he was obliged to hear so many would-be dramatic sopranos. What my friend didn't realize was that we needed an agent. Busch didn't regard the audition as very important, and that was that. I sang with him afterward and reminded him about it, and we laughed over it. There was no reason why he should have paid any attention to me then.

My friend was a very devout Catholic. One morning she announced that she had arranged for me to sing the following day at ten in church. She made me do Denza's *Ave Maria* for the services. There were lots of children there and the next day they sent me flowers. It was the first time I had ever sung in a Catholic church. I thought it most beautiful.

Then we went to Munich, and there I heard my first performance of Puccini's *Gianni Schicchi*. We heard no Wagner at all,

40

The Early Manuscript

When you realize how much Wagner I sing now, sometimes for months only Wagner, isn't it surprising how few Wagnerian performances I actually attended during that period?

My friend suggested Italy, and the mere thought excited me. She had Rovereto, first of all, on her mind, especially the cloisters.

"I was brought up there, Kirsten," she said. "Let's go to visit them. You won't regret it. They're beautiful."

We went and stopped there overnight. We saw the little cloisters where she had been brought up. They made a deep impression on me. I also heard an opera there, Giordano's *Andrea Chenier*. The artists were from La Scala of Milan. Nothing outstanding. Then we went to Venice and roamed around enjoying the sights and sounds of that dream city. After that, three days in Rome and more tours and thrilling sights. But no opera for us. Finally we reached Milan on the way back. It was just our luck to arrive one day after La Scala had closed with *Aïda!* But how much I saw of Italy in those seven days! We went sight-seeing all day long. It was too much to swallow in such a short time.

Then we went to Cologne and heard *Mârouf*, Rabaud's colorful Oriental opera, and Richard Strauss's *Der Rosenkavalier*, which was more important. I had already heard this lovely music in Sweden. After that we hurried back to Norway.

Chapter Five

AN important new chapter now opens in my life. I came home and immediately went into rehearsal for *Lohengrin*. There were to be only a few rehearsals in all, the first performance being scheduled for the twelfth or thirteenth of June, 1929. That was a crucial day for me. It was during that performance of Wagner's *Lohengrin* that Henry Johansen saw me for the first time. He always insisted that he fell in love with me the moment he saw the new Elsa come out on the balcony in the second act. At least that's what he said. I don't vouch for it. Men are all romantics at heart. I have reason to believe him, though.

Mr. Johansen was one of the sponsors of the opera season. Well, immediately after the performance the soloists, myself included, held a party in the Grand Hotel of Oslo. It was about one o'clock and we were all feeling gay. In the midst of it all one of my colleagues came over to me and said, "I would like to introduce you to a friend of mine who admires you very much."

We had engaged a special separate room for our little party. Mr. Johansen was in the large dining room outside, where members of the audience had gathered for a celebration of their own. I went with my friend to be introduced. He was most gallant and quite simply told me he liked my singing. He then

The Early Manuscript

invited us all to continue our party at his home which was nearby.

I was in a daze that night. I can't explain it otherwise. We all trooped over to that large beautiful house that was later to become my home. Something unusual, quite trivial in itself, happened. Mr. Johansen had a chair in that house that no one occupied but himself. He strictly forbade everyone else to use it. Some of my friends knew about this. Naturally I did not. Well, the moment we arrived I fell into this very chair and made myself quite comfortable. Mr. Johansen said nothing. He let me sit·there and even came over, sat on the arm of the chair and spoke to me. My friends who knew this chair to be the holy of holies in his household, immediately realized something unusual had happened. You can imagine my own feelings when I learned about the chair later on.

Mr. Johansen invited me to dinner the following day. I accepted. My brother, who was present that night, often twits me about it, reminding me of things that afterward amazed me. I can't explain it, except that it was probably love at first sight with both of us. We were together the following three days, at dinner, at the opera, and with mutual friends. On the third day he proposed to me. Still in a daze, I accepted. He told me he was a widower. I told him I was separated from my husband and that the required time of one year had elapsed, so that according to Norwegian law I could get my divorce any day. All I needed was my husband's agreement to it. He suddenly looked concerned and said he hoped he was not coming between me and my husband. He said he didn't want that. I assured him the separation was final, that everything had been at an end between me and my husband long before he came along.

There is one other detail to add about that episode. It shows how vivid an impression Mr. Johansen had made on me. The night after that performance of *Lohengrin,* shortly before I met Mr. Johansen again for dinner, I had written my husband and asked him for a divorce.

43

Henry Johansen was then engaged in the same business as his father before him: lumber, which is so vital to Norway. He had been educated in London for a commercial career and had married very young. He had four children, two twin boys and two girls. He had a commanding position in many large companies in Norway and was chairman of the boards of directors of some fifteen of them, from lumber firms to companies producing wheel belts. He was also an official in the ownership of the Grand and Bristol Hotels in Oslo. Among his properties was the only plywood or veneer factory in Norway, a beautiful plant in Kristiansand, which was to become and remain my real home. Even then we spent nearly as much time there as in Oslo.

As I said, I had promptly fallen in love with him that very night of *Lohengrin* at that little party in his home. In writing to my husband I admitted quite frankly that I had met another man and fallen in love with him. Anyway, I felt I didn't belong to him anymore and that it was only my right to expect him to grant me the divorce. I was being perfectly honest about it.

When Mr. Johansen proposed I told him I had already written my husband. I assured him there was no hope and no desire on my part to be reconciled. I had long thought I would never fall in love again. I had insisted on it time and again, talking to my family at home. They had laughed at me. And here I was falling in love with someone who had been totally unknown to be before that *Lohengrin* performance three days earlier and who scarcely knew who I was. He was hearing me sing for the first time. We were perfect strangers to one another, though I learned later that his children had often heard me sing in light operas. At that time Annie, who has since come to America and has made it her home as a naturalized citizen, was the only one of his children I became acquainted with. The others were in school in Switzerland and England.

And then I sang my first *Tosca* in Norway, along with the *Lohengrin*. Everybody began to notice that I was a new person

In musical comedy *Her Excellency* (1927).

With Karen-Marie Flagstad in *The Cousin from Batavia* (1927).

Two costumes from *Der Orloff* (1928).

The Early Manuscript

on the stage. They said they didn't recognize the former Kirsten Flagstad. They knew I could sing, they said, but they had never dreamed I could act. As I have already pointed out, I had suddenly become conscious of drama as a living reality when I left my country, and I had brought that new freedom back with me. My shyness was all gone, and those who knew me saw the change immediately.

I'd like to say a little more about Mr. Johansen's proposal and what followed. We were dining at the Bristol, which was one of his hotels—that is, he had an interest in it. It was an early dinner. We sat there and talked and were very formal. We were not using first names. Suddenly he put his hand over mine and said, "Well, Madame Flagstad, you love me, don't you?"

Just like that! Before I knew what I was saying, I gasped, "Yes!" and he thought it was wonderful.

At first we didn't let anyone in on our secret, not even my parents, though they soon began to suspect how matters stood.

Then I got the letter from my husband. I had been waiting anxiously for it. He said he was sorry I had come to such a decision, but he understood fully. He was willing to grant me a divorce and even put it in so many words, "I agree to divorce, and so forth," on a separate sheet of paper, so I could make legal use of his consent. But, as luck would have it, he had forgotten to have the affidavit notarized! I'm sure it was his honest intention to give me my freedom then and there.

When I went with the document to the proper authorities, they asked me, "Are you going to marry again soon?"

I said I had no immediate plans but that I would like to be free to wed by Christmas.

So they said, "Why don't you write your husband again and ask him for a more regular affidavit?"

I acted on their suggestion and wrote. But I didn't hear from my husband for months after that. I began to fear something had gone wrong. Finally I felt there was no real hurry so I went back to Göteborg to sing, confident that the notarized agreement would come in due course. At length the letter from my husband arrived. It gave me a jolt. He didn't want to give me my freedom. He had changed his mind. He had decided to wait until the full period expired. One year must elapse in Norway if both parties agree and two if they don't. After that no one can stop a divorce. The period would not expire until May 30, 1930. The authorities suggested that I take the case to court, but I decided not to and bided my time.

Meanwhile I met all of Mr. Johansen's children that winter and spent Christmas with them. Mother and Father took strongly to Mr. Johansen. For that matter, my whole family did. My brothers and sisters all adored him and they all became the closest friends. When I was not in Norway he would ask them to come and visit him. What he loved most was to have them speak to him of my early childhood. From the very start his devotion to my family was deep and sincere.

It was during the season of *Lohengrin* in Oslo that the long arm of the Metropolitan Opera House reached me for the first time. After a performance of *Tosca* the manager came up to me and said, "Well, my dear young lady, guess who was here to-night? The director of the Metropolitan in New York. He asked to send you his very best greetings." I was quite thrilled and asked him what the director's name was.

"Why, Otto Kahn!"

The next day the Oslo newspapers phoned me and asked, "Are you really going to the Metropolitan, Madame Flagstad?"

I was taken completely by surprise. "Why do you ask?" I said.

"Because everybody knows Otto Kahn heard you yesterday at the opera."

I said, "Oh that! Why, Mr. Kahn merely sent his greetings to me and all the others." Well, they didn't get any story out of me because there was no story to give them.

Three months later when I was in Göteborg and already engaged to my husband, I got a letter from Eric Simon, the Metropolitan's European representative, asking me to send him

46

The Early Manuscript

criticisms, lists of roles, and pictures. Frankly I wasn't very impressed. First of all, I had never dreamed of coming to the Metropolitan which, after all, seemed like the top of the world to singers everywhere. For us at home it was like reaching for the moon. Besides, I wasn't very ambitious, as you know, and, anyway I never had the faintest thought of its happening to me. Most of all, I was happily engaged to the man I loved and I had my work to do in Norway. There was still another thing. I didn't have pictures of myself in many roles. No one had ever asked for pictures before. We didn't do that sort of thing at home. Nobody chased after autographs or anything like that. As for the reviews, that meant translating, and more work, and anyway what does it matter to New York what a critic in Oslo or Göteborg says about a singer?

I did not answer Mr. Simon. Three weeks later I got another letter urging me again to send what he had requested. It took me two weeks to gather up enough energy and courage to have some reviews translated. I sent them along to Mr. Simon with a few postcard pictures of myself. That was the last I heard of that. I shrugged my shoulders and never gave the matter another thought. I've since asked about it at the Metropolitan. You know, Otto Kahn died before I finally came over here. When I brought the subject up in a talk with Edward Ziegler, then assistant manager, he remarked, "I remember it all very well. It was Otto Kahn who wanted you over. I recall saying to him, 'But who's ever heard of Kirsten Flagstad here?' Kahn insisted on my getting in touch with you. So I wrote Simon to write you. When we didn't get any answer from you, I urged Simon to write again. Still no reply from you. Finally I guess it was just a question of being too late."

I suppose if I had taken a keener interest and answered Mr. Simon on time I might have come to the Metropolitan five years earlier than I did. On the whole I don't think that would have been very wise. When I finally joined the company I was a maturer artist in every sense and knew a great deal more about

THE FLAGSTAD MANUSCRIPT

Wagner than five years earlier. So it may have been good sense rather than mere lack of ambition that delayed my answering Mr. Simon.

I've heard that Oscar Thompson, the New York *Sun's* music critic and the editor of the magazine *Musical America,* claims to have "discovered" me. Mr. Thompson wrote a very nice article about me in his magazine, at the time of his "discovery," and sent it to me.

Meanwhile I was in Göteborg singing. I remember we did Puccini's *La Rondine* and that I didn't like it at all. Somehow I never quite warmed to that opera, in spite of my fondness for Puccini. But the management had decided to give it, and there was no help for it. Often you are obliged to sing music to which you are completely unsympathetic. That is part of the job, as you know. There was some compensation in the fact that we dropped the last act of *La Rondine* and filled out the bill with Debussy's *L'Enfant Prodigue,* or *Prodigal Son.* My role was Leah. Oh, but that was beautiful music, and brimming over with true feeling! It went so much deeper than *La Rondine.* Then I did Eva in Wagner's *Die Meistersinger.* That was my second Wagnerian role. It thrilled me so. Eva is such a beautifully romantic part to act and sing! I've often wished they would ask me to sing Eva here, but they never have. I love the role, and it helped deepen my interest in Wagner, which wasn't very great at that period in my life.

My fiancé came to see me quite often in Göteborg. He drove down, and I would go up to see him whenever I was free. My daughter and Mr. Johansen's girl Annie were then in a boarding school in the country together. Later she and Annie came down to Göteborg to pass Easter with me. While there they saw a new opera that none of us liked, Ernst Krenek's *Johnny Spielt Auf.* It had imitation jazz in it. Whether I liked it or not I was under contract and had to sing it. It was my last performance that year and not a very pleasant memory.

Then I was free again. It was drawing towards the end of

48

The Early Manuscript

April. Mr. Johansen and I had decided not to get married in Norway. My fiancé wanted to go to Karlsbad, where he spent a vacation every summer. We took his eldest daughter with us, crossed over and drove on to Karlsbad. We motored through Germany and spent some time in Vienna, where I heard quite a fine *Tristan und Isolde*—my first. I regard that as another important Wagnerian experience in my life in view of what was to come later. I was gradually getting the *hang* of Wagner. Have I said it right? But do you know what happened at that performance? I got terribly tired after the first act. Frankly, and this may sound strange, it was just too much music for me for one evening, especially since I didn't know it. Mr. Johansen wanted to stay to hear it through, so I gave in. And do you know what he said to me?

"This is something *you* could never sing, young lady."

I was just as convinced as he was and replied, "I believe you are right, Henry. It's much too big for me."

Well, we stayed in Karlsbad for a while and then drove over to Belgium. In Brussels we met one of his sons. He was studying the lumber business just as his father had in his youth. We waited four days for my papers to be strictly and legally in order. The news came on the thirtieth. They telegraphed it down to me from Oslo. I was free and could marry again! So the next day we rode to Antwerp and were married in the office of the Norwegian consul general. Mr. Johansen's son and daughter were present. Then we crossed over to Norway, and motored up to Kristiansand.

I was married again! The beautiful house where I had innocently occupied his sacred chair that night after *Lohengrin* was my home. I was now supposed to give up singing as a profession. I didn't have to earn my own money any more, and I thought it was time to give it up, anyway, except perhaps to sing at an occasional concert. I was fed up with singing, I tell you. It had been hard, unrelenting work. Besides, my husband didn't want me to sing, either. He said so. He preferred to have

THE FLAGSTAD MANUSCRIPT

me traveling about with him and being plain Mrs. Henry Johansen. I assure you I would have had no regrets if it had remained that way. I felt I had earned a long rest. But it was not to be as we had planned.

Sometime later in the fall the Philharmonic of Oslo asked me to sing. I consulted my husband. He said he had no objection so long as I wanted to. I had done no singing for three or four months, and did I have a hard time working my voice again! It was then that I made an important decision: that whether I sang publicly or not I would at least keep my voice in good shape, always. Then something else happened. The prima donna who had succeeded me in Göteborg, also a Norwegian, fell sick, and there was a telephone call.

"Won't you come to help us? We're in a pinch! We need you desperately! We're giving Jaromir Weinberger's *Schwanda* in eight days and you've got to come and sing for us!"

It was tempting. Of course it meant the end of all my lovely plans of a quiet married life. But I suppose there's no point trying to fight against one's destiny. After talking it over with my husband I went to Göteborg. We discovered we both liked the idea.

As a matter of fact, I found out soon enough that he was thrilled every time I sang. In one way he didn't want me to sing, for my own sake and for his too, because he wanted me constantly with him. But when I did sing he was the proudest man alive, as if he had himself created my voice.

Of course *Schwanda* wasn't my opera, exactly. But I got quite a lot of fun out of it. It is an amusing work, and some of the music is lively and sparkling. But my artistic style had been developing in another direction.

Then the managers bothered and pestered me some more. They said they would put on Händel's *Rodelinda* if I would come and sing it. You can understand how tempted I was. It is such beautiful music! The part is difficult but unusually fascinating to act and sing. Well, I didn't even dream of resisting

50

The Early Manuscript

the offer. I sang Rodelinda and my husband came to hear me. After the performance he took me aside excitedly and said, "Do you remember what I said to you in Vienna, Kirsten?"

I said, "Yes, that I could never do Isolde."

And he said, "Well, I'm positive now that you can sing Isolde!"

By a strange coincidence less than two weeks later I was invited by the directors of the National Theater in Oslo to do Isolde the following June. My first reaction was a flat refusal. I explained that I needed plenty of time to study the score and see for myself what it was all about. Besides, I was scheduled to sing in *The Creation* of Haydn in Göteborg, and I didn't dare to start learning Isolde as long as I had to keep my voice so light for Haydn. Fourteen days went by with nothing more said about it. Then I accepted, prodded by the thought of a difficult assignment. Exactly six weeks in which to learn Isolde! I wasn't to sing at the first performance. Nanny Larsen-Todsen was scheduled for that, which was billed for early June.

I studied Isolde with Mother. It was to be my first opera in German in public. Mother and I spent two hours daily on it. Of course there were cuts. Still, an immense amount of work remained to be done. I sang with all my lungs and I felt my voice growing bigger every day under the new pressure. My sister and sister-in-law would come in and listen and even act as prompters when I tried to do it all by heart. In the middle of it all we would call a recess and have coffee and cakes and sandwiches. We had a lovely time with Wagner's music, we four, during these little vocal sessions together during the whole of May. They are among my happiest memories away from home.

Mother continually expressed surprise at the way my voice had grown. Incidentally, she had never coached me before in an opera, though she had coached hundreds of others throughout her life. *Tristan und Isolde* was our first opera together, and I owe a great deal to Mother and the sound training I got during those afternoons in May. When I reminded Mother that she had never coached me before, she refused to believe it. It was her idea she had, though when she stopped to think of it she admitted I was right. I had done all my operas by myself. Of course during that Opéra-Comique season she used to accompany at rehearsals. But that was not the same thing as coaching.

Tristan und Isolde was new to all of us. We plunged into it like an exciting adventure. None of us really knew anything about it before we started. How I loved it! I noted down all the difficult German words I didn't understand. With a dictionary I made up a long vocabulary and memorized it perfectly. I've done that with all my Wagnerian operas since. I have always been that way. I make up my mind about what I am supposed to know, write it down, make a careful list, and learn it. In addition to the music of Isolde, I read through all the other parts as well.

All this went on in my new home during my husband's business hours. You can understand why those were such happy days for me, having my mother, my sister, and sister-in-law with me in my new home day after day and knowing that my new marriage had in no way separated me from my own family. My husband and I led a rather simple home life, although we often gave parties. It was a large house, of course, beautifully furnished. Mr. Johansen was widely known, and we both enjoyed having friends around us as often as possible. I had new responsibilities, and don't think it was a simple routine.

Fortunately the servants who had been there for years were quite familiar with things around the house, and that made my job easier. Of course Mr. Johansen had lived for years as a bachelor and the servants had practically run the house. I lent a hand but was not very active. I tried to learn bit by bit. His friends and my friends increasingly became mutual friends. My family came often to visit us. We would sit around and talk. My husband would ask my brother to bring his cello and my younger brother would play the piano. I would sing and my sister would sing with me. Mother sometimes played the organ

The Early Manuscript

for us. Mr. Johansen had had a small organ installed in the large hall. It is quite high. And he planned to install a huge pipe organ there someday.

My daughter and Annie came down from school and resumed their studies in Oslo. We thought it best to have them near us. The boys got married shortly after we did and went on living in Oslo. Mr. Johansen's other daughter traveled a great deal, going to London and Paris. In the beginning I thought them all just a little spoiled, so I was perhaps a bit hard with them. But their father had urged me to look after them and manage them as I saw fit. I did the best I could and they were really very nice and respectful. I saw less of the boys. And then grandchildren began to come.

It was a new life for me, complete and satisfying in every way, and I could very easily have done without the singing. I would have been perfectly happy, happier than I had ever dreamed, if it had all gone on that way. To be perfectly honest, I never really returned to music. It sort of came to me. It found me comfortably settled in my new home and refused to let bygones be bygones. There was that emergency telephone call from Göteborg. That started the ball rolling again. More and more requests followed that. Then I found out how much my husband really liked my public singing. So I slowly slid into it again. And of course the Isolde was quite a personal triumph for me. Such a big role! The biggest I had had up to then, and the sublimest of all. Isolde's music all told takes one hour and thirty minutes of actual singing, and what singing!

53

Chapter Six

AT the time I was singing Isolde for the National Opera the famous Swedish singer Ellen Gulbransen heard a performance. She was married to a Norwegian. Gulbransen had been the Brünnhilde at Bayreuth for eighteen years, up to the world war—an unequaled record. On the night we gave *Tristan und Isolde,* she came to my dressing room and said, "Well, all I can say is that it's a crime your staying here at home and not letting anybody else hear you."

I laughed and she went on. "You should go to Bayreuth, Madame Flagstad."

I didn't take it very seriously. I was positive there wouldn't be any chance for me there and it had never remotely entered my mind. I was quite satisfied singing in Norway. Why struggle? I had work enough to do. There was my family. Why should I strive for something else?

But Gulbransen wasn't satisfied with my explanation. She went ahead on her own and wrote to Winifred Wagner and got back word that if I would come down for an audition she would be glad to see me. So, with trembling knees, I went down to Bayreuth—alone. I had my husband's approval and he had assured me it would be an educational experience, in any event. There was no festival at Bayreuth that year. Well, in July, 1932, I came and sang at the Festspielhaus for Winifred Wagner and

The Early Manuscript

Dr. Heinz Tietjen, the director, who conducted and managed stage business. Dr. Tietjen was the head of everything. Frau Wagner was very nice to me and talked a lot about our mutual friend Ellen Gulbransen. She asked me to come in and see her after the audition.

Three other singers were scheduled for auditions before my turn came. I watched one of them carefully, a tenor. I noticed that he was acting his arias out. That gave me a problem.

"What am I going to do?" I said to myself. "Shall I be bold enough to act or shall I just stand there in one spot with my hands at my sides and sing?"

I decided to take a chance on acting. I chose Isolde's Narrative from the first act of *Tristan* and I started to get busy and wave my arms around. And the trouble started. Professor Kittel, one of the chief coaches there, was accompanying me. He was a very able and wonderful person. We had gone through the music before. There was a cut in the middle of it that I didn't know and we had arranged to leave it out. But of course, when we came to it, he forgot all about the cut and played the part he wasn't supposed to play. So right in the middle of my arm waving, I had to stop and excuse myself and explain to everybody that I didn't know that passage. I felt wretched. I was sure the interruption had made a bad impression on everyone, including Frau Wagner.

Well, when the Narrative was over, I wanted to sing the Liebestod from the last act of *Tristan*, but they said simply, "No, no, that's sufficient!"

"Ah," I repeated to myself, "That's sufficient! Well, I'd better go back to my hotel, pack my trunks and go home to my husband and Norway. That's the end of Bayreuth for me!"

Then I went in to see Frau Wagner, as she had suggested. And I heard a different tune from her. They liked me very much!

"But why was I asked not to sing the Liebestod?"

THE FLAGSTAD MANUSCRIPT

It wasn't necessary. They had heard enough to decide for themselves. So that was it.

"You are the first one I've ever heard use the first-act Narrative from *Tristan* in an audition," Frau Wagner said to me. "Everybody who comes here sings the Liebestod!"

Later I was asked whether I would like to sing at the Festspielhaus for them. I replied I should love to. There was only one difficulty.

"For the next two years we have engaged everybody we need," I was told. "Some smaller roles are still available, but that's all. Of course you have to get into the Wagnerian tradition, which obviously you don't know very much about."

Naturally that was true. Where could I have picked up the Wagnerian tradition?

"You need the polish of language. You need the grand manner and style," they said. "If you will come here and be satisfied with singing a few small roles, you could spend the rest of your time profitably studying the other things—the bigger roles—with Professor Kittel."

I agreed eagerly. It was all too wonderful to turn down.

They engaged me to sing the Third Norn in *Götterdämmerung* and Ortlinde in *Die Walküre*. In addition, I was instructed to have Eva in *Die Meistersinger* and Sieglinde in *Die Walküre* ready as understudy. This was for July and August, 1933. I was told to come early. I was highly excited over it all, and the whole setup down in Bayreuth impressed me deeply. Everything I saw and heard fascinated me and deepened my interest in Wagner and his operas. It was like a new world opening to me. Frau Wagner herself took me around and showed me things, especially the magnificent stage. I drank in the atmosphere greedily. I wanted it to remain with me in Norway as an inspiration.

That same evening I left Bayreuth, having been there only twenty-four hours in all! It was one of the most crowded days in my life, and also one of the most crucial. I hurried home with the good news. My husband was naturally overjoyed to hear of

56

The Early Manuscript

my success and we began to make preparations almost at once.

In August we gave *Tristan* again in Oslo. Alexander Kipnis, later one of my associates at the Metropolitan, was then the King Mark. He had been invited to come up and do that role in Oslo. He was evidently so impressed by my singing that he came to my dressing room to talk to me about it. He spoke to me in German. I was still very shy in that language, though I knew it quite well. I think he got the impression I didn't know German. He even tried English with me, and I knew English fairly well then, but I was even shyer in it than in German. Anyway he was very kind about it all, and later I heard from friends that everywhere he went after that he talked about the Isolde he had heard in Oslo. Mr. Kipnis is responsible for lots of things that happened after that. I met him again the following year in Bayreuth.

After that *Tristan* was out of the way, I set to work on the two roles I was supposed to sing at Bayreuth, as well as the two understudy parts. That year went by. I even started to study the *Siegfried* Brünnhilde. That had been a suggestion of Dr. Tietjen's. His advice was that I study the Brünnhildes by starting with *Siegfried* and finishing with *Götterdämmerung*. Mother and I worked on them together. These operas were also absolutely new to her.

I had sung Isolde in June and July and then did nothing till the middle of August. During that period my voice seemed to grow just by resting. When I sang Isolde again I discovered that it had not only grown but that it responded to my wishes with much more ease. Moreover, it had deepened to a darker color. This had probably come from all that heavy work, studying *Tristan und Isolde* in six weeks, and so forth. There was another result which had me worried for a while. In studying and singing Isolde my back had developed so tremendously from all the heavy breathing that my dresses actually burst apart. They had become too tight for me in the shoulders. Mind you, I had not put on any additional weight. My lungs had expanded so. I could hear the difference, as well as feel it in my back muscles.

THE FLAGSTAD MANUSCRIPT

Of course, all the while I realized that if I could manage the Brünnhildes later I would probably be invited back to Bayreuth every summer. But the thought did not make me any more ambitious. I was never ambitious, really. After my Bayreuth audition Dr. Tietjen had asked me, "Do you want to come to Berlin and the Staatsoper and get into the repertory and sing all these roles?" I had said no. He was astonished and wanted to know my reasons. I said, "Why should I? I'm happily married and I like staying in Oslo."

This takes us to June, 1933. I went down to Bayreuth early that month and started to work and work and work, mostly with Professor Kittel. Then came the stage rehearsals. They were an ordeal. There was a huge rock on the stage for the third act of *Walküre*. We had to run up and down on it. And was that something! We rehearsed every day, again and again, climbing up and down that rock. Besides, I attended all the other rehearsals for my own pleasure and instruction.

Soon I began to feel right at home in it. I was really in love with Wagner from the start. It was a season rich in musical experiences for me, bounded on all sides by the genius of Richard Wagner. I had Wagner day in and day out. Then came the performances and they went marvelously, my two small roles and all. They sharpened my appetite for more. When it was over, I was invited to come back the following year and do Gutrune in *Götterdämmerung* and Sieglinde in *Walküre*. Dr. Tietjen repeated his offer to have me come down to Berlin, adding, "If you can come to Berlin in May next year, I will coach you for Sieglinde."

It was too tempting to resist. I accepted eagerly. Both Mother and Mr. Johansen had come down to hear me in Bayreuth. We had a little celebration there over my debut. My husband seemed happier and prouder than ever over my success. We returned home together and I relapsed into a calm and peaceful home life.

Meanwhile Mr. Kipnis had been talking to the manager of

58

The Early Manuscript

the Brussels opera about me. I received a letter asking me to come down to sing Sieglinde on May 24. I accepted willingly, despite the fact that I had never done Sieglinde before. I remembered Tietjen's kind offer, and decided to pay him a visit in Berlin and take him up on it before going to Brussels. On the strength of that, I accepted the invitation, assuming the company was to be the regular Belgian troupe. Fourteen days before the scheduled performance, I went down to Berlin expecting to coach with Tietjen.

As luck would have it, Dr. Tietjen had either lost interest in me or had too much to do. For one thing he had a Strauss festival on his hands. So, instead of being coached in Sieglinde, I heard lots of Strauss operas—a whole solid week of them! That was early in May. Of course I love Strauss's music and had a terribly good time during the festival. But I didn't see Dr. Tietjen once. I talked with him on the telephone, and he promised repeatedly to find time to see me. But he kept putting me off, and finally I knew there was no hope of last minute coaching with him for the Brussels performance. I was very disappointed. That was to be part of my Bayreuth work, anyway, and he had already shown me things about *Die Walküre* that proved highly useful.

Tietjen or no Tietjen, I went on to Brussels and then made another discovery. The performance was to be given by a visiting German opera company. That put me even more on my mettle. All of my colleagues were to be German and fully in the tradition. They had done *Siegfried* the night before. And Lauritz Melchior had been in that cast, the same Melchior who has been my associate in so many Wagnerian performances in America.

There was a rehearsal of *Die Walküre* that very day. When I came on the stage I was suddenly terror-stricken. I found myself regretting my own daring and promptly forgot everything Sieglinde was supposed to do in the first act. Of course, I knew it well. I wouldn't have gone on at all if I hadn't. But these were

59

THE FLAGSTAD MANUSCRIPT

all seasoned Wagnerian artists around me. I just plain forgot Sieglinde's stage routine. There is really a lot of business to do in that first act when you come to think of it. We hadn't gone far when the man doing the part of Hunding in the opera whispered in my ears, "Listen, how often have you sung Sieglinde, anyway? Something's wrong here. You have either sung it too often or not at all. Which is it?"

I whispered back to him, "I'll tell you after the performance, if you don't mind." I didn't dare tell anyone before the performance that I had never done the role before.

Then came the performance! As I explained before, when I have an audience to sing to and no one to interrupt as at rehearsals, I am complete mistress of myself. The performance went extremely well. I had recovered all my confidence.

When it ended I confided laughingly to the man singing Hunding that it was my first Sieglinde.

"Oh, aren't you the smart one, though!" he said skeptically.

He meant that I was just pretending. After all, I hadn't asked to become a guest. The manager didn't know whether I had ever sung Sieglinde before. He hadn't bothered to ask and I hadn't bothered to tell him. That was my privilege. The reviews were very good, not exceptional, but very good considering all the circumstances.

I met Mr. Melchior for the first time while he was rehearsing *Siegfried*. I had attended the rehearsal, and we were presented to one another by the manager. He was very helpful and encouraging, and as usual in excellent humor. As a matter of fact, Mr. Melchior had been a vivid memory to me from the time I had heard him sing *Tannhäuser* in Oslo in 1919. When we later met on the Metropolitan stage, Mr. Melchior had completely forgotten that we had ever met before. I suppose I was just another Wagnerian singer in that special season of German opera at Brussels. You can't blame a Lauritz Melchior for forgetting an obscure Norwegian soprano who was doing her very first Sieglinde in Brussels.

60

The Early Manuscript

Early in June I went to Bayreuth for my second season. I sang Gutrune and Sieglinde as promised and scheduled. I took part in several stage rehearsals of *Die Walküre*. Everything went smoothly. The experience was very stimulating and I felt a growing maturity as a Wagnerian singer. There was another event in which I participated that was unforgettable. The previous year, on the anniversary of Siegfried Wagner's death, when they always have a special musical evening in the old theater, I had sung some songs by Richard Strauss. This year there was a performance of Beethoven's Ninth Symphony, with Strauss himself conducting. I sang the soprano solo. That was one of the great thrills of my musical career. I wanted so much to meet Strauss. But he came and hurried immediately away before anyone could approach him for an introduction.

The event was memorable, however, for another reason. The old choirmaster—I believe his name was Riedel, though I'm not sure—came to me and said, "I've heard, conducted, and coached the Ninth Symphony more often than I can remember, but never in my life have I had such a soprano soloist!" I'm sure he merely meant to be nice, but it was one of the most beautiful compliments I ever received. Of course, I had had loads of experience in the great choral symphony of Beethoven. I had sung it twenty-five times in my life—this performance was the last.

Chapter Seven

THEN came the first real offer from America. Fritz Reiner wrote asking me to come to Philadelphia to sing three performances of *Tristan und Isolde* in October. He had never heard me, but he professed to be satisfied with reports about me. Unfortunately I couldn't go. Who knows how different my career in America would have been had I accepted? I had already been engaged to sing *Tannhäuser* and *Fidelio* in Göteborg in September and November. I asked Göteborg if they could possibly release me from *Tannhäuser* so I might go to America. They gave me an emphatic "No." It was nothing more than a passing thought, anyway. America was still very remote. But not for much longer!

At the end of the Bayreuth season something else happened that started the Metropolitan ball rolling all over again. An amazing cable from Mr. Simon arrived, asking whether I would be able to sing dramatic roles like Isolde and Brünnhilde during the coming season at the Metropolitan. He warned me to keep quiet about the offer for reasons he couldn't then specify. It had come like a flash of lightning! The first thing I did before answering the cable was to telephone the news to my husband in Oslo, and ask him what I should do.

"That's fine!" he said.

"You really wouldn't mind my going to America?" I asked.

The Early Manuscript

"Why, no," he said. "I'll go with you!"

And I was supposed to have given up singing when I married him! First it was a little singing in the home, then an occasional recital, then the opera in Göteborg again, then Bayreuth and after that Brussels, then more Göteborg, and now the Metropolitan. My prospects of a serene married life without professional cares had vanished forever. I suppose it wasn't my destiny to end my career then. But who could have predicted what lay ahead?

I wrote Mr. Simon I was interested. He wrote back promptly. I was to come down to St. Moritz in Switzerland and sing for Giulio Gatti-Casazza, the Metropolitan's general manager, and his chief conductor, Artur Bodanzky. I must be prepared to sing the three Brünnhildes, besides Isolde and Fidelio. There were just six days in which to get ready! After a last talk with my husband, who gave me great encouragement, I left for St. Moritz the evening following my last Gutrune. In the meantime I had started to study the *Siegfried* Brünnhilde. I didn't know it by heart yet, but I had learned a good deal about Brünnhilde, though practically nothing about the *Götterdämmerung* Brünnhilde. I had only started to study that. I went at once to Professor Kittel and explained my difficulties.

"What shall I do now, Herr Professor?" I asked him.

"Well," he replied, "we can go through the last scene of *Götterdämmerung*."

That's the big Immolation Scene when Brünnhilde dashes into the fire on her horse after a last great outburst over Siegfried's dead body. Professor Kittel wanted me to know it so that at least I could sing it from the score.

As for Isolde, this is really amusing: I hunted all over Bayreuth for a score of *Tristan* and couldn't secure one!

"Don't you keep a single *Tristan* score in Bayreuth?" I asked.

"No, we're not giving *Tristan* this year," they said. It was a bit hard especially since I was supposed to keep it all a secret. Another problem was getting a score of *Fidelio,* which I had only sung in Norwegian in concert form. Of course, I knew it, especially the great aria, but not well enough to sing it in a few days. And no score available at the moment! Finally I got the Liebestod from *Tristan* as a separate piece of music. When I stopped to take inventory, I said to myself, "Well, this looks pretty hopeless, but, come what may, I'll go down to Switzerland. If they don't want me it's all right too."

So I came to St. Moritz. Mr. Simon met me and I reminded him that he had written me several years before. He had no recollection of our correspondence.

"But how did you get hold of my name?" I asked him.

"Alexander Kipnis has been talking about you," he said.

That was the second time Mr. Kipnis' "talking about me" had borne fruit! Then I learned the real reason why I wasn't supposed to say anything about the Metropolitan offer. It seems that Frida Leider wanted to get rid of her Metropolitan contract. She was determined to leave. Gatti-Casazza didn't like to retain people who didn't want to stay. But before releasing her he wanted to be sure the Metropolitan could get someone else to fill the breach. The Viennese soprano Anni Konetzni had already been engaged, but she could not stay beyond the first six weeks. They needed a soprano for the rest of the season. Accordingly Mr. Simon had been scouting around for dramatic sopranos when Kipnis reminded him of me.

One other singer had been invited to that audition in St. Moritz—Elisabeth Delius. The two of us arrived together about six o'clock that day. We had met on the train in a casual way, though we were formally introduced by Mr. Simon himself on our arrival. Mr. Hermann Weigert, who was going to play the piano accompaniments, called at my hotel. He said he wanted to go through the things I intended to sing. I protested.

"Please, not now! I'm so tired. I've been on the train since five o'clock this morning, and it's been a frightfully hot day."

"Just the same you'd better go through it," he insisted.

I didn't have a piano in my room, so we went to his *pension*

The Early Manuscript

and there I had to sing in the salon. People gathered around to listen. I was terribly ill at ease, shy, and dead tired.

Mr. Weigert asked me what I planned to sing.

"I'm asked to sing such and such," I replied, "and to be perfectly honest with you, I don't know it. But I can sing Sieglinde. . . ."

He cut me short. "Nobody wants to hear you in that! Can you sing the Todesverkündigung?"

I said I could but only from the score. I didn't know it by heart.

"Well, let's try it," he said. He played and I shivered away at the score.

Mr. Weigert got more and more annoyed. When that ordeal was over, he said, "Can you sing *Götterdämmerung?*" I replied meekly that I could, but with score. And *Götterdämmerung* went the same way.

"Is there anything at all that you know by heart?" he growled.

"Yes, *Tristan!*"

By then I was annoyed too. After all, they had asked me to come here on terribly short notice and I hadn't had the time to prepare these things. Mr. Weigert already thought the case hopeless, and made no bones about showing it.

"I can sing 'Dich theure Halle,' " I suggested.

He thought it was a good idea, even if they didn't need me for that.

Then he asked, "Do you know 'Ho-jo-to-ho' from *Die Walküre?*" I said I did.

"By heart?"

"Yes."

"Sing it, then!"

He was being so disagreeable, I thought, and I so fatigued! But instead of losing heart I got more and more furious at the way he was treating me. I said to myself, "I'm going to show him!" I let go completely in the Valkyr cry and he nearly fell

THE FLAGSTAD MANUSCRIPT

off his seat. It was quite a triumph for me, and do you know what he said?

"You're going to be engaged right away! Don't doubt it for a moment."

He had changed his tune completely. He looked like a different man. But he was still worried about my not knowing the other selections by heart.

The audition took place the next day at ten in Mr. Gatti's hotel. It was a great big salon with heavy furniture and even heavier drapes, the kind of place in which it is always difficult to sound to good advantage. We had a brief rehearsal with Mr. Weigert. Elisabeth Delius had a gorgeous voice and knew everything in Italian and German, including all the big Wagnerian roles. Beside her I was nothing at all. It didn't worry me because, as I said, I was not ambitious and it didn't matter too much to me whether they liked me or not. While going through the "Dich theure Halle" I noticed a Swiss fifty-centime piece on the floor. I picked it up and said to myself, "This is for luck."

I'm not at all superstitious; still I like to feel that the little coin has brought me good fortune. I had it set in my bracelet later, and treasure it.

Well, Gatti finally came into the room, accompanied by his wife—the former Rosina Galli—Mr. Bodanzky, and Mr. Simon. They were ready for the audition. Mr. Bodanzky asked what I proposed to sing. I said so and so. He didn't want to hear Sieglinde or Elisabeth. He said quite gently, "We don't need you for that, Madame Flagstad. What else do you know?"

"Todesverkündigung," I said. "But I've got to use the score because I don't know the role."

Mr. Bodanzky replied, "That's all right. Go ahead."

That made me feel a lot better. So I sang it. Then he asked me if I knew *Fidelio*. I told him about my trouble getting the score on such short notice. Anyway, I sang the aria as best as I could. Miss Delius also sang the *Fidelio* number and the Todesverkündigung.

The Early Manuscript

Mr. Bodanzky next asked me to do the Narrative from the first act of *Tristan*. I told him again about my failure to find a score in Bayreuth, which seemed to amuse them. I realize it must have sounded like a string of alibis.

"But I can sing the Liebestod," I volunteered.

He said, "Oh, no, everybody can sing the Liebestod."

Then he asked me to sing the Ho-jo-to-ho. And again I let loose in the Valkyr cry.

But Mr. Bodanzky said, "You sang flat. Sing it again."

I sang it again.

"Once more."

I sang it once more.

"That's right," he said simply. Then he got Miss Delius to sing it.

"Now let's hear your Elisabeth," he said, turning to me again.

He seemed to be getting more and more interested. Finally, he asked Miss Delius to sing Brünnhilde's Immolation. She did. Then he asked me to do it.

"But don't sing the whole thing—start towards the end."

By then I was feeling quite happy over the way the audition was going. Gatti appeared to be pleased with me. Mr. Bodanzky, though, looked very serious and forbidding.

With the final scene from *Götterdämmerung* the audition was over. Mrs. Gatti came over and said very nice things to me. They asked us to wait while Mr. Gatti, Mr. Bodanzky, and Mr. Simon went into a conference. We sat down with Mr. Weigert and waited three-quarters of an hour. Elisabeth Delius turned to me like a good sport and said, "They're going to take *you*."

But I wasn't at all sure. I was glad, though, that at least they knew about me now. Mr. Gatti and Mr. Bodanzky rejoined us. Mr. Gatti looked at me and exclaimed cordially, *"Auf Wiedersehn!"* That was all. I said to myself, "What does that mean, I wonder?"

We went into the street and stopped in a nearby restaurant for lunch—Mr. Simon, Miss Delius, and myself. She had worn

67

THE FLAGSTAD MANUSCRIPT

an evening dress for the great occasion, while I had on a simple dress with jacket. When we reached the restaurant, she said, "I'm going to my hotel to change into another dress. Will you wait?"

I said, "Of course."

After she left, Mr. Simon opened up. "Well, now I can tell you something. You're engaged by the Metropolitan. You'll get a contract within fourteen days."

When Miss Delius returned to the restaurant and we began to have lunch, she said with a courageous smile, "Well, Mr. Simon, I'll tell you what's happened before you tell me. They've engaged Madame Flagstad. Isn't that so?"

Mr. Simon said it was and added, "They liked you very much, too, but—well, you know it yourself—you are much too heavy. You don't mind my being frank, do you? You'd have to take off something like thirty pounds before you came to the Metropolitan."

She was one of those persons with very short necks, packed thick. She didn't seem to mind at all and was very sweet about everything. I felt badly about it. I tried to convey it to her but she laughed it off, saying, "Why should anyone feel that way when I don't really?"

She was one of the best losers I've ever met. It was really a joy knowing her and watching her take her defeat with such fine sportsmanship.

I was surprised to see Bodanzky later that afternoon. I came a little late, and found him playing cards. He looked up and said, "Don't you go and get fat now. Learn those roles. Find yourself a good coach and learn them as fast as you can. Then come to America. The quicker the better."

I told him I had an engagement up to the end of December and could be at the Metropolitan early in January, not sooner. He asked me what and where I was going to sing. I said *Tannhäuser* and *Fidelio* in Göteborg. He thought it was good that I

68

The Early Manuscript

was to sing *Fidelio,* but he urged me to study it in German immediately after.

"Do you suppose you can find time to go to Prague and study these things with Professor Szell?" he asked. I told him I'd try.

Later I cabled home to my husband. I still wasn't allowed to say anything about the engagement. They were afraid that if Frida Leider knew they had found someone to replace her she might change her mind. She wasn't released yet. I went back to Norway as fast as I could and didn't confide my secret to anyone but my husband till the day the contract arrived, which was just two weeks later, as Mr. Simon had said. I let the Norwegian papers have the story. And of course they thought it a great honor for me. My husband telephoned my mother.

"Come over at once—we've got a big surprise for you!"

Mother came as fast as she could. I don't know what she expected to be told.

"You're the first one to know, Mother," said my husband, and he broke the news. My mother was overjoyed to the point of tears.

I set instantly to work. First, of course, there were the performances in Göteborg. For the second time I tried to get released from my contract.

"I've done you so many services before," I pleaded. "You can do me this one favor in return. I need the time badly for these roles. Every day counts." All they said was, "Oh, you can do it, anyway. We know your ability." They refused to release me.

Preparing those Metropolitan roles was something. I had to use every available moment. I traveled around with my husband on long trips in his car. While he drove I would take my Wagnerian score out and sing the whole opera through. I found it a very good way to study. He was very patient and considerate about it and pretended to like every note of it. I just had to master those roles; that is, the three Brünnhildes, Isolde (with-

69

THE FLAGSTAD MANUSCRIPT

out cuts), and Elsa, and later Fidelio (after the Göteborg season) and even the Marschallin in *Der Rosenkavalier*. During the Göteborg season a conductor in the company gave me some help.

In the midst of the Göteborg engagement I went to Prague for ten days and studied intensively with Professor Szell, who was very severe with me. Not a single complimentary word until the very last day. Then he remarked, "I'm going to write to Mr. Bodanzky and say that he doesn't have to worry about your not knowing the roles in time."

But how stern and harsh he was with me during those ten days! He would get so irritated over the most trivial mistake. I got quite scared at times. We spent one hour a day together on my Metropolitan roles. In-between I stayed in my hotel room and put in as many hours of study as I could possibly stand without collapsing. When I could I went to the German opera in Prague, where he directed. I've since sung with Professor Szell in Prague—one *Tristan*. I didn't hear any Wagner while I was studying with him, but I did take in *Les Huguenots, Don Carlos,* and *Fidelio*. I heard Hilde Konetzni in *Don Carlos* and Rose Pauly in that opera and in *Fidelio*.

When the ten days were over I returned to Göteborg. I sang four *Fidelios* a week. In-between I worked either on the Brünn-hildes or Isolde. Every moment was jammed with work and study. What terribly hard work it was! You can imagine how I used my voice! I felt it growing stronger and larger under constant pressure. I gained quite a lot from singing *Fidelio*. What a score that is! A perfect artistic holiday for singers, musicians, and . conductors. Nothing surpasses *Fidelio* in music, nothing! It is pure and human all the way through and it brings out the best in the sincere artist. It was quite a contrast going from a *Fidelio* performance at the opera to my Wagnerian studies at home. They are two completely different ways of singing. Meanwhile Mr. Simon arranged a broadcast for me in Copenhagen. I went and sang some arias and enjoyed doing it.

The Early Manuscript

I had already done a little broadcasting, nothing much really, in Oslo. The Copenhagen appearance was my first big broadcast, and it helped prepare me for my radio work in America.

We come now to the end of December, 1934, when I left with my husband for America.

Chapter Eight

WE sailed on a Swedish boat and arrived on January 8th. We had a whole week of terrific fog before we arrived. Boats were idle for days. We lay in quarantine for thirty-six hours. Suddenly late one afternoon we started to move again. The fog lifted for a few moments and a great shout went up on all sides. There before us, like a scene in *The Arabian Nights,* was Manhattan, all lighted up! The fog was like a curtain that had gone up on an opera scene. I was never so impressed in my life. That sight of Manhattan rising through the mist, with all those lights glimmering, was overwhelming. I had read about it and seen pictures of it. But they were nothing beside the real thing. Then the fog closed over it again. But the curtain had gone up, you might say, on my New York debut.

My first thought was to see Gatti-Casazza and find out just what my duties were to be. I also wanted to see Edward Ziegler and naturally Mr. Bodanzky too. My husband and I went to the opera house together. We gathered there in Mr. Gatti's office about lunch time the day after we arrived. Of course I didn't dare speak English. I merely said yes and no, although I followed the English conversation easily enough. I used some German phrases where I could. I discovered I was four weeks early. Mr. Bodanzky said I was to start working with Mr. Weigert, who had been the audition accompanist at St. Moritz. I was

72

The Early Manuscript

entrusted to his care for Wagnerian coaching. Mr. Bodanzky also asked me to be ready to take part in an orchestral rehearsal of *Götterdämmerung* on January 15th. He requested me to be made up and in costume. I was the only one in the cast who had not previously sung in the opera. Since they had never seen me on the stage before, naturally they had no idea what I looked like in dress make-up.

Well, I spent that week studying. There was time for little else. Sight-seeing was out of the question. Then came the rehearsal. Paul Althouse was the Siegfried. It must have gone well because the men in the orchestra applauded me. Mr. Bodanzky himself stood up and shouted, "Brava, Flagstad!"

We had to sing the duet three times. During the second going over Mr. Bodanzky left the pit, turned the baton over to Karl Riedel, and went and sat in the rear of the house to hear how I sounded from there. At that time I took the high C's regularly. The orchestra stood up and cheered me. I was thrilled. And so was my husband, who was seated in the orchestra. As the singing went on I noticed that more and more people kept slipping into the auditorium.

That was the beginning. They had begun to recognize me. Mr. Bodanzky said to me later when we had become good friends, "I knew you had a good voice but I never expected anything like this."

He told me the others felt the same way. Mr. Bodanzky suggested that I start with Sieglinde in *Die Walküre*. The *Götterdämmerung* rehearsal had been for a much later performance. You see, some singer, even if she isn't the specific one cast for the role, has to sing at the rehearsal to make it complete, so they used that particular one to try me out. The part was Gertrude Kappel's but they gave me the rehearsal. She didn't need rehearsing, anyway. It was all part of an opera house's routine. The *Götterdämmerung* rehearsal occurred on the fifteenth of January.

I was told that Mrs. Pierpont Morgan Hamilton—later to

THE FLAGSTAD MANUSCRIPT

become my good friend Becky—was among those sitting in on that rehearsal. Well, a day or two later my husband and I attended an evening performance at the opera. We were standing apart in one of the lobbies, quite alone, knowing no one, naturally. I had been so busy working that I hadn't even had a chance to meet anyone. Mrs. Hamilton came over to where we were standing, and said rather hesitantly, "Aren't you the lady who sang in the *Götterdämmerung* rehearsal?"

I said I was, still very shy about my English. She was very gracious. I soon had the pleasure of knowing her well. She has been a most faithful admirer and, I discovered, quite a remarkable musician. Mrs. Hamilton had heard my Gutrune in Bayreuth and put a cross after my name in the program book.

Then came my debut on February 2nd as Sieglinde. It was a Saturday afternoon and the opera was broadcast. Although I had had no rehearsal, I wasn't a bit nervous. The moment I faced the audience I felt all the stimulus I needed and everything went smoothly. Once on the stage it made no difference to me whether it was Oslo, Brussels, or the Metropolitan. People are the same everywhere and they come to the opera to be moved. That's all the incentive I need. And oh, the crowd that came to see me afterward! Of course such things had happened to me before, but never on such a scale. What a demonstration! People rushed to the dressing room. There were flowers and photographers and more flowers.

I hadn't even dreamed that anything like that could happen to me. I had been used to success of a kind and somehow I always knew I would make out all right in America. But not this. I never hoped or expected to become famous. And the critics were all so very kind to me. There again, I was used to getting good notices, so that wasn't so much of a surprise really. But the general reaction swept me off my feet. There had never been anything like it for me. I was terribly happy about it all, of course. Standing on one of the greatest stages in the world—

74

The Early Manuscript

actually singing a leading role in the Metropolitan Opera House —that was the real thrill.

At first I hadn't regarded it as such an astonishing thing, that is, my being there at all. Maybe that's why I wasn't the least bit nervous. But what happened really overwhelmed me. Then came the *Tristan* performance on February 6th. I believe that really made me here. It confirmed the first impression. After that I felt the American public and I understood one another.

There was another pleasant moment during the intermission of the *Walküre* performance. Milton Cross had said beautiful things about me on the radio. And Geraldine Farrar, who took part in the intermission program, also talked sweetly about me to the radio audience. That was new to me because I wasn't used to radio as a vehicle for personal compliment. I added up all these experiences and I saw what it meant to be a success at the Metropolitan. I would probably have been a great deal more excited before my first Sieglinde had I suspected what it would be like. Naturally my husband was there in the house when I sang. I think he was satisfied. He is fearfully nervous when I sing. He told me frankly how scared to death he was that afternoon I made my debut. I don't remember what he said when it was over. But I'm sure it was nice. I'm sure he was proud of me. I remember the look on his face. That told me everything.

My next role was the *Walküre* Brünnhilde, again without rehearsal. You can imagine how difficult it was. I was studying and studying in-between, always studying and working with Mr. Weigert. He was just too wonderful for words, so patient and thorough. I had never done Brünnhilde, though I had been working on the role for some time. I had been coached a little by Mr. Wymetal, the stage manager, but only in a general way. When I found time we worked together on stage business, but that wasn't very often. Well, it went somehow and again the public and critics liked me.

Right after that Brünnhilde I suffered an attack of laryngitis and was obliged to cancel a couple of *Tristans*. The attack also prevented me from singing the *Siegfried* Brünnhilde. I could scarcely talk, let alone sing. I was terribly unhappy over it. And worst of all, I lost a good part of my hearing from that laryngitis. The effect on my hearing lasted two full years! For a long while after the attack I couldn't even hear the orchestra. I had an awful time. I tried to cover myself up as best I could. I ruined my nerves doing it. I managed somehow, but it was simply horrible. Luckily, I have perfect pitch. If I hadn't, I could never have done it.

And remember, sick as I was, I still had to sing *Götterdämmerung.* I had been in bed all the time. My husband had to sail the evening before. Just before he left he said to me, "I'm glad I'm going now because I couldn't live through your *Götterdämmerung* tomorrow." He was positive something was going to happen. He knew what my illness had done to me. But then he was always that way, scared about every note I took. We had a stage rehearsal the evening before. During the rehearsal one of my ears went "click" and opened. I could hear! I was overjoyed, but not for long, alas! The next day something in the ear closed again.

Well, bad hearing or not, I sang the *Götterdämmerung* Brünnhilde. I heard miserably. I came out after the first scene and had no idea what I had been singing. I asked my colleagues how badly I sounded. They and Bodanzky knew about it. Everybody was so sympathetic and co-operative. It was really a miracle how I did it. Then I was asked to sing Elsa in *Lohengrin,* which I did for the first time at the Academy of Music in Brooklyn on March 5th. I had already sung it in Norwegian six years earlier, as you know. Of course I had to relearn it in German, but that was becoming a habit, so it didn't bother me much. I had sung it in all about seven or eight times, so I knew my way around in it.

Then I sang *Tristan* and *Walküre* again, and after that came Elisabeth in *Tannhäuser,* on March 15th. Then Kundry in *Parsifal,* which I learned in eleven days. They had come to

Tosca in Göteborg (1929).

Desdemona in *Otello* (1929).

Aida (Göteborg, 1930).

Elisabeth in *Tannhäuser*
(Göteborg, 1934).

The Early Manuscript

ask me about it, if I could possibly accomplish it in time. All I said was, "I don't know. Ask Mr. Weigert. He's the only one who knows."

They did and Mr. Weigert thought it possible, yes even in eleven days! Remember I had all my other work to do. On April 17th I did my first Kundry and everybody was again very kind about it. I could never have done it if they all hadn't been so confident that I could.

How did I feel about it all, singing this sublime music? How did it affect me? It's hard to say. In the beginning it was mostly rehearsals and more and more things to study and remember and do. I lived between studying and singing at the Metropolitan. I was only happy that I was able to go through the roles. Perhaps I never had time to stop to think just what they meant to me, that is, how they satisfied my need for expression. They were a job to do and I did it, as I always had. I couldn't feel anything personal about them under that increasing pressure of work and study. The true feeling of artistic satisfaction came later, when I was sure of the roles and they had in a way become part of me.

Sometimes the critics wrote that I was too static on the stage. That was merely my habit of listening to what the others were singing. I like to know a whole opera if I can. I had studied my own roles, that's all there was time for, but not the others. I tried to make up for it during actual performances. I distinctly recall in *Walküre* when Schorr began Wotan's long narrative how I listened and learned new things each time. I must have appeared silly and stiff to some people. I really discovered Wagner during my first years at the Metropolitan. My previous experience had been purely rudimentary. As I said, I used up all my time studying my own parts during my first year. I knew what the operas were about, of course, but I didn't know then every word and tone in them, as I do now. After all, I couldn't take in everything. There is so much, really! But there was tremendous satisfaction in it all. My personal life at this time was

77

THE FLAGSTAD MANUSCRIPT

work and work and work and nothing else. I made a few friends whom I saw quite a lot, chiefly Norwegians.

Then came my first real American broadcast on April 21st. That deserves to be mentioned. Of course, I had already been on the air for my debut, but this was the real thing, you might say. It was in Detroit. I was accompanied there by a lady from NBC. The first thing she asked me was what dress I was going to wear.

"To what?" I asked.

"Why to the broadcast, of course."

"Oh, any dress will do for that, won't it?" I said.

She looked dumbfounded.

"I'm afraid you'll have to wear an evening dress," she said.

"But why?"

Then I found out. It was perfectly simple, but perfectly incredible to me. There was to be a visible audience of four thousand people! That was a shock. I don't like audiences at broadcasts and I have never become quite used to the American practice. I like to sing either to a seen audience or into a microphone, but not both. At a broadcast you must really divide yourself. And it doesn't help being self-conscious. It confused me horribly at first. The whole thing was spoiled for me by the presence of all those people. If only they could eliminate studio audiences! How much easier it would be! The audience ruined it for me both ways, as artist and as listener. When I broadcast, I don't need the stimulus of applause, and when I listen I am annoyed by the applause.

I should like to tell one thing more about that broadcast in Detroit. Mr. Knudsen of General Motors had asked NBC if I could see him and his family afterward. NBC already knew that I didn't like social events of any kind and left it entirely up to me. My train was to leave for New York one hour after the broadcast. I told them it wouldn't be possible to see Mr. Knudsen and his family after the broadcast because there wouldn't be time. Besides, I didn't like the idea. I wanted peace

78

The Early Manuscript

and quiet after the broadcast. Every artist deserves to be left alone after a performance. They insisted things would be so arranged that I would reach the train in time. Finally, I agreed.

When the broadcast was over I came down to the big reception hall. Tables were loaded with sandwiches and drinks. Before I knew what was happening, I was shaking the hands of about two hundred people! That was Mr. Knudsen's "family." Nobody gave me a thought except to shake my hand. What did impress me terribly was that Mr. Knudsen actually got the train to wait forty minutes for me! Forty minutes delay so that I could shake two hundred hands. It was unbelievable. A policeman on a motorcycle escorted us at high speed to the train, with the siren screaming through the streets. My, that was thrilling!

We arrived at the station. Hundreds of people seemed to be waiting for us. "Have you really been waiting only for me?" I asked breathlessly. They assured me they had, and looked at me as if I were someone important. But you can be sure the train was not held up for me exactly. It was only Mr. Knudsen's influence and General Motors that did it.

My concert work began to assume more importance as time went on. Edwin McArthur had written me after my debut, offering his services as concert accompanist. I hadn't been thinking of concerts or anything of the sort and referred the matter to NBC. Later when recital arrangements were being discussed, I asked NBC whether Mr. McArthur was considered good. They said he was very good, but that there were many other first-rate accompanists. Mr. McArthur came to see me and played some accompaniments. He was quite young, still in his twenties, and extremely alert. It had been decided that I should give some concerts the coming fall, and my desire was to include several Norwegian songs. Mr. McArthur played some of this music for me. I was deeply impressed. He seemed to know everything about it, and that more than anything else won me over right at the start. There was a second consideration. Being as tall as

79

he was, I thought I wouldn't look so big beside him on the stage. Mr. McArthur is over six feet. I didn't want an accompanist who would make me look like a giantess.

Since then Mr. McArthur and his charming wife have become my close friends. I consult with them both on most of my business affairs, and they have been very considerate and helpful. Mr. McArthur has given me sound advice about America and American customs. My husband was extremely fond of both of them and always felt I was being left in excellent hands whenever he was forced to return to Norway alone. Mrs. McArthur has been a practical and sympathetic companion. I don't know what I would have done without her.

To get back to my recital plans. I was told I would have to prepare four different concert programs for the coming season. Mr. McArthur made many good program suggestions and showed me lots of good American songs that he thought should be included. I have always liked American songs and done my best to do them justice through a fair selection for my programs.

Well, I took all that material home to Norway with me and worked out four full concert programs. I can't tell you how I worked on those programs. And I thought I was going home to a vacation and rest! It was much harder than I had suspected. I had been overconfident about the material. I soon discovered that while I knew my Schubert, Schumann, and Brahms, I didn't know them by heart, which naturally was necessary. I thought it would be so easy to do so many of the songs I had known and sung all my life. But I found out that without the music before me, I knew next to nothing about them. Moreover, I had done only a few concerts in my life, so I knew precious little about concert style, tradition, and routine. Of course I had made many appearances with orchestra. But that's something else.

That summer I was supposed to sing in South America, but, do you know, I had to cancel it. My nerves were so shattered from overwork. I was never so tired in my life. It took me two

The Early Manuscript

months to recover. If people so much as talked to me I would burst into tears. Having a nervous heart besides, it affected me doubly. It wasn't a very happy summer.

I should like to say a word about my return to Oslo. That was really a great triumph for me. Everybody seemed so proud of me and made a lot of fuss about my success in America. Some friends arranged a big dinner for me. There were lovely speeches and all that. The following morning a messenger arrived from the King with my first decoration and a request that I wear it. Naturally the papers carried stories about me. There were interviews and pictures. Everyone made me feel like a Norwegian heroine returning from some great adventure overseas. For a while I traveled through England and Belgium with my husband. He had business to attend to in both countries and I went along with him. Then we came back to Oslo and I buried myself in those four concert programs.

There are a few more things I should like to say about that first season at the Metropolitan. Everyone I met and associated with was thoughtful and co-operative. From Mr. Gatti to the members of the chorus they all made me feel at home and did their best to help me out. The prompter was extremely patient and helpful. After all, I didn't exactly know those new parts when I first sang them. My colleagues aided me wherever and whenever they could. And Mr. Bodanzky himself—well, I can never say enough about him and what he meant to me. It was a terrible loss when he died.

Gatti-Casazza, the little I saw of him, was charming and encouraging at all times. *Parsifal* was his very last performance as Metropolitan impresario before he retired and returned to Italy. I remember he came to my dressing room and said nice things to me. He gave me a silver-framed picture of himself and seemed highly satisfied with all that had happened since that first meeting in his hotel at St. Moritz. He gave an interview to reporters when he left. If you remember, he was quoted as saying, "I have given America two great gifts—Caruso and Flagstad."

THE FLAGSTAD MANUSCRIPT

No greater praise has ever been given me, even though I know Gatti was just being kind. Another flattering compliment paid me in America I shall never forget. At a flower show held in the Grand Central Palace a flower was named after me. I was asked to attend the ceremonies and I was thoroughly delighted. My flower belongs to the Amaryllis family. I keep it at home and watch it religiously. Every April it bursts into bloom. But, alas, I am so rarely home in April!

In the meantime I had signed a contract for the following year with Herbert Witherspoon, who followed Gatti as general manager of the Metropolitan Opera Company. Mr. Witherspoon died suddenly of a heart attack and Edward Johnson, who had been so fine an artist on the Metropolitan stage, succeeded him as director. Mr. Johnson sent me a telegram immediately after Mr. Witherspoon's death proposing that I sing *Norma* the following season. Well, I got myself Bellini's score and tried ever so hard. There are lots of recitatives in *Norma*. Not knowing Italian, I didn't find it so easy. I translated the Italian words from the German version given in the text.

The role of Norma is nearly as large as Isolde. It means a terrific amount of work. But that wasn't my problem. I felt I couldn't master Italian in time for the performances. I worked hard and faithfully at the role. I loved it so. Bellini's music has such a rare purity. When I returned the following season I sang it for them as a test. I asked them to be sole judges whether I could sing it or not. I didn't want to trust myself. The judges were Mr. Johnson, Ettore Panizza (the conductor), and the assistant manager, Edward Ziegler. They professed to like my Norma very much, but they all agreed I needed to get deeper into the Italian style.

Mr. Dellera was called in to go through the whole part with me. We did so one day for three hours. I am sorry to say I lost all interest after *that* session. All sorts of things were asked of me in preparing the role. First, there were to be cuts and transpositions. I should have a cry in my voice here, and I should

The Early Manuscript

glide up and down there. Nothing of the sort was in the score. Everything was to be changed.

So I said to Edwin when Dellera left, "If only they'd ask me to sing Italian opera the way Elisabeth Rethberg does. She sings it clean and the way it is written in the score. I'm absolutely against the way they want me to do *Norma*."

What with one thing and another, chiefly my distaste for tampering with a composer's intentions, I lost interest in *Norma*. I discussed it later with Mr. Johnson when I came back from my concert tour. I emphasized that I couldn't do Bellini's *Norma* the way I was being told to. It went completely against my temperament. I said I would have liked doing it the right way. He agreed. On the whole, I think it was wise of me not to get mixed up in Italian opera. It was better to remain exclusively in the German wing. I really don't miss doing a lot of operas. *Musical America* once asked me a question. "Which non-Wagnerian role would you like to sing if you were given your choice?" I couldn't answer. Wagner was sufficient for me.

I came back to America on September 26th, this time with my daughter. I plunged immediately into concert work and found myself enjoying it more and more each concert I gave. At the beginning the critics didn't like me very much. I didn't sing German *Lieder* the way they were used to. I didn't have warmth. I lacked style. I went on studying harder and harder. Since then they have found more to praise. Now they even say beautiful things about my concert work.

Then there was the traveling and traveling. Concerts after concerts. And gradually I found myself discovering musical America. Somehow living in Europe and listening to people speak contemptuously of musical taste in America, you never get the true picture. Why, America was far ahead of Europe in many ways! It astonished me to find how many people went to civic concerts and lectures and how many took all kinds of music courses. Thousands and thousands of people came to my

THE FLAGSTAD MANUSCRIPT

concerts, even in the small cities. This was by no means true of Europe, not on this scale!

And then I made another pleasant discoveiy. Americans were not smug in their tastes. They liked unusual things. I learned the meaning of the word "unhackneyed." I remember I wrote it down and thought it such a funny word. These people actually liked "unhackneyed" things. For instance, they liked "unhackneyed" Norwegian songs. Of course, everybody knows and loves Grieg's "A Dream," "The Swan," and "I Love You." But when I came to sing a less familiar song like Grieg's "Water Lily," I was amazed to see that they liked it better than any other song I sang! "Water Lily" was requested more than anything else I sang as an encore.

That made me bolder in arranging my programs. It's the greatest stimulus to a singer to have her public take so readily to unfamiliar things. I started to add more and more lesser known songs to my programs. In my last program in Carnegie Hall, which I repeated in Washington, Boston, and Chicago, I let my own pleasure decide for me in the choice of songs. How they were received! It was simply amazing. And the unfamiliar songs of Hugo Wolf and Brahms that I sing—it is the same story again. As I said, Americans are very responsive to unfamiliar things and are eager to learn new things rather than hear the "hackneyed" things over and over again.

That has been one of my most agreeable experiences here: how appreciative you all are of good music, whether you've heard it before or not, and how well you are trained in the schools. I felt ashamed when I thought of the way things were done at home. We in Europe had supposed we were the last word in culture. And then to discover that it wasn't true at all, but that here in America people were really showing the way. That was a great thought to carry back with me to Norway.

My first season in San Francisco came at that time, followed by my second season at the Metropolitan, where I had to learn and learn and learn and work and work and work all the time.

84

The Early Manuscript

That was a difficult season! I was tired. My bones ached so! I couldn't understand how my voice endured all that punishment. I still didn't hear very well. My family doctor in Norway had warned me about overworking, fearing I might lose my hearing entirely. But I couldn't help it. The job had to be done! And I had my pride! I went on working and overworking, and I have been at it since. And the strangest thing of all is this: my hearing, instead of getting worse, actually got better. That's another argument in favor of hard work!

There is only one practice in America I have not been able to get used to. I know that what has happened to me here could never have happened in any other country. But you show your appreciation in a very different way from what I was used to there. You make a kind of public property of your celebrities. What was terribly hard on a person of my quiet habits was the difficulty of having any private life of my own. It was all right to have so-called "fans" and admirers. But when your admirers wouldn't leave you alone and demanded to see you and shake your hand, I think it was overdoing it.

I dared not leave my New York apartment. I lived practically guarded against intruders. Everything was looked after. I hardly dared go shopping or so much as take a walk on the streets of New York. Only the movies were perfectly safe. There it was dark and no one recognized you and hurried over to shake your hand. I dreaded going to the opera. People saw me and felt compelled to come over and talk to me. I knew everyone meant well. That was just the tragedy of it. But did they stop to consider the ordeal for me? Strange ladies came up to me for autographs or told me their whole life stories. It was all very difficult, being spotted in crowded places and, as you say, lionized.

That is why I wanted to give up several times. I got so worn out. I felt as if I were haunted. I knew there were artists who liked it and couldn't live without it. I found it awful.

85

THE FLAGSTAD MANUSCRIPT

I wish people would understand. Let me tell you a story. Not long ago I rode up on the elevator of my hotel. Charlie Chaplin entered it on one floor. As much as I wanted to look at him, I turned my back. I respected his privacy.

That's the way I'd like to be treated.

PART TWO *The Later Manuscript*

Chapter Nine

HIS second part of my story will be both simpler and more complicated than the first, and also more painful to me as a person, as a woman, and as a wife. To do it right I must begin in the year 1940. I had definitely made up my mind to retire from opera, but to do so by degrees. My plan was, first, to give up singing opera in America, and, then, gradually, to give it up altogether.

Of course, people always refused to take me seriously when I announced my intention to retire. They tease me now about how I had made up my mind to sing that one season at the Metropolitan in 1950–51, declared so publicly, and then changed my mind. The truth is I am womanly enough, weak enough, to yield to the insistence of friends, and human enough to be swayed by a public that will not let me go. But I have always wanted to retire. I have always wanted to go home and lead a quiet life, surrounded by my family, a few friends, and a little private music. Those were my feelings in 1940.

There was something more. I honestly thought I had given so much of my time and so much of my art, used my talents as best I could, that I was sure the good Lord Himself would have agreed I had earned a rest—a long rest. I had a feeling that I had done all that could be asked of a person of ability, however modest that ability might be. And modesty aside, I frankly be-

THE FLAGSTAD MANUSCRIPT

lieved I had accomplished in a short space what it had taken others twice the time to accomplish. And I had sung all the roles I wanted to sing. There was no desire and very little incentive to move on to new things. I was convinced I had had enough.

Besides, I was tired. I was suffering from a form of anemia which my doctor assured me was largely due to overwork. The strain had also given me a prolonged siege of insomnia.

In every sense, physical, psychological and spiritual, I needed a complete change. I was exhausted to the verge of hysteria. The more exhausted and ill I became the more I knew that home and husband and children were the only cure. I will admit this, however: I wanted to do a little more singing in Europe before I withdrew entirely from opera. I had done comparatively little work there, other than in Sweden and Norway. I felt, too, that Europe would be less fatiguing than America to an artist like myself. Now that I have divided my seasons between Europe and America, I know that to be a fact.

Working and living in America takes twice as much out of a public entertainer. I believe it has something to do with people wanting you too much, occupying your time; and I mean both the fans and the friends. So very much is asked of you that in the end you never have any time for yourself. Now, I love my American friends and am proud of their love and friendship for me. One result was that I had a bad conscience about them —because I am not able to be with them, to accept and return their hospitality, as I would have wished. The demands on you are so great in America, that is, when you are working hard and almost without interruption. Then there are the telephone calls! If only I could somehow have made all these wonderful friends and admirers understand that after I had been with them in the beautiful harmony of the concert hall or opera house I needed desperately to be left to myself. In Europe they are less exacting. They may worship their favorite artist—but

90

The Later Manuscript

from a distance which allows the artist a restful margin of privacy.

I was tired too of all the things that go with fame: the publicity, the newspapers, the photographers, the pressure of fans. What a blessing it would be, I thought, to escape this once and for all, in exchange for the quiet of home.

So, in 1940, to all intents and purposes, I was already saying good-by to America. I did not sign any further contracts. I had all my Metropolitan costumes, wigs, everything belonging to me, packed, together with my books and pictures, in a huge crate to take back to Europe with me. I had absolutely no intention of ever coming back to America—certainly not to sing opera. Whatever I possessed here was going back with me to Norway, to my home.

I had still another reason, selfish, perhaps, but again very human. My daughter Else was returning to Norway with me. Now, Else had already fallen in love with an American boy named Arthur Dusenberry, and being a determined person like her mother, she made it very clear to me that it would be useless to try to discourage her.

"Come home with me, Else," I said to her, "you'll have plenty of time to think it over and decide later."

"I'll do that, Mamma," she said, "if you promise to let me come back to Arthur."

There was nothing I could do but give my word. I saw that she knew what she wanted and frankly I admired her taste. I had met Arthur, a manly, clean-cut, and hard-working American boy, and I liked him. Still, I had always hoped that Else would marry a Norwegian. In my mind was this secret thought that once Else was back in Norway with me, she might forget Arthur, meet a fine Norwegian lad, marry him, and remain with me in our country. I must admit that hope wasn't too strong in me. I knew Else was determined to marry Arthur, but I didn't realize how determined she was till she announced to me that she would spend her one year in Norway in a housekeeping school. My daughter's ambition, as it had been mine, was to be a good wife and nothing more. She never showed any inclination toward an artistic career, and I must confess I was extremely happy that she didn't.

So Else and I were all set to leave America on April 20, 1940. We had booked passage on a Norwegian ship, the *Bergensfjord*. Everything was packed and ready to go. I was definitely leaving America—I thought for good, and I hoped the same thing for Else. . . .

It was now the evening of April 8th. I was on a train bound for Cleveland with the Metropolitan cast of *Tannhäuser*. Sitting with me in my compartment were Lauritz Melchior and his wife "Kleinchen" and Herbert Janssen and his wife. The conversation had turned to my approaching departure for Norway and home. They had all known of my plan for some time.

"But why must you go back to Europe just now?" asked Mr. Janssen.

"Because Norway is my home," I said, "and I'm homesick."

Mr. Melchior turned to me.

"Kirsten, there's one thing you may not realize. At any moment now the Germans may occupy your country as well as mine."

I remember how that stunned me. For some reason I had never even thought of such a possibility; perhaps I had been working too hard, perhaps the thought of retiring had become so strong it overshadowed everything else that was happening in the world. I don't know. I do know that when Melchior said that it shocked me to realize that perhaps he was right. Whether it was wishful thinking or not, I tried not to take Melchior's prophecy too seriously.

"Well," I replied. "I'm going home no matter what happens. I'm through in this country. I want to quit as a singer here and give whatever singing I do from now on to Europe. Then I want to retire for good and become a plain ordinary housewife again, which is what I should have remained."

The Later Manuscript

That was the very first time I had heard anyone so much as hint that my country was in danger of invasion. And how strange that I should hear Mr. Melchior say what he did on the very eve of the occupation of his country and mine. I didn't like what was happening in Europe. I was bewildered and heart-broken by the news that reached us here, and I suppose like so many other people I felt it could not continue—that it had to end soon with the return of peace and tranquillity. I suppose much of my ignorance came from the fact that neither my country nor the America that had been so good to me was as yet involved in the conflict.

The following morning, there was a knock on the door of my compartment. It was Melchior. The train had stopped before we reached Cleveland and he had already purchased a morning newspaper.

"I have something to tell you, Kirsten," he said, "something very painful. Denmark and Norway are at war with Germany."

I shall probably be accused of cold selfishness when I confess what my very first thought was on hearing that dreadful news. Maybe it was wrong, and maybe it was only human. It was a thought that remained with me amid all the emotional turmoil of that day. It was simply this: *I might not be able to go home now! The Germans would prevent me!* I realize that at that moment I should have thought of what was happening to my poor country. My feelings as a Norwegian should have silenced my feelings as a homesick wanderer and wife. I *know* that should have been my first reaction. But I want to be truthful about it. All I could think of that day was, "You can't go home now!"

As we left the train at the station outside Cleveland, I saw that Kerstin Thorborg and her husband were crying. Both were Swedes. Their country wasn't affected, yet they wept—wept because they felt so strongly for Melchior and me. That entire day they stayed with me at the hotel. I never cried, not the way they did; my eyes were full of tears, but somehow they didn't flow over. Knowing that I was scheduled to sing *Tannhäuser* that

THE FLAGSTAD MANUSCRIPT

night, friends from all over America called me on the telephone. I was deeply touched to know that their thoughts were with me on this dark day in my country's history. My daughter Else telephoned to ask if I knew anything more than she did.

"But, Else," I said, "I don't know anything."

I did know something: that I had to sing Elisabeth in that evening's performance, but how I was going to do it I hadn't the slightest idea. "What now? What now?" I kept asking myself. My whole body had gone hard. I tried to suppress my personal feelings and concentrate on those of the role. I felt numb. And, again and again, in a haunting refrain, came the thought, "I can't go home now."

I remember going like an automaton to the opera that night in Cleveland. Ten thousand people were gathered in that vast auditorium. When I arrived the first person to meet me was the conductor, Erich Leinsdorf, who expressed his feelings warmly for what was happening to my country and Melchior's. I shall never forget the remark he made about the performance.

"Think of it," he said, "we are six different nations appearing in this beautiful opera by a German composer, while these dreadful things are happening to our countries in Europe."

The audience felt with us that night; the atmosphere was tense with unspoken thoughts, and I was sure that in the stirring ovation that Melchior and I received there was a great deal of feeling for the two little countries that were now being overrun by an unprincipled army.

At this point I must relate the first of several painful experiences that came to me in the wake of the war. It was now April 9th. I was booked to sail on April 20th. I had promised to give a concert in Brooklyn for the Norwegian Hospital on April 16th. This promise I had given at least two months earlier. My program had long been made up, consisting of *Lieder* by Schubert, Brahms, and others, one or two Wagnerian arias, and a group of Norwegian songs. Early in March I had given an exclusively Norwegian program in Town Hall. I had wanted that to

94

The Later Manuscript

be my special concert, the farewell of a Norwegian visitor to her generous American friends. My manager had agreed to the arrangement, and to me that Town Hall recital, because of the personal and national note, was more of a leave-taking than my last appearance at the opera. I wanted it to be my good-by as an artist and a friend. It had also satisfied a long-standing ambition of mine to sing a program made up entirely of my country's songs. I had done what I could to make my Norway dear to my American public.

And now this other concert was a few days ahead—with its announced numbers by Richard Wagner and other German composers. I began to get nasty letters from Norwegians asking how I could sing "enemy" music at a concert for a worthy Norwegian charity. They might have realized, don't you think, that the program had been arranged weeks earlier. Moreover, I was being accused several days before I set foot on the stage of the Brooklyn Academy of Music. Well, on came the concert of April 16th. The house was completely sold out. Something like six thousand dollars was netted for the Norwegian Hospital in Brooklyn. What's more, I was made an honorary member of the hospital committee. All considered, it was a moving and symbolic event in the life of the Norwegian community here. All the Norwegians of any prominence in that area were there. Even Ambassador Morgenstierne came, and so did the consul general. What I should like to make clear is that I didn't have to be prompted to sing or not to sing certain numbers. Only one Norwegian group had been originally listed. After the intermission, when I started on my second group, which was to be of German songs, I made the following statement from the stage:

"Ladies and gentlemen, in view of recent happenings, I think all of us will be happy if I make some changes in my program. I shall therefore announce each number as I go along."

Instead of the scheduled German numbers I sang several songs in either English or Norwegian. How could I possibly know

95

when the original program had been put together that Norway would be occupied in a few weeks? And why should anyone presume to dictate what I should sing? Couldn't I be trusted to know what was best under the circumstances?

I found it terribly hard to do that concert, I mean emotionally hard. The sorrow of all those Norwegians was such a tragic thing to see and feel. Yet it was a very dignified affair. There was no special applause for my change of program, and I didn't do it with the obvious intent of a gesture. They accepted it as a matter of personal taste and judgment. Ambassador Morgenstierne made a touching speech expressing the anguish and the hopes we all shared. As he spoke I could understand why many people in the audience wept.

I shall never forget the end of the concert. While I stood on the stage with my piano accompanist, Edwin McArthur, the audience and I began to sing our national anthem, "Ja Vi Elsker," which means "We love." I could not get beyond the first few notes. My voice broke into sobs. Edwin, who did not understand the language, cried even more than I did. It is this very sentimental young American who knows me better than anybody else in this country. He has been with me from the beginning of my American career, and he will be with me to the end, steady, reliable, and watchful of everything that concerns me. After the concert I went for the first time to the Norwegian Club of Brooklyn. There I met a great number of my compatriots, among them Ambassador Morgenstierne himself.

I had to explain to a *Herald-Tribune* reporter who came to interview me the next day that those vases and vases of flowers in my Dorset Hotel apartment were from my Norwegian compatriots.

"You would have cried to hear them singing our national anthem," I said. "I am an optimist and hope Norway can triumph against the Nazis. But there are so few of us Norwegians, I can only hope."

The Later Manuscript

That interview appeared in the *Herald-Tribune* on April 18th. . . .

Then came a cablegram from my husband—my first word from him since that fateful day earlier in April. All it said was:

STAY WHERE YOU ARE. I AM ALL RIGHT.

That was all I was to hear from him for several months. As far as I remember, the *Bergensfjord,* on which I was to sail, stayed in its American dock. I next went to my manager, Marks Levine, and told him I couldn't go home.

"How about continuing your concert work?" he asked. "That is, if you care to keep busy this summer. Everybody will be happy to have you on their programs."

"All right," I answered. "Go ahead and book me if you can. But I must have at least two months vacation—beginning now. I'd like to go to California with Else."

I was convinced that the Germans had already appropriated all my husband's possessions, as well as everything that belonged to me and my family. I remember saying to Mr. Levine, "I suppose I'll have to go on making money for everybody now."

"What about booking you for concerts next season?" he asked.

"You can book me if you like," I said, "but I would like to sing as much as possible in the Norwegian section of this country."

Mr. Levine shook his head.

"There's no money in it. They couldn't pay you."

"That really doesn't matter, Marks," I said. "Not this time. I have a feeling I want to be with my own people at a time like this."

"All right, then. I'll book you all through North and South Dakota, and I'm sure you'll want to sing at St. Olaf's College in Northfield, Minnesota."

"Absolutely," I said. "And wherever else the songs of Norway may bring hope and courage to Norwegians."

97

THE FLAGSTAD MANUSCRIPT

Here again I must say, it wasn't the usual kind of patriotism that made me want to do that. I simply had this strong urge to be where my countrymen were; where my native language was spoken. I think it was plain, honest-to-goodness homesickness. . . .

"Now, what about the Metropolitan?" Mr. Levine asked.

"Very well, Marks, I'll go back there too."

So this tireless and tactful manager, who has been a devoted and steadfast friend too, booked me for the entire season to come. My opening engagement was to be at the end of June, as soloist at the Lewisohn Stadium of New York, to be followed by concerts in Washington, Philadelphia, San Antonio, Chicago. But, first, I wanted that two-month vacation. I needed it badly, because of my acute fatigue and anemia—and the nervous strain of worry and waiting. Well, on April 25, 1940, I made one more appearance, as soloist at the annual forum of the New York *Herald-Tribune*, where I remember Wendell Willkie was one of the speakers, and that same evening Else and I took the train west.

Chapter Ten

WE went first to the Grand Canyon; then on to Hollywood and Santa Barbara, California, where we spent fourteen wonderful days of rest, sunshine, and being together. May 17th is my country's Constitution Day as well as my daughter's birthday; so on that day Else and I commemorated both events with a glass of champagne, sang our national anthem, and—it shouldn't be hard to guess the rest—cried like babies. When the two weeks were up, we went to San Francisco to stay with my good friend Mrs. Milton Esberg. Else then went back to the ranch in Montana, where Arthur was working, and before long it was time for me to move on to New York for my Stadium appearance.

I must have expected what happened next. While I was in New York a letter arrived from Else. Very gently, but very firmly, she said she had made up her mind to marry Arthur Dusenberry; that she wasn't interested in traveling around with me from city to city, from concert hall to concert hall. Did I approve? I did the only thing there was for me to do—I gave my consent, and my blessings. Arthur, I decided, was everything any mother could want in a son-in-law, loyal, serious-minded, but with a healthy streak of American humor. And very much in love with my daughter—and she with him. There was only one problem—Else wanted me to be at the wedding;

THE FLAGSTAD MANUSCRIPT

and of course I wanted to be there too. Now this wasn't so easy, because of the heavy schedule ahead. I looked over my bookings with Edwin, and decided that the only time for the wedding, if I were to be present, would be after the Chicago concert. That meant Else would have to get married in two weeks, which was rushing things.

"If you can be married on August 10th," I wrote, "I'll be able to come."

Then I telephoned her.

"Mamma, that's just too fast!" she said.

"Well, if you can manage it, I'll be there with you. I can't possibly make it later. Edwin and I will be on tour."

I also told her that if the concert in Chicago was postponed on account of rain, the marriage would have to be put off a day or two. Else agreed to the arrangement. She wanted me to be there, and I wanted her to be happy. I frankly thought she was too young—barely twenty—but I was confident she would be happy with Arthur. Well, our train was one and a half hours late, but Edwin and I arrived in time for the wedding, and left the same evening for our next concert on the Coast.

Then, suddenly, right in the middle of my tour, came a series of insistent cablegrams from my husband:

WHY DON'T YOU COME HOME? I AM WAITING FOR YOU.

I showed the cablegrams to Edwin, whose good judgment has so often served me well in the years of our association. What he then advised me to do was afterward repeated by everyone else I consulted.

Among other things he said, "You must not write to Norway that you are earning money."

"But why?"

"Because they might force you, through your husband, to send money. Anything you say in a cablegram or letter is dangerous now. You've got to be very careful."

100

The Later Manuscript

So I sat down and composed an answer to Henry's cablegrams that I thought was the peak of diplomacy:

PREVIOUS CONCERT COMMITMENTS OBLIGE ME TO STAY HERE FOR THE PRESENT.

I hoped Henry would understand—that he would somehow guess why I didn't say more and what I was trying to say in that one bare sentence.

I must admit I was terribly frightened by the things people said the Germans would do to my family if I didn't watch what I did and said. There were all sorts of ways, they warned me, that the Germans could take advantage of my name and position. I was simply scared. When I returned to Norway, my husband assured me that I could have written him quite freely without fear of reprisal. So, at any rate, he believed at the time.

Finally, I received a rather hard and bitter cablegram from my husband and this time I knew I just had to go to him. I immediately called up Mr. Levine.

"I can't stand it any longer, Marks," I said. "I've just got to go home. My husband cables me that he doesn't understand what's keeping me."

And of course, I was longing for him more than I can say. Regardless of what anybody says, I was terribly in love with my husband. This was the longest separation we had ever had, because previously I had been going back to him every summer. I longed for him, but I longed for my family and country too.

Now Mr. Levine, besides being a gentleman, has always been a profoundly understanding and tender person. He not only knew my husband well; he knew what our relationship was like and how much in love we were with each other. So he said to me, "All right, Kirsten, go back, since you feel so strongly about it. I'll cancel all your Metropolitan engagements—everything. But you must remember one thing. If you do this, people in America

THE FLAGSTAD MANUSCRIPT

will say you broke all your contracts to go back to a country occupied by the Nazis."

That stopped me. I had never broken a contract in my life, and I didn't like the idea of beginning now, under such conditions, no matter what my personal desires were. I was so unhappy over the position I had been put in—how unhappy no one will ever know. I was torn desperately between two duties. I finally put my own wishes aside, and decided to stay till I had filled all my American engagements. Everything I was booked to do, including my appearances at the Metropolitan, would be finished on April 17, 1941. No one could then say I had broken my word.

I asked Mr. Levine to arrange for my departure by plane on that date, if at all possible. Now, I want this to be very clear. My passage on the clipper was booked at least three months in advance, and Mr. Levine made all the necessary arrangements. After I expressed my determination to go home, I had nothing further to do with how I got there. It has been charged that I resorted to bribery to secure passage on the plane. I never bribed anybody; in fact, I had no contact at all with anyone connected with the flight overseas.

I must say that the prospect of flying brought on the most frightful and prolonged siege of insomnia I have ever had. I don't believe I had one real night's sleep from the day my passage was booked to the day three months later when I boarded the plane. I had only flown once before, and the experience had frightened me sick.

In the meantime my stepdaughter Annie had arrived from Norway, in October, 1940, reaching San Francisco by way of Russia and Japan. There she wasn't permitted to disembark, because she carried a visitor's visa, and they were no longer honoring such credentials. I was again in San Francisco when the vessel docked one morning. I remember I kept wondering why Annie didn't come off the boat. Finally, I had to promise

102

The Later Manuscript

the authorities that my stepdaughter would either leave the country in six months or apply for a quota admission, which she eventually did.

No sooner was I alone with Annie than she gave me a message from her father. It was the same thing: he wanted me to come home and he couldn't understand why I didn't. Knowing what a sensible girl she was, I gave her my reasons.

"But it isn't at all that way, Kirsten," she said. "There isn't too much pressure, at least there wasn't when I left."

The truth is the real pressure hadn't started. Open warfare had ended, and the cruel repression didn't begin till sometime later. Frankly, I was pretty much relieved by my talk with Annie about the situation in Norway, at least about one aspect of it. However, it was from her that I really first learned of the inner turmoil there: that Norwegians were now arrayed against Norwegians. I came to realize what I had not even suspected, that a civil war was going on in Norway that might become as serious as a real war.

But, then, how could I have surmised all this? I had been plunged in work; I knew next to nothing about politics, and while I had been reading the newspapers I suppose I had been lulling myself into a false optimism about what lay ahead. That longing to see my beloved country had again become so strong that I kept saying to myself, "Wait and be patient! This will all end soon." I couldn't see into the future, and I probably didn't want to see anything, other than being home again. It isn't easy for me to express my exact feelings at that time. I have lived long enough to know that if you really want to, you can push all the disagreeable things away from you. For instance, I went on assuring myself that whatever was happening, it was something other people were taking good care of. Somehow I didn't feel it was my job to be involved in these matters. I was a public entertainer, not a fighter or politician.

I had a jolt on Thanksgiving Day of 1940. Annie and I were

103

both in my suite at the Waldorf-Astoria, when she suddenly announced to me that she had put in a call to Norway.

"So Father can talk to you," she explained.

"Oh, no, Annie!" I cried out in dismay. "That's the worst thing you could have done to me!"

She looked very disappointed.

"I'm sorry," she said, "I thought that you would be happy and Father too."

Well, the call had already been ordered, and I agreed to take it, and thanked her for her kind intentions. I was invited by Edwin and his wife to dine with them on Thanksgiving Day. There was no telling, of course, when the call might come through. Transatlantic calls were not as easy to make at that time as they are now. We began to wait for it at twelve midnight. Finally, at six, on the morning of Thanksgiving Day, the phone rang. I picked up the receiver and immediately I heard the voice of my husband Henry. The shock was as great to him as it was to me. Neither of us was prepared to talk to the other. So great was the emotion on both sides that we couldn't say a word. We just cried. And in the midst of his crying he kept repeating one thing.

"Kirsten, why don't you come home?"

And I kept answering, "I've still got to sing."

"But who told you to do that?"

I then reminded him that after all he was the first to urge me to remain in America. I told him I was trying to do what I thought was the wisest thing under the circumstances, and that I couldn't possibly come home before April. I remember his reply to that very clearly. "That might be too late."

Which, of course, could mean anything at that time. Whatever it was Henry had in mind, he was convinced that something was going to happen which would prevent my leaving America. I know it left me feeling more wretched than ever. I cried and cried all Thanksgiving Day. I was so wrought up emotionally

The Later Manuscript

I didn't dare go to dinner, and of course I went on blaming Annie, sobbing over and over again, "That was the cruelest thing you could do to me!"

I still feel the emotions of that day, and it is so difficult to make others understand what I was going through. I had wanted to say so much to my husband, and I was frightened into silence by what everyone had been warning me. I wrote to him, and I couldn't think of what to say; everything seemed dangerous or silly or stiff. I wanted to set his mind at rest about so many things and I didn't know what I was free to say to him on the phone or write in a letter or cable. Hanging over me was the haunting dread that the Germans might hold my family as hostages and compel me to send money to Norway. I was confused and I tried so hard to do what was right in every respect. Least of all did I want to hurt my husband by any action of mine. More than ever I knew I had to go home.

At length, NBC called up to tell me that the only route I could take was by way of Bermuda, Portugal, Spain, over France and Germany, and on to Norway. I had no choice but to instruct them to go ahead. Passage was tentatively booked for April 19th. I was told that the date couldn't be sure because members of the diplomatic service were being given right of way, along with the mail, and the place reserved for me might be needed. Actually, I didn't know till the evening before I boarded the clipper that I was definitely leaving.

Now I should like to return to the subject of my relations with the Norwegians in America during this period. While I was in San Francisco, I was invited to a private party at the home of the Norwegian consul general. I remember that his wife was very active in Norwegian Relief. Among other things, she told me she had been collecting money, but what most interested me was that she and a great many members of the women's clubs were knitting garments to be sent to Norway.

THE FLAGSTAD MANUSCRIPT

"I don't think they need those things just now," I remarked.

"You're quite right," she replied. "But they will eventually need them, if the war continues. And, anyway, we have no facilities to ship them over now."

Somehow that conversation stayed in my mind. About that time I was asked by one of my American friends if I too would knit something for Norwegian Relief. I did, and it was auctioned off and brought quite a lot of money. Later, in Chicago, the head of Norwegian Relief, an American minister of Norwegian descent, came to ask me if I would give a concert for his organization, and I said, "Certainly." So, they hired the Chicago Opera House and I gave the concert in January. Up to that point, except for the nasty letters I received before my concert for the Norwegian Hospital of Brooklyn, everything had been cordial and inspiring. It had been a rich and rewarding experience to be with my countrymen, and a great need in me was satisfied, at least in part. Then came something different.

One day a gentleman from a Norwegian publication paid a visit to the offices of NBC and spoke with Miss Elsie Illingworth, one of their booking agents, about the possibility of getting me to do a concert in Carnegie Hall, also for Norwegian Relief. Miss Illingworth called me up and asked whether I wouldn't like to do it, and my immediate reply was, "Of course I would, and shall."

With all my previous bookings, it was rather difficult to find a spot in my schedule for the event, but I believe March 3, 1941 was the date we agreed upon for it. Then Miss Illingworth came to see me.

"Very peculiar people, those Norwegians, Madame Flagstad," she said.

That was news to me.

"Why is that?"

"Well, here you are all set to give a concert for Norwegian Relief, and they have some strange ideas of their own about how it should be given."

The Later Manuscript

"Please come to the point," I said.

"All right. They wanted to lower the admission price for Carnegie Hall."

"Why do they want to do that?"

"So the Norwegians would be able to buy tickets. They say they can't afford the high prices of Carnegie Hall."

"What did you answer to that?"

"I hope I said the right thing. I told him that the concert wasn't for Norwegians alone—that, in fact, it was more for the Americans, and that the more money we raise the more there would be for Norwegian Relief."

"That was good. And what did they say to that?"

"That the concert was for the Norwegians."

Apparently these people did not understand or would not understand. Wasn't the purpose of the concert to raise as much money as possible for the aid of our unhappy country? Well, they wanted the prices lowered, and that was that.

Miss Illingworth finally said to them, "I'm sorry, but Madame Flagstad is in no position, morally or professionally, to have the price of her concert tickets lowered. What would other organizations for which she has given benefit concerts say?"

The fact is that a great many of my Carnegie Hall concerts were for benefits of one kind or another. As a rule, prices for these events were raised above the standard scale, and the women's committees usually received a handsome contribution for their worthy causes. And no matter how high the prices were, my fee was always the same. Now, if I were to sing at lower prices, how would the others running benefits feel about it, and wouldn't those who had purchased tickets for these other benefits have a right to protest?

Mr. Levine and his office were ready to run the whole thing for nothing in order to provide Norwegian Relief with additional funds. At length, after considerable persuasion on the part of the NBC people, our Norwegian friend consented to keep the standard price scale for the Carnegie event.

THE FLAGSTAD MANUSCRIPT

"But on one condition," they said. "If we can get the Crown Prince and Crown Princess to be present at the concert."

That made me good and mad. First, they were trying to run something they knew absolutely nothing about. Evidently they doubted my ability to draw a concert audience in Carnegie Hall at regular prices, though I had had sold-out houses since I began to sing there. Can I be blamed for putting my foot down?

"I'm sorry," I said to Miss Illingworth. "Tell them there are no conditions when I sing. I want to sing at this concert, and I want as much money as possible to go to Norwegian Relief. It has to be done my way."

"They are so difficult to handle, Madame Flagstad," she said, "but I'll try again."

It was no good. They repeated their new refrain: "We'll consent to the regular prices if the Crown Prince and Crown Princess agree to come."

And that wasn't all.

"We must also insist," they said to Miss Illingworth, "on approving the program before the concert."

That was the last straw.

"This is more than I can take," I said to Miss Illingworth. "I'm singing for a Norwegian benefit in Chicago. They have said they are going to take care of everything. They have not interfered in any way. They have said not one word about my program. Will you tell me why in this other case a concert that will undoubtedly make a great deal of money for Norway should be interfered with?"

"May I tell them that?"

"Tell them every word of it," I said. "Tell them this too: that I have decided not to sing for them at all. I'm prepared to pay Carnegie Hall the fee for the booking, if necessary—I'm finished with them. I can't do a concert under such conditions."

Needless to say, NBC agreed with me, though it worried them.

108

Sieglinde in *Die Walküre* (Metropolitan debut, 1935).

Isolde (1935).

The Later Manuscript

"You know what this is going to mean?" they asked.

"I'm afraid I do."

And, of course, that's one of the twisted and distorted weapons they have been using against me. For the upshot of that painful and wearisome episode was that they began to say, "Kirsten Flagstad refused to sing for the Norwegians." Was it my refusal, or was it really theirs, as it turned out? I have explained all this in court in Norway to everybody's satisfaction. And when Edwin came over to Oslo and they asked him about it, he repeated word for word the whole regrettable story as I had already told it.

Having finished with this unhappy episode, I went on to Chicago and gave my benefit concert for Norwegian Relief—one of the most moving and satisfying concerts of my whole career. Something like $6,000 net was raised, and every dollar of it went to Norwegian Relief. The audience was with me from start to finish, applauding one number just as warmly as the next. I sang what I thought they had come to hear, and I wish to say this: I never thought that singing arias from the operas of Wagner had anything to do with the Nazis.

Those who have not been overfriendly to me never mention that concert. They prefer to repeat over and over again that I never did anything for Norway. I was not interested in quarreling with them, but they might, in elementary fairness to me, at least mention that Chicago concert. And the Norwegian gentleman was not only there; he came up to me afterward and said, "It went very well, didn't it?" I said "I think so," and that was all. I have since read a book containing a passage in which all the blame is put on me for the fact that the Carnegie concert never took place. Is that fair?

I should add that after my Chicago concert I went to a little reception where the head of Norwegian Relief, the Norwegian-American minister, presented me with a gold charm consisting of a tiny gold album on which were inscribed these words:

THE FLAGSTAD MANUSCRIPT

A token of appreciation to Madame Kirsten Flagstad, Norwegian Relief Concert, Chicago, January 17, 1941.

Inside this little album are small photographs of my husband, my daughter, my father, and my mother. I put them in later myself.

110

Chapter Eleven

I MUST now take up another charge that has been loosely made against me: that several Norwegian officials contacted me personally to urge me not to go home and that I disregarded their pleas. There is absolutely nothing to this accusation. To begin with, I don't believe any of them knew that I was going home. Several of my American friends knew, of course, and so did one or two Norwegians—not connected with the government. The fact is, except for my professional contacts, I had not been very intimate with the Norwegians here. Of the few with whom I had spent considerable time, one was a prominent Norwegian in the whaling business, not a refugee. It must have been sometime in March of 1941 that I visited him and his wife at the Waldorf-Astoria. The subject of my impending departure for Norway came up. I told them how my husband had been urging me to return, and I remember my friend's wife said to me, "Why must you go to Henry? Let him come to you."

They both knew how much I wanted to be with him.

"In the first place," I said, "you can't order Henry around—he's not that kind of person. In the second place, I want to go home. I think my place is there."

Then her husband spoke up.

111

THE FLAGSTAD MANUSCRIPT

"After all," he said to his wife, "maybe it isn't such a bad thing to have some good Norwegians left in Norway."

Those were his exact words.

"Then you agree there's nothing wrong in my going?" I asked.

"The only thing I have to say," he replied, "is: don't go in April. Wait until June. I'm convinced everything will be over by then."

That, of course, conflicted with what Henry had said—that April "might be too late." I was more confused than ever. Henry had evidently thought Europe would be in an even worse state later and I wouldn't be able to get through. My friend in the whaling business seemed equally certain that the situation would be stabilized by June and that it would be safer to go then. A prominent American also advised me to wait until June. In fact, most of my friends kept asking me, "Why don't you stay here?"

They all seemed concerned about my personal safety, rather than anything else. However, none of them strongly urged me *not* to go home, once they knew how very much I wanted to. What they did advise me to do, again and again, was to postpone my going. I must repeat this emphatically: there were no so-called orders by representatives of the Norwegian underground that I remain in America. If they objected, it never came to my attention. Early in April, while I was waiting to leave by plane, I did receive another warning about going, this time from a very distinguished American statesman. While I was in my suite in the Waldorf Towers one day the phone rang. It was Herbert Hoover. He said he had just learned that I was stopping at the Waldorf too, and that he wanted very much to talk to me. Would I come for tea? I told him I would be honored. Without suspecting what he wanted to see me about, I went down to his apartment, quite thrilled to be meeting the former American president.

112

The Later Manuscript

"I hear that you are going back to Norway," was his first remark after exchanging a very cordial greeting.

I said I was.

"My advice to you is: don't."

"May I know why, Mr. Hoover?"

From the things that were said when the war ended—that it gave prestige to the Nazis for me to return, that I could be of more service to my country here in America, that it would damage my reputation in America—one would have thought Mr. Hoover was appealing to my patriotic sense. But that wasn't the case at all.

"This is why," he said. "Norway is today worse off than any other country in Europe. There is great hardship in store for you if you return."

I was naturally disturbed to hear such words straight from the lips of one of the world's most noted authorities on such matters. But despite my deep respect for the knowledge of this great man, I could not bring myself to accept the information. . . . I shook my head.

"I'm happy to tell you, Mr. Hoover, that that isn't quite true. My stepdaughter recently came over, and I have her word for it that conditions aren't as bad as many people think."

"I'm sorry to disagree with you, Madame Flagstad," said Mr. Hoover. "I happen to be in a position to know. I suppose you know that during the first world war I had a great deal to do with relief for Belgium and other countries. If you recall, the British maintained a very strict blockade of occupied Europe and it was virtually impossible to get anything through. Take my word for it: your country is worse off than any other at the present moment. You would do best to remain here for the time being."

"Mr. Hoover," I said, "I know you have my personal safety and my country's well-being at heart, but I am sure that you have been misinformed about present conditions in Norway."

That didn't stop him, however.

THE FLAGSTAD MANUSCRIPT

"Madame Flagstad," he said, "they are practically starving right now. I have it on the most reliable authority that people are dying of hunger in the streets of Oslo."

"Oh, no," I said, "that just isn't so!"

"... furthermore, they have no clothes. . . ."

"Mr. Hoover, that can't be true," I said. "From what I know about Norway and the standard of living there, I would estimate the clothes situation to be about as follows: if the average Norwegian were suddenly told he couldn't buy any more clothes, he would still have a supply to last him at least three or four years. It's simply impossible for me to believe what you are telling me. Norway worse off than any other country in Europe? What about Poland, Mr. Hoover?"

I don't believe he answered that. I do want to stress that his purpose in warning me was that I would suffer all sorts of hardships if I went back, and I was indeed grateful for his concern over my welfare. And I remember I later said to myself, "If Mr. Hoover's information is correct, I have still another reason for returning home." If my people could stand whatever it was they were being forced to endure, I could stand it too.

That became my attitude, and it is still. I never once thought and will never think of saving my own skin. Anxious over the present European situation, many of my friends are already warning me again.

"Why don't you stay here? The situation is very critical."

My answer is still, "No." Whatever my Norwegian people can take, I can take too. I am now being told that if war comes, it will overwhelm Norway first of all, and once again my beloved land will be occupied by an invading army.

"I have never tried to avoid anything," I say to these well-meaning friends. "I don't believe in trying to escape. I have never run away from anything that had to be faced. I may be wrong, but that's the way I am."

I honestly believe I would be a traitor to my country if war came and I stayed here for reasons of self-protection. What

The Later Manuscript

would it have been like if everybody had fled Norway to save their own skins? And if I had remained in America, what exactly would I have been expected to do here? I gave that concert for Norwegian Relief, and I knew pretty well from my talk with the consul general's wife that they would not be able to send help over till the war had ended.

"We will need it then," I said. And of course we did.

I shall now discuss the troublesome issue of Ambassador Morgenstierne.

I should have preferred making no reference at all to him, but since he has spoken against me time and again, I have no choice but to give my side of the story. Most of the trouble has to do with just what happened at my concert with the Baltimore Symphony Orchestra in Washington in 1940. Now, as I recall, I had sung either four or five times in Washington within the year. I distinctly remember that one of the concerts was at the famous Watergate. Now this is very important: my program was all Wagner. I didn't know it at the time; but I learned later, while looking through a book of clippings that someone sent me, that Mr. Morgenstierne was present at that concert. In any case, I never heard him make any kind of protest against that program. Why didn't he? And why did he come to my next concert in Washington if Wagner's music had suddenly become an insidious affront to the Allied cause? Whether Mr. Morgenstierne liked that second program or not is irrelevant. I should like only to point out that *it was not arranged by me.*

Now, it so happened that the German chargé d'affaires occupied a box beside Mr. Morgenstierne's. Quite understandably he was embarrassed, and even outraged. But in Washington many things of that sort happen merely by chance. America was not then at war with Nazi Germany. Could tickets have been refused the German official? In any case, how was I to blame? Surely Ambassador Morgenstierne knew I did not control the sale of tickets. Was I supposed to know everyone in the house

THE FLAGSTAD MANUSCRIPT

that night? As a musical artist of some standing, isn't it sufficient for me to prepare myself for a concert and to try to give my very best at all times?

Ambassador Morgenstierne did not give me the benefit of the doubt. He chose not to. He would seem to have taken it for granted that the German chargé d'affaires was in that box next to him on my invitation. And from that supposition he concluded that I must have had help from the Germans to secure my visa for Portugal. The presence of the Nazi official at my concert was, accordingly, a gesture of gratitude on my part for services rendered by the Third Reich, and, presumably, a token of my sympathy for the enemy. The theory was easy and pat, and I'm afraid a great many people believed it.

Mr. Morgenstierne has since been assured time and time again, by private sources and government officials alike, that his conclusion was wrong. But I suppose that, having once announced that as his belief, he is reluctant to give it up. To this day he is convinced that that was why and how I got my transit visa, when the simple truth of the matter is that it came through without anybody's help.

Why did Mr. Morgenstierne feel like this about me? There is a theory among some Norwegians whose judgment I respect that Mr. Morgenstierne had resented my being called "the best ambassador Norway ever sent to America." That may have been too much for both a man and an actual ambassador to take without a certain twinge of jealousy. That is their theory. There was something else that may possibly help to explain his attitude toward me.

My mother and my sister were with me in 1938, and I remember I was giving a recital in Washington. How I managed it at all I don't know, because I had a terrible cold that night. A message was brought to me that Mr. Morgenstierne was in the house and wished to see me during intermission. Feeling as ill as I did, I begged to be excused. Later when I returned to my hotel with Mother and my sister, Mr. Morgenstierne telephoned

116

The Later Manuscript

to inquire about my health, and I remember he was very charming about it all. Yet, a short time later I heard that he had complained to a friend of mine that I had treated him badly by refusing to see him.

I know that Mr. Morgenstierne was extremely distressed by what was happening in Norway, and in his rightful bitterness may have been a trifle hasty. I could not help feeling that he might have been more considerate of me as an honorable woman, a true Norwegian, and a reputable artist.

My original plan was to go not to Norway, but to Sweden, where my husband would come to meet me in Stockholm. Once in Sweden we could decide whether I should continue my journey home or not. I had been assured here that I would be able to get my Swedish visa in Berlin, while I was passing through. I assumed that having obtained my visa I would immediately take a plane to Sweden. Meanwhile all the other visas needed for the journey were obtained, all except the one for Portugal. That was delayed. Just what happened I did not know at the time. I must insist on this, because I believe it is very important in this whole muddle of accusation and misunderstanding.

Because the Portuguese visa was held up longer than the others, an NBC representative went to the Norwegian Legation to request that they ask the Portuguese consul to do what he could to secure the visa in time for me. The Norwegian Legation cabled our government in exile in London for instructions, and the answer was that they were opposed to my going back home through Germany. So the Norwegian Legation was obliged to refuse NBC's request to intercede on my behalf. It so happened that the visa came through on time, and I suppose that's why I never heard till after the war that my government was against my going back by way of Germany. Perhaps I should have been told and perhaps not. But I want to be explicit on that point. I knew nothing about it. This is the truth and anyone who states otherwise is lying.

THE FLAGSTAD MANUSCRIPT

It is possible, though I am not at all sure, that this whole incident may have given Ambassador Morgenstierne the story that I got my Portuguese visa with the help of the Nazis. That may also explain why he went so far as to accuse me in the newspapers of having traveled on a German passport. That, of course, just wasn't so. I am now convinced that it was this unfortunate difficulty over a visa with the Norwegian Legation—of which, I repeat, I knew absolutely nothing—that caused most of the subsequent disturbance.

I must not forget to mention one more detail, I believe a very important one in view of some of the things that were said later. It is this: I had a return trip ticket to come back from Lisbon by plane in September. In my very last talk with Mr. Levine, he had asked me to let him know before June 15th if I planned to return to America. I gave my promise that I would do so.

"However," I said, "if conditions in Norway are as bad as some people have been saying they are, I might not be able to come back."

"That goes without saying, Kirsten," said Mr. Levine.

"And it is also likely that I might not want to come back."

"I understand perfectly. But what shall I do about the coming season? Is there any point in booking you?"

"That's up to you, Marks," I said. "If you book me, you do so at your own risk."

"That goes for the Metropolitan too, I suppose?"

"I'm afraid so. All I can say now is that I'll let you know definitely by June fifteenth."

It has been held against me by some people, including a distinguished New York music critic, that I broke my contract with the Metropolitan. I wish to assure them that this is not true. There was no contract, and I never broke anything. I knew, and Marks Levine knew, how slender the chances of my coming back were. How could I possibly sign a contract on such uncertainty? Yet against that small possibility of coming back, *I purchased*

118

The Later Manuscript

my return ticket by clipper from Lisbon. Beyond that I made no commitment of any kind.

When I finally departed by clipper on April 19, 1941, I carried away with me a beautiful memory of my last Metropolitan performance, a memory of my American public that warmed me during the six years of separation that lay ahead. Edwin conducted and the opera was *Tristan und Isolde.* The date was April 14th, a Saturday afternoon. I recall the long and resounding ovation, in the midst of which Lauritz Melchior, my Tristan, finally appeared, and, raising his hand to the audience, announced that I was leaving by clipper in a few days to visit my husband in Norway.

"I think we should all wish her a happy journey," he said, "and a happy journey back."

I could hear the cheers from all sides, and my name being shouted again and again.

"Flagstad! Flagstad!"

I came out once more and silenced the crowd with a motion of my hands, indicating I wanted to say something. It wasn't easy to find the right words at that moment. I said, "I am very happy to be going home, but I shall be even happier to return to you."

I was so choked up I could say nothing more. When I left the stage and all those wonderful people, I was crying like a baby.

Chapter Twelve

IT WAS not till I reached Portugal that I had my first intimation that something was wrong—that is, as regards my husband's position in Norway. NBC had made a reservation for me at a hotel, but apparently nobody paid any attention to it. So I walked up to the desk of another hotel in Lisbon, and as I registered the room clerk remarked, "Oh, you're Norwegian, aren't you?"

I said, "Yes, why do you ask?"

"Why, there are three Norwegians sitting out there in the hall," he said.

"I wonder if I know any of them," I said. "Would you kindly tell me their names?"

He mentioned them.

"I know who they are," I said.

One had been a consul general in Italy. Another was a colonel in the Norwegian Army, and a third was a businessman. I thanked the clerk and went into the hall, where I found them having cognac and coffee. I introduced myself, something I have very rarely done in my life, and they invited me to sit down and join them in a cognac and coffee. I was so happy to be with some of my own people in this strange country, and to be talking Norwegian again. I felt so much closer to home. All three of them were extremely charming to me. We talked about many

The Later Manuscript

things and then one of them, who was holding a copy of the Norwegian paper, *Aftenposten*, remarked that there was something about my husband in it.

"I see Mr. Johansen has been appointed to the board of directors of the Wine Monopoly of Norway," he said.

Sensing nothing beyond the bare statement, I merely commented, "Is that a fact?"

In one voice, they said, "Yes," in what I thought was an odd tone.

"He ought to be a good man for the job," I said, "because, you see, he knows quite a lot about wines and liqueurs. He's president of two large hotels, you know."

And in that same curious tone, they replied, "Yes, we know that too."

There was a long pause now, and I felt a bit uncomfortable for the first time. Finally, one of the Norwegians, I believe it was the colonel, said very seriously, "The fact is, Madame Flagstad, your husband is not in very good company these days."

I bristled a little.

"What do you mean by that?"

He mentioned the name of a man—a name faintly familiar to me.

"What's wrong with him?" I asked.

"Well," was the reply, "he's an N.S. man."

Now that stood for the party headed by Quisling, and it was no secret to me or to anyone else that my husband had been a member of it for many years before the war broke out. Up to that moment I'm afraid I had not fully realized what membership in Quisling's Party had come to mean. I had felt it, yes, and I had secretly feared its new significance, but again, I had pushed the thought from me. It was only now among these Norwegian refugees that I knew something was very wrong. I had frankly never given much thought to Henry's membership in the Party, and when I did, I dismissed it as a kind of paper

THE FLAGSTAD MANUSCRIPT

membership. I suppose I was at fault for not grasping sooner how bad a thing it had become.

However, my hosts said nothing more about my husband that day. We sipped our cognac and coffee and talked of music and other matters.

I can't recall now why I was delayed in Portugal. I believe I had to obtain some more papers. In any event, two days went by, and I must say that, thanks to the colonel and the business-man of that little Norwegian group, I had a very agreeable time in Lisbon during my stay.

After that we crossed over to Spain, where I spent one night in Madrid. Then we moved on to Barcelona and from there flew over France, descending only once, to pick up the mail. Finally we came down at the Berlin airport about eight in the evening. That is where, many of you have no doubt read or been told, I was supposedly met by Adolph Hitler with an armful of flowers. Where that tender little fabrication originated I have no idea. It too went obediently into the sinister picture that several people in various parts of the world were piecing to-gether of my imaginary activities during the war years.

I was waiting to board the bus that takes people to and from the airport, when an official of the airline asked me if I had a hotel in mind.

"Yes," I said, "the Adlon."

"Have you a reservation?"

I said I had. That was supposed to have been made directly from Norway, and I assumed everything had been taken care of. But a call to the hotel brought the same response as in Lisbon. There was no reservation for me.

"Not even under the name of Johansen?"

"No, nothing."

"What do I do now?" I asked the airline official.

The man mentioned another hotel.

"They have rooms there, if you care to go. It will cost you twenty marks."

122

The Later Manuscript

"That sounds all right," I said. "I'll go there. Thank you."

The official finally got me a cab, which was by no means easy, and I went to the hotel and registered. Further disappointment was in store for me the next day. There was no message of any kind for me—nothing whatsoever. And I confess I felt very strange and uneasy in Berlin, and knowing nobody at all. I left the hotel early that day, because I wanted to be sure to get to the Swedish Embassy in time for my visa. It was absolutely impossible to get a taxi, so I walked. After what seemed several miles, I reached the address I had been given, only to learn that the Embassy had moved. I finally located its new home, and of course it was closed for the day.

I went once more to the Adlon. Still no message or word of any kind. I now began to worry about whether I would get the Swedish visa after all. I resumed my walking tour and called on the Norwegian Travel Bureau, which was on Unter der Linden. As I entered the office, I received another jolt. Up on the wall, in prominent display and size, was a photograph of Quisling. I noticed, too, that some of the people in the travel bureau wore the membership button of Quisling's Party in the lapels of their jackets. The whole dismal picture was becoming clearer to me.

"Is it possible to get a plane to Sweden?" I asked.

They laughed.

"If you stand in line, you might get one in five weeks, provided you're lucky."

"This is very depressing," I said. "How do I get to Sweden?"

"When do you plan to leave?"

"Tomorrow," I said, remembering that I still had to secure my Swedish visa.

I can't quite explain the uneasy feeling I had in the office of the Norwegian Travel Bureau. I thought they treated me very curiously.

I am not an early riser, and I got up rather late the next morning, but rushed over to the Swedish Legation at once. I was met by a very curt young lady.

THE FLAGSTAD MANUSCRIPT

"I'm supposed to collect a visa here," I said.

"That will take you exactly three weeks," she said.

"But how can that be? It was all arranged for me a long time ago. Instructions were cabled from America, and I was assured the visa would be here waiting for me when I arrived."

Very emphatically, she replied, "That's impossible. I'm afraid I can't be of any assistance to you."

I saw she was a person you couldn't argue with. But why she was angry with me I have never been able to understand. Whether it had anything to do with the political situation I don't know, though I doubt it; I only know she seemed to be very angry with me.

"Come back tomorrow, if you wish," she said.

"But I would like to leave tomorrow."

"You can't go to Sweden without a visa. I'm sorry, Madame."

"What am I to do?"

"That's your problem, not mine."

"What if I decide to go to Norway, instead. . . ?"

That was my only alternative.

"In that case you will need a visa allowing you to pass through Sweden—a transit visa."

"Can I get that?" I asked.

"Yes," she said, "but you'll have to have your ticket first."

"I'll get that today," I said.

I keep wondering about that girl and her strange behavior. The fact is she didn't even look to see if my Swedish visa was there. She never even asked anyone else in the office about it.

"I'll make out a transit visa for you tomorrow," she said.

"Thank you."

"Do you have your permit to re-enter Norway?"

"I have my Norwegian passport, of course."

"That's not sufficient. You must obtain permission from the Germans to re-enter Norway."

"Not I," I said. "I'm a Norwegian."

"That doesn't matter. You still need a *Reisevermerk.*"

124

The Later Manuscript

"Where do I get that?"

"From the police. But first you must go here."

I took down an address she gave me, thanked her and continued my walking tour of Berlin. By then my heels were half worn down from walking and running. The place I went to proved to be an emigration office. When I arrived, I found hundreds of people on line waiting to secure permits and visas of one kind and another. After standing in line for two hours, I reached the table where an official was answering inquiries and issuing forms.

"I would like to go to Norway," I said.

"Have you a transit visa for Sweden?"

"Not now," I replied, "but I'll have it tomorrow morning."

Then he looked at my passport.

"I see nothing in your passport to indicate that the police know you have entered Germany," he said.

"Why," I said, "do I need that?"

The official seemed to understand that I was having difficulties.

"I'm sorry," he said, "but you'll have to go to the police with your passport and you've got to go personally. If you do that now and get back fast enough we'll give you a *Reisevermerk*."

He then gave me an address and instructed me how to get there quickly. I took a streetcar and was soon at police headquarters, where I learned I was guilty of another irregularity.

"You have been very slow in registering," they said. "You are one day late."

"But I had no idea...!"

To make a long story short, they made the necessary entry in my passport. Frantic with nervousness and dread that something else would be found wrong, I rushed back to the emigration office and received my German transit visa to pass through Sweden. That much was done. I still needed my Swedish visa. The following day I returned to the Swedish Legation. There was no trouble at all this time. I was taken care of by two polite

THE FLAGSTAD MANUSCRIPT

Swedish gentlemen, to whom I related my encounter with the curt young lady.

"Have you any idea why she was so nasty to me yesterday?" I asked. "She didn't even look to see if my visa was there."

They shrugged their shoulders and one of them said, "You mustn't mind her, really. She sometimes gets those fits. I'm certain she meant nothing personal."

This was my second day in Berlin. I was now scheduled to leave by train the following morning at 10:15. I returned to my hotel, so exhausted I could have screamed. I was in my room resting when, suddenly, the phone rang. It was a lady.

"Is the name of Director Sigurd Larsen familiar to you?"

I said it was.

"Who is he?"

"Mr. Larsen is director of the Grand Hotel in Oslo," I answered.

"We have a message to communicate from him: 'When will you arrive in Oslo?' "

I gave my reply: "Sunday at noon, if possible. I have my ticket."

"That's all I want to know," said the lady on the telephone. "Good-by."

That was my very first sign from Norway.

I wasn't allowed to receive a telegram. I couldn't telephone and I couldn't send a cable. I felt completely helpless. I decided to have something to drink, called the room service, and said, "Please let me have a double sherry." They brought me what must have amounted to half a bottle. I drank it down, felt more relaxed, and played solitaire the rest of the afternoon. That night I experienced my first air raid. The alarm sounded and I followed the other guests into the cellar. We were not hit.

The next day I was on the train leaving Berlin and very happy that I had come this far. I was still in Germany, though, and anything could happen. At Sassnitz a ferryboat was waiting to make the four-hour crossing. Swedish and German ferryboats

126

The Later Manuscript

alternate at that place. I can't tell you how glad I was to see the blue flag flying on this one. It was Swedish. I went on board and, for the first time since entering Germany, began to feel safe. After we docked at Trälleborg, I took the night train and arrived in Oslo the following day, pretty relieved, I must confess. And there, at the station, waiting for me was my husband Henry.

I need scarcely describe the meeting or what our feelings were like. We had not seen one another for nineteen months, and all those nineteen months I had been away from my country and my home. Neither he nor Larsen had told my family I was coming, or when. So, the moment we got home, I telephoned my mother, who couldn't believe it was me. And, of course, she came over at once, and we all spent a wonderful evening, Henry, Mother, his children, and I, talking, talking, talking. I was home.

I had promised Marks Levine that by June 15th I would let him know whether I would or could return to America. Actually I knew much sooner than that. I had only been in Norway a few weeks when I said to myself, "I'm not going back. This is my home, and I can't leave it as long as the war lasts."

Nobody forced me to stay, not even my husband. It was my decision alone. I stayed because I wanted to stay and because I felt I should stay. That I was forbidden to leave never even came up. That is the simple truth. I had been yearning for my husband, my family, and my people, and now that I was with them I could not think of leaving them again. I'm afraid I didn't think of the Germans at all at that moment. I suppose I had been homesick too long.

And during those first few days, I saw that people in Norway were not actually starving and that they were not walking the streets in rags. It is possible that, at least for a while, I did not want to see the other side of the picture. Perhaps I lulled myself again into a belief that things were not so bad and that in any case the situation was only temporary. I never for a moment doubted that our side—the side of the democratic world—would triumph over the Nazi evil in the end. I had complete faith in

THE FLAGSTAD MANUSCRIPT

those who were doing the job. Like millions of others, I had no choice but to sit it out. There was nothing I could do, nothing my background and temperament had prepared me to do, but to wait. Yet, can anyone knowing how deeply I loved my proud and independent country doubt that I too suffered to see her chained to an alien tyranny?

After those few days in Oslo my husband and I went to our home in Kristiansand, where I was to live so long in virtual seclusion, seeing very few friends, going to very few places, and playing the tedious and watchful game of waiting for events to decide our future. Perhaps selfishly, I tried to ward off unpleasant thoughts of what might be going on outside the narrow circle of my personal life. It was so good to be home—secure from the exhausting routine of concerts and operas and crowds, secure from that demanding master, Career. I needed a period of tranquillity and I was determined, even at the cost of self-delusion, to have it. It was not to be, as it happened, and I soon realized how foolish it was to believe I could remain politically detached for long. A few days after I arrived, my oldest stepdaughter came to visit me. She came to the point at once.

"You must ask Father to leave the Party," she said.

"I suppose I should," I replied. "But it really doesn't mean very much to him. He never was active, you know, and I don't think he's had any recent contact with it at all. He never mentions it."

"I know he's not active, but he's got to leave the Party."

"It's that bad, then—being a member?"

And she said, "Yes."

"Then I certainly shall speak to him at the first opportunity."

"You must," she said. "It will be a relief to all of us, including himself."

As a political conservative Henry had joined the Party several years before in the belief that it was the businessman's best defense against radicalism in Norway. That had been his choice, and as I said before I never meddled in politics. My own world

128

The Later Manuscript

was bounded on one side by my husband and family and on the other by my music. Even if I had wanted to, which I did not, I could not have found either the time or the energy for political activity.

I knew I had to speak to Henry for his own good and my own peace of mind. Moreover, ever since my talk with those Norwegians in Lisbon, I had become frankly curious about one or two things. So I asked my husband point-blank whether he was planning to resign from the Party. He was neither surprised nor hurt, but acted as if he had been waiting for me to introduce the subject.

"The fact is, Kirsten," he said, "I've been wanting to leave the Party all along. I'm just waiting for an opportunity to get out quietly, and I think it's coming very soon."

"Why, what's happening?" I asked.

"You know that I was made a director of the Wine Monopoly."

"Yes," I said. "You were criticized for it by the Norwegians I met in Portugal."

"Well, it isn't for that reason," he said. "I've really nothing to do with it. It's only politics. I went to one meeting, had a few conversations, and then stopped going altogether. It's nothing for me. I'm going to resign from the board, and when I do I will turn in my resignation from the Party too. I think that's the only way to do it."

"I'm sure you know what's best, Henry," I said.

"I want to warn you, however. It may be dangerous to resign right now, but I know I've got to do it. Even though I am completely inactive, it's unfair to all of you to have people think I approve of what the Party stands for. And you know that's not so."

The opportunity Henry was waiting for finally came two months later, in July. He had gone to Oslo to attend to some business, and in the meantime I had asked my Danish sister-in-law to stay with me in Kristiansand. She had just lost her mother

THE FLAGSTAD MANUSCRIPT

in Denmark and was unable to make the trip over to that country to attend the funeral. Since she was very depressed about the whole situation, I thought it would do her good to stay with me for a while. One morning the two of us jumped into a car that belonged to my husband's factory, and drove up to a place, a kind of châlet, Henry and I had in the country. When we got there I asked the chauffeur, who was driving back to the factory, to come and fetch us after a few days. We stayed there alone.

On the trip back to Kristiansand, I asked the chauffeur to stop at an inn at a bend in the road so that my sister-in-law and I could have a drink. They didn't have quite what we wanted, and when we returned to the car, my sister-in-law, who is a charming and good-humored person, said, "Now that Henry is a director of the Wine Monopoly, he ought to have a law passed to make all these restrictions easier, so people can get a drink when they want one."

"I don't believe he is a member of the board any more," I replied.

You see, although Henry and I had not spoken of it, I had a suspicion of what he was doing in Oslo. Well, at that very moment the chauffeur, who was listening to our conversation, interrupted to say, "You can ask him right now, Madame, for here comes Mr. Johansen himself."

And there was Henry. I hadn't expected him back from Oslo quite so soon, and his car just happened to pass that bend in the road when the chauffeur saw him. We waved to him and he stopped. I got into his car and drove with him the rest of the way back. I could tell from his face that he was bursting with news. I couldn't wait to hear.

"How did it go?" I asked him the moment we were alone.

"That's why I came back so soon, Kirsten. I've resigned as a director of the Wine Monopoly."

"And the Party?"

"I've resigned from that too. I got here as fast as I could be-

130

The Later Manuscript

cause I didn't want to be in Oslo when they received my resignation."

"Is there anything to be afraid of?"

"You can never tell," he said. "I thought it best to be out of sight when they read it."

A half-hour later, as we drove into Kristiansand, I asked Henry if I could tell my sister-in-law the news.

"She might as well know too," was his reply.

So I told her, and we all felt very relieved, though a little anxious over what might happen in the next few days. However, nothing did happen. They evidently accepted the resignation without inquiring into Henry's motives. That was in July of 1941, and I even remember the precise day, the seventeenth.

Later that summer the people in Kristiansand were punished by the Nazis, I never found out for what, though. The punishment consisted of nothing more than the loss of our radios. I believe Kristiansand was the first place in Norway to be penalized that way. The order was that all radios should be delivered within a specified time to the police. In many cases the police came to take them away and to search for any that might have been hidden or "overlooked." Any radios Henry and I had at home were all taken down to headquarters. Only Party members and the Germans themselves were exempt from the ruling.

The order did not affect Oslo till a month later, when it was declared unlawful to possess a radio there too. In the meantime, because his car bore an Oslo license, Henry saw no reason to turn in the radio with which it was equipped. But one day our factory chauffeur reported that he had been ordered to remove the radio from the car.

"But it's an Oslo car, and the order doesn't apply there," said my husband.

"They said it's got to go," replied the chauffeur, "and they were very emphatic about it."

"Let's inquire of the manager," said Henry.

The chauffeur went back to the factory, where this man was

THE FLAGSTAD MANUSCRIPT

head of Henry's office, and, as it turned out, the only remaining member of the Party in the whole factory. When the chauffeur explained the situation to him, the office manager replied, "Tell Mr. Johansen he can keep his radio if he renews his membership in the Party."

That was the first positive sign my husband and I had that the others knew he had left the Party. Of course he never applied to be re-admitted. He had washed his hands of the whole business, once and for all.

"She kept her servants and had a comfortable time of it in her two houses."

I am told this charge has been made repeatedly about me by certain people. What should we have done with the two houses? Given them to the Germans? Would that have helped the war— to deny ourselves the comfort of a home that had always been ours and relinquish it to the enemy? Just what would have been gained if we had abandoned those two houses? Why don't people think of such things before they make accusations? And, then, exactly what am I being charged with? We never gave any parties there. I have heard it said that in Kristiansand our friends refused to have anything to do with us. The fact is we had no friends in Kristiansand, with the exception of a pianist who came over to the house from time to time to play for me.

The same thing was true of our home life in Oslo. Other than an occasional musicale which we held for the family and one or two friends, there was no social activity. Emil Stang, chief justice of the Supreme Court of Norway, was a guest at one of those gatherings. It couldn't have been such a terrible place to be invited to.

As for Henry, he looked after his business and went to his meetings with members of the firm. Once in a long while we went out for supper. More and more of our time was spent at Kristiansand, just the two of us. Often, when Henry went to Oslo for a few days, I drove up to this country place of ours,

132

The Later Manuscript

and life there was quite uneventful. Naturally, I was a little bored, after a year or two. So, when an invitation came from Switzerland I accepted eagerly. I sang two seasons in Zürich, two or three months at a time, and I must confess it was a wonderful relief to get away.

Chapter Thirteen

BEFORE going to Switzerland for my first season, I stopped in Stockholm to give a concert. I was anxious to go to Stockholm for a very special reason: I wanted the chance to write my daughter Else and my stepdaughter Annie, from Sweden to America. As for the concert, I am sad to say it was not a success. I didn't know until the day it took place that the Norwegians, many of whom had fled from Norway since the occupation, were doing everything they could to ruin it. Among other things, they had protested to the Swedish newspapers about me. The substance of their protest was on this general principle: that if anyone got out of Norway without difficulty, at such a time, and could return without difficulty, it could mean only one thing— such a person must be a member of Quisling's Party. No one else could get the permission of the Nazis to leave, so they said. Which was ridiculous, of course. Business people were traveling back and forth all the time without being members of the Party. Then a vicious letter arrived at my hotel in the mail the morning of my concert, again full of malicious and baseless accusations.

You can well imagine my feelings when I walked out on the stage of that concert hall. The house was only half full. Outside the Norwegians were standing around the box office urging people to boycott the concert. Well, I started my program with

134

The Later Manuscript

four arias from Handel's *Rodelinda*. The reception was so cold I shivered. So, I said to myself, "Oh, I'm going to win them over!"

The next group was a cycle of songs by Grieg, *Haugtussa*. As I began singing them I could feel the ice melting. By the time I was finished, the audience had completely warmed up to me. After the intermission, I sang several German *Lieder* by Brahms, Schubert, and Strauss. By then the crowd was so excited they insisted on my repeating Strauss's *Wiegenlied*.

I will never forget that experience—to have an audience which was completely against you turn completely for you. I won them over entirely—all of them, that is, but the critics, who, with one gallant exception, were positively slashing the next day. Why? I suppose they had decided from the furor raised by my Norwegian compatriots that I must be a traitor to my country.

"She comes out," wrote one of them, "loaded with diamonds."

This was the same critic who said I had no voice. That was his privilege, of course. The shock for me was something else. For the first time I realized something that had not quite dawned on me before, that some people now had a strong personal feeling against me. A picture had been built up in their minds, from hearsay and rumor, of the sort of person I was and what I believed in. They never once bothered to ask for the proof of this picture. Maybe I had been naïve, for it had never occurred to me that anyone could ever make such irresponsible statements about me. I had done absolutely nothing wrong—either then, before, or later. No official accusation of any kind was ever made against me later when there was every opportunity to uncover any misconduct on my part. I never for a moment felt conscious of doing, saying, or even thinking anything unpatriotic.

I was very disturbed, of course, and I began to wonder if I would run into similar feelings in Switzerland, but, there, everyone, critics and public alike, were wonderful to me. I don't remember the slightest hint from any source whatsoever, that I

THE FLAGSTAD MANUSCRIPT

was anything but a good Norwegian and an artist who respected her work and her obligations.

Once I was safe again on neutral ground I put in a call to America and had a pleasant and reassuring talk with my accompanist Edwin McArthur. They invited me back to Zürich the next year and I went, but when they asked me to return for a third season I said no. The experience had been a welcome change from the eventless waiting and inactivity at home, but it had proved a little taxing, too—the traveling in wartime and so forth.

It was really very difficult. For both those seasons in Switzerland my husband's firm had taken care of all of the details of the trip. Of course, one had to ask the Germans for permission to get a visa, and this the company evidently found easy enough to do for me, both times. When I thought I might go back a third time, the Germans refused. On each trip the Swiss visa had to be picked up in Berlin, on my way to Zürich. So, in 1942, my sister and I went down to Berlin and stopped at the Adlon Hotel. From there we went immediately to the Swiss consulate to ask for our visas, not caring to remain in Berlin any longer than necessary. After a routine search, the consulate reported, rather impudently I thought, that there were no visas for us. "Sorry," they said.

"I was told it would take one month," I protested, "and it is now three months since the application was made."

I thought they were rather nasty about it.

"That's very unfortunate," they said. "You'll just have to wait. It may come any day."

"How can I be sure?"

"You might come and ask tomorrow."

I did, and that went on for twelve days—twelve days in Berlin of all places at a time like this! On the second or third day I became rather desperate, wondering who there was in this cold and unfriendly city that I might know. I thought immediately of Max Lorenz, the singer, but I had no idea where he might

136

The Later Manuscript

be stopping. So I wrote him in care of the Staatsoper, asking him to communicate with me. He never did. I found out later that the reason he didn't was that he happened to be in Italy at the time. So there we were, my sister and I, stranded in Berlin, aliens of an occupied country, and completely helpless. I went pleading to the Swiss consulate.

"Couldn't you telephone to the theater in Zürich? I've got to sing for them and they're expecting me."

They coldly assured me they could not telephone under any circumstances, and of course, being an alien I couldn't telephone or wire Zürich myself. I was allowed to send a letter, but I thought it best not to. It might take too much time, and meanwhile the visa might come through. To make matters worse, every three days we had to renew our permission to remain in Germany. That meant queuing up in an awful place, waiting, waiting. . . . Finally, one day, when our turn came at the end of that wearisome line, they said, "We can't let you stay any more."

"But what are my sister and I to do?" and I explained our situation.

"Very well, we'll give you permission for three days more. But that's all."

Then one evening I was at the Adlon, playing solitaire as usual, when the telephone rang.

"There are two gentlemen here asking to see you."

"Yes? What are their names, please?"

"Kammersänger Lorenz and Kammersänger Hoffmann."

Up they came, and I knew our troubles were over. Max Lorenz communicated at once with his agent, contact was made with the proper authorities in Switzerland, and the next day the visa was waiting for us at the consulate. When I arrived in Zürich I was asked to make a report about the treatment I had received at the Swiss consulate in Berlin. I told them quite frankly what had happened, and I understand the man responsible for my needless delay in Berlin was properly disciplined by his government. Thanks to him my sister and I were stuck in

THE FLAGSTAD MANUSCRIPT

wartime Berlin for twelve days. That was no fun! All we did during that time was to play solitaire, drink a bottle of wine with our meals, and fret ourselves into a state of nervous suspense.

On the way back from Zürich, we thought again we were going right through. Arriving in Berlin late in the evening, we stayed overnight with Max Lorenz and his wife, and were ready to leave the following morning. So we thought. At the station we were greeted with the news that the ferryboat to Sweden had been bombed that night. Again, we were stuck. Back in Lorenz's apartment, we thought we would try to get back by way of the ferry in Denmark. That, of course, meant a Danish visa, so off we went to the Danish consul. That took another day. Our next step was to go to the Germans and have the new place of exit stamped on our passports. Then this other place was suddenly closed off. A third way out of Germany was being considered, when Lotte Lorenz said, "I think I'd better try to get you out by plane."

And with lots of difficulties she finally got us booked on a plane to Copenhagen, but not before we had secured still another exit permit. At last we boarded a train in Copenhagen, and overnight we were home again, with a deep sigh of relief.

The next year I went alone to Switzerland. Much as I dreaded the prospect, there were no obstacles this time. I went to Berlin, picked up my visa, and moved right on to Zürich. I had some trouble getting back, however. The transit visa permitting me to travel back through Germany did not reach me in Switzerland till three weeks after I had planned to leave.

The following year, 1944, I thought of going to Switzerland for a third time, but the Germans turned down my application for an exit permit to leave Norway. When I so informed Zürich, they promptly cabled:

WE FEEL CERTAIN WE CAN HELP YOU GET THAT VISA, IF YOU AGREE TO COME.

The Later Manuscript

"No," I cabled back, "I'd rather stay where I am."

I suddenly realized I wasn't too anxious to go this time. I thought of all the possible complications, and I must have remembered, too, that exactly one week after I reached home in July, 1943, things started to get really bad in Berlin. The heavy bombing had begun.

So I stayed on in Norway, leaving only once after that, 'to return to Sweden for a concert in Malmö. That was an all-Wagner program with orchestra, and the critics this time were unusually kind. There was one moment of uneasiness, but it passed off quickly. The Finnish conductor of the orchestra said to me when we met, "You must know our concertmaster. He was first violinist of your orchestra in Oslo. He fled your country a short time ago."

He mentioned his name. I was overjoyed to hear of his safety.

"Of course, I know who he is," I said. "He played several times for me in the orchestra. I'm so happy to hear he's all right. Isn't he a splendid musician?"

"An excellent one," said the conductor, "but he's still a little bit shaken."

"I can well understand that," I said. "I'd like very much to say hello to him. Could you let him know?"

"Gladly."

That was some time before the concert started. I waited and waited, but no concertmaster.

"What's wrong now?" I said to myself.

The concert began, and the first thing I noticed was that our concertmaster was playing just as beautifully as ever. When it was over, I seized his hand and thanked him. I looked into his face and saw that he was very serious.

"I want to talk to you," I whispered, and he nodded mechanically. But he did not come to see me.

I was more puzzled than ever, though I was beginning to sense something, something I had run into before. He did come up later.

139

THE FLAGSTAD MANUSCRIPT

"How are you?" I said. "I'm so happy to see you here and all right."

He was very distant. I don't recall that he said anything at first.

"Your friends have been worried about you in Norway," I went on. "And now I can tell them that you are happy and well in Sweden. Is there anything I can do for you in Norway?"

"No, nothing," he said quietly.

"There must be some relatives I can call up for you. . . ."

I told him how my brother had been helping one of his colleagues who was in desperate need. That seemed to make all the difference in the world.

"There are one or two persons. . . ." he said, almost eagerly now.

Anyway he was smiling, and I remember how relieved I was that whatever suspicion had been forming in his mind, had vanished. I regret to say there is a rather unpleasant epilogue to this story. After the war the concertmaster returned to Oslo. The day after I was made an honorary member of the Musical Guild of Norway, a lady expressed her surprise in the newspapers that I should have been so honored. Just what she had against me I wasn't sure. Perhaps she was swayed by some of the ugly rumors that were circulating about me. But she was the wife of that concertmaster, and it hurt. . . .

After that I kept more and more to myself. I sang a great deal at home, and nowhere else. I had a number of gramophone records which we played constantly. Life went on quietly, one day pretty much like the next. There was nothing to plan, and no point in planning if there had been. Gradually my eyes opened to the full horror of what was going on. As the war got worse so did the Germans. The dreadful uncertainty of it all began to move closer. Things were now happening to people around us. More and more men and women were seized and sent to concentration camps. Someone we knew would be arrested; then someone else. There was this endless and feverish

140

Brünnhilde in *Die Walküre* (1935).

Leonore in *Fidelio*.

The Later Manuscript

inquiry about names, names, names. Who was picked up, who had disappeared, who had been shot. We grew more and more depressed, and a sick feeling of futility would come over me at times. We could never look further than the twenty-four hours ahead, and sometimes even that seemed remote.

Then, one day, my stepson, who had been pretty active in the underground, slipped away to Sweden with his family. It was this boy who Prosecutor Sundför later charged deserved five and a half years in jail for his business activities in Norway during the war, this same boy who had risked his life in the resistance movement. Of course he was acquitted.

We are now in the early part of 1945. I remember my husband had gone to Oslo and I had taken my maid and driven up to our little country place. For three weeks I did nothing but ski.

One afternoon I picked up one of the newspapers of Kristiansand and turned sick. There on the front page was a list of sixteen persons who had been executed that very morning in reprisal for the slaying of a leading member of the Quisling Party. Among those names was that of a brother of my stepdaughter's husband, a prominent lawyer. Some of the others were known to me, either personally or by reputation. I shall never forget how I sat down and was terrified and furious.

"Why do they do such things?" I said to myself.

Sixteen good, useful lives for the life of one member of the hated Party of collaboration!

Almost at that very moment, the general manager of the Kristiansand factory, a very sane and thoughtful person, rang my doorbell, as he usually did after lunch. I could understand why he looked so pale and shaken.

"I'm sorry, Mrs. Johansen," he began. "I have bad news for you."

"Yes, I know," I said, "I've already seen it in the papers."

"It isn't that," he said.

THE FLAGSTAD MANUSCRIPT

I could see there was more sorrow in store for me that day. I said nothing, and waited.

"Your husband was arrested last night."

"What!" I cried. "But why?"

"None of us can figure it out."

"Have you had word from Oslo? Have they done anything to him?"

"Stake has already telephoned from Oslo."

Stake had been my husband's chauffeur and was now a sort of general assistant—an extremely devoted and thorough person. A stanch and fearlessly patriotic Norwegian too.

"What did he say?"

"That they came into the house, asked for your husband, and placed him under arrest. Stake says Mr. Johansen protested and said, 'What is this? What is the charge against me?' But they wouldn't give him any explanation."

Apparently there was nothing my husband could do but go along with them. However, it seems he insisted on driving to the place of questioning in his own car and had his chauffeur go along with him, thinking that after the matter had been cleared up he would go right back home again. So when they arrived, he asked the chauffeur to wait outside the building in the car. The chauffeur waited till six the following morning and then drove the car back alone.

It has often been said that my husband was taken to a concentration camp. That is not true. He was confined in an ordinary jail in Oslo, and kept prisoner for eight days. He told me later they questioned him ceaselessly—in the middle of the night, at early morning, whenever they thought they could best draw out of him what they suspected he knew. Three other prisoners shared a tiny room with him. A few days after Henry's arrest the police also locked up Stake. He too was subjected to the same ordeal of questioning, but finally both of them were released.

Those were eight terrible days and nights for me. Of course

142

The Later Manuscript

I thought the worst—that Henry would disappear and nothing more would be heard of him. And the more I thought about his arrest, the more bewildering it became as to why they had seized him. I began to wonder what he might have been doing without my knowledge. . . . After the great relief of seeing him home again, one question burst from me, "But, why you, Henry?"

"I can't tell you now, Kirsten," he said. "I'll tell you the whole story when the war is over, and I don't think we'll have long to wait."

But he never got the opportunity to tell me. He did reveal this much: that as he entered the place where they questioned him, he saw two of the hostages whose names were on the list of those executed the next morning. My husband said he went over to talk to one of them, but a German soldier stepped forward and stopped him.

Is it wrong to confess that I was happy beyond words to have my husband back—alive? If I had ever been nice to him before I now became twice as nice. If I had ever failed him, I was now determined to become the ideal wife. I had been so terrified at the thought of losing him.

After the liberation, when an investigation of the execution of these sixteen men by the Gestapo came before the court, one of the Gestapo men on trial was asked this question by the prosecutor: "Henry Johansen was arrested as a hostage at the same time. Why wasn't he executed along with the others?"

"He was too old," replied the Gestapo official.

"Didn't you know that he was one of the biggest collaborators you had?"

"If he was, we didn't know it," was the answer.

Norwegians in America have made a great many people believe that my husband's arrest was prearranged, a sort of frame-up to clear him later with the Norwegian authorities as a reward for his alleged collaboration. This is all nonsense. I know Henry had a hand, if only an indirect one, in helping

143

THE FLAGSTAD MANUSCRIPT

people in distress because of the occupation. I know personally that he contributed money to such people—not directly, but through the faithful and patriotic Stake. It was Stake who saw to it that this money reached the right people for the right purpose. Stake would ask for money, and Henry never hesitated giving it to him. There was an unspoken agreement between them. Stake never told him what it was being used for, and Henry never asked. They both thought it safest to do it that way. But Henry Johansen was never a traitor.

I shall always have one thing on my conscience, however, and that is this: in all the newspaper reports of my husband's subsequent arrest by the Norwegian authorities, they never spoke of him as merely Henry Johansen. He was "Kirsten Flagstad's husband." I believe, and I am not alone in this belief, that had he never married me and had he been just another businessman who went on doing business in occupied Norway, no one in America would ever have heard about him and his arrest. What is more important is that even in Norway he might have been treated with more consideration if he hadn't received all that publicity on account of my name. He was made tragically conspicuous only as my husband. I shall always have this guilty feeling that Henry might have been spared that agony of humiliation and notoriety had he been married to someone else. There would never have been all that fuss, all that sickening exaggeration and the front-page prominence, if Henry Johansen had never attended that fateful performance of *Lohengrin* and fallen in love with Lohengrin's bride.

Chapter Fourteen

PEACE finally came to Norway and the world, and we were all so grateful and happy. Henry was in Oslo when the good news came, and he drove right down to Kristiansand to rejoice with me. That was the eighth of May. The thirteenth of May was a Sunday. As we so often were in the habit of doing, we took a walk together through the garden, over to the factory, and from there down to the sea, looked around and talked, and then walked up to the office, where Henry wanted to look at some papers. On the way back we strolled through the garden along the main road, and suddenly we saw two cars at the main entrance, just outside the garden. My husband looked troubled for a moment, and said, "I wonder if. . . ."

Just then the men in the cars sighted us, and we now saw them coming toward us with drawn revolvers. Since great numbers of people were being arrested at that time, an extra police force had been recruited, and I'm afraid that many of these deputy policemen didn't know what they were doing and often acted hastily and overzealously. The men handed my husband a warrant. He looked at it carefully and then turned to them. I remember his words very clearly.

"You have no right to arrest me," he said. "I am not a member of the NS."

THE FLAGSTAD MANUSCRIPT

Their only reply was, "You'd better follow us."

My husband saw that there was no use arguing with them. They had their instructions and they were probably in a hurry to move on to other business.

"Very well," he said. "May I get my coat?"

They shook their heads.

"You cannot go into the house."

My husband turned to me.

"Will you please telephone—"

One of the men cut him short.

"Not another word! Come along!"

That was all Henry was ever able to say. To whom he wished me to telephone, and what else he might have desired of me, I never knew, though I felt certain his message was intended for Stake. I kissed him there in the garden of our home, and he was taken away. It was all over in a flash, as if I had dreamed it. I won't try to show how very hard it was for me, the anxiety, the humiliation, the bewilderment at what was happening. I never saw him again.

I believe a new Kirsten Flagstad was born that day. I'm afraid whatever softness there was in me vanished forever. I could sense a hardening in all my human feelings. Because of that harsh episode in the garden and what followed I sometimes think I no longer have any nerves. I have lost something, definitely—perhaps the innocence in life that I once had, or, rather, the feeling of innocence toward life. I have become suspicious and mistrustful of others. I remember I had a new kind of feeling, like ice around me, or an iron girdle. I discovered too that I couldn't cry any more. But I was as strong as a bull physically, and of course that helped me to hold out.

After his arrest, my husband was taken to a detention camp that had been converted from a Nazi concentration camp. What happened to him there I shall never know completely. I did

The Later Manuscript

hear, however, that the new jailers had learned a great deal from their predecessors. That Norwegians could subject other Norwegians to that sort of treatment I found hard to believe. I didn't want to think that of any of my countrymen. People admit now that much of what was done during those feverish first days of restored liberty was wrong.

I suppose it is easy to understand why many people acted as they did. There had been a fearful terror and repression. There had been reprisals and disappearances, and a black hopelessness. And now people were drunk with their recovered freedom, with victory over a ruthless enemy. It could not be helped if a little of the captor's ruthlessness had entered the captive. But for me, loving my husband as I did, and knowing him for the gentle soul he was, it wasn't easy to think of him up there in the hands of men who felt they had a score to settle—men who were ready to believe every charge made against those who had been seized in the first wild fervor of the liberation.

Although many of the people in that camp were soon brought out for trial, my husband remained there. This was done on the orders of Prosecutor Ingolf Sundför. Our lawyer Trygve Bendixen was permitted to talk with him, and that was all. Again and again, Henry pleaded to be let out so he could explain everything; and we waited and waited, expecting him to be set free the moment the misunderstanding had come to the attention of the authorities. But it was all in vain. Sundför was firm. Even when Henry became ill, gravely ill, he was not permitted to leave. Only when it was too late was he removed to the hospital.

When we first heard that Sundför was to handle the case, none of us, not I nor the lawyer nor Stake, believed for a moment that the appointment was a coincidence. That he should be made prosecutor seemed unfair to us for many reasons. Many years before the war Sundför had lost an important case against Henry and freely accused and denounced him in the

147

THE FLAGSTAD MANUSCRIPT

newspapers. So we protested the appointment of Sundför, and gave our reasons. The government reply was prompt and courteous. It admitted that the choice, under the circumstances, might not be a happy one, but nothing could be done about it. It was too late, the letter said.

Chapter Fifteen

PRISONERS of my husband's classification were allowed to communicate with their families once a month, and only by open post card. A maximum of fifteen lines was permitted. These were double post cards. Henry wrote on one side, and my reply had to be written on the other. The first one reached me the second week of July. There was very little for me to read, however, because the censor, for reasons of his own, had blacked out most of Henry's writing. I could see that the message started with "G" and ended with "Dagen," which means "day" in Norwegian. My birthday was July 12th, so I am sure the censored message was the highly subversive Norwegian birthday greeting, "Gratulerer med Dagen." However, that was the only card from Henry that the censor saw fit to touch. I am certain there was nothing more than the simple greeting on it, so that it could only have been a case of childish meanness on somebody's part.

Now during the war I had received letters from Frédéric Horwitz, my Paris agent for European concert and opera bookings. It had been Mr. Horwitz who acted as my representative for the two seasons in Zürich in 1942 and 1943. Shortly after my country was liberated I heard from Mr. Horwitz again. He was stationed once more in Paris, and he wrote me reminding me that it was his firm that had introduced me to Switzerland.

149

THE FLAGSTAD MANUSCRIPT

"I assume we are to continue as your agents and that you are prepared to sing again," he said.

That was the very first step of my return to active professional life. Up to the time I received Mr. Horwitz's letter I had no idea of singing again. I had put that all behind me. I didn't dream I could summon the energy and determination to start all over again. My first impulse was to say no. And then I reread Mr. Horwitz's letter. Suddenly I realized there was a counter-impulse, half hidden at first, that was stronger than my first reaction. I began to feel I had no right to turn down the offer. This was based on practical considerations. I had begun to think that it was just possible we—Henry, I, the family—might lose everything. There was still no way of telling what the outcome of the court action in the property matter might be. Lists were being prepared of all our possessions, joint and individual. I and the others might be left penniless. I could not help thinking it might be a good thing to begin earning money again. . . .

In his letter Mr. Horwitz asked me, among other things, if I would do a special Red Cross concert in Paris. He listed proposed dates and so on, and gradually I began to feel the old excitement coming back. But, first, I wanted to consult Henry. That had always been my practice, and I wasn't going to abandon it now. So, I delayed answering Mr. Horwitz's letter till the next opportunity came for me to communicate with Henry. It came, of course, with the next double post card from him. On the back of it I wrote him that my European agent had asked me to come back.

"Should I start my career again?" I asked. "What do you think?"

Again, a long wait till the next double post card arrived. Henry's reply was brief and to the point. "By all means get out as fast as you can and start working again."

That gave me tremendous confidence. I realized it was all I needed as incentive. Now that I had his approval my conscience was clear. I felt safe to go ahead. I must repeat once

150

The Later Manuscript

more—I would never have done anything without my husband's consent. That was how I was brought up, that was how I viewed marriage, and that was how I loved Henry Johansen.

After receiving Henry's encouraging reply, I began making inquiries about securing a passport. Because the old ones were no longer valid, everyone had to get a new passport. In no time at all, I began to see the hand of Sundför again. On one pretext or another he interfered at every point to prevent me from leaving the country. Mainly, his argument was that the financial affairs of myself and my husband were so entangled that I might be needed in Norway to help straighten them out.

In despair I finally wrote Mr. Horwitz that I was afraid we had to forget all about my singing again, at least for the time being.

"I can't get out of Norway," I wrote. "They are holding up my passport."

Not a bit discouraged, he went on writing me about the many places that were asking for me. I could choose my own program, he kept assuring me. Was I interested? And in almost every letter the same refrain: "What about that passport?"

I would answer that I couldn't plan so far ahead, not quite now; that I didn't know when I would be able to leave the country. I suppose I was stalling for time. I didn't want to give up all hope, and yet I couldn't promise anything definite. I knew I couldn't go on saying, "I don't know; I'm not sure; maybe, but let's wait another week." It finally became so complicated that I gave up.

Then came the news that Henry was ill, very ill.... Our lawyer had gone to visit him and reported that his condition was so bad he had been given a bed in the camp infirmary. My first thought was to get him out of there and into a place where he could be properly taken care of. Sundför was approached again, and his answer was "No." Renewed and earnest applications were met with the same answer.

I must confess to something that was then regarded as highly

151

THE FLAGSTAD MANUSCRIPT

irregular: Henry succeeded in smuggling out two letters to me. In one of them he wrote for the first time that he was not feeling well, though he gave no details. In the other he said I had been behaving well. Reports had reached him, he wrote, of how Stake and I were standing up for him.

"If I live," he ended the letter, "everything is going to be all right again. Believe me."

Not that Henry had any suspicion of how ill he was, at least not at that time, which was about the middle of February, 1946. After those two letters, I received no further word from him— not even the usual double post card. I wasn't worried, however. I felt certain that he had recovered from whatever it was that had been bothering him. No news, I told myself, was good news. Well, toward the end of April, while I was home in Kristiansand, the telephone rang one evening. It was Stake.

"I think your husband must be in a hospital in Oslo called Ullevold."

"What makes you think that?"

"This is why, Madame Flagstad: you know, when a person enters a hospital they always ask the name of the nearest relative. Well, somebody at that hospital in Oslo just telephoned the office. They wanted to know where you were staying and what your telephone number was."

"That means Henry is there, Stake!" I cried. "It must be very serious."

"I'm going to find out for sure."

Stake made inquiries, and that was how we found out that my husband was no longer in the concentration camp, but in the hospital. The moment I knew, I left for Oslo. That was the first of May. I remember the date because we passed May Day demonstrations in the small towns on the road to the capital. I went at once to the Grand Hotel. Shortly after I arrived a young Norwegian composer named Doerumsgaard communicated with me. Doerumsgaard is a gifted song writer and arranger whose name has been on many of my programs. I've

152

The Later Manuscript

forgotten why he wanted to speak to me, perhaps about a new song, but I recall he asked about my husband and I told him how troubled and mystified I was.

"I can find out about your husband," he said. "I happen to know the head doctor at that hospital."

"Would you do that for me? I'd appreciate it so much. The reports are all so vague and confusing. I'm awfully alarmed."

The following evening, I was in my hotel room with my sister and sister-in-law. In a few minutes we were going out, for want of anything better to do, to see a play. Just then the young composer rang up from downstairs and asked to see me. When he entered my room, I could see at once that he had serious news for me. I asked him to come into the bathroom, so the others wouldn't overhear.

"Well?" I asked.

"You should have been informed a long time ago. . . ."

"Please tell me what it is—how bad is it?"

"Unless a miracle happens," he said, "your husband will be dead in two months."

"Not a word to the others," I said, feeling suddenly very weak.

I took quick hold of myself, not wanting to spoil the evening for the others. It struck me hard—the abruptness of it, and the cruelty of not having been told sooner. The young composer left, and somehow I brushed off his visit to my sister and sister-in-law. I said nothing to either of them about Henry. I had to think things over, and I wanted to act perfectly natural while I was doing so. So the three of us went to the play as if nothing had happened. . . . Several years later, I heard that same play over the radio. It was some time before I realized that it must be the one I had seen that dreadful night in Oslo. Even so, I couldn't be sure. . . . I shall always be grateful to Doerumsgaard for finding out and telling me the way he did. I don't suppose it is easy for a boy of twenty-four to do what he did.

I must have telephoned Stake the moment I got back to the hotel from the theater. You see, he was so very close to Henry

153

THE FLAGSTAD MANUSCRIPT

and me, I owed it to his loyalty and devotion to inform him first. I waited until the following day to let my family know. I then called my oldest brother and asked him to telephone Mother to come up to his place, where I would join them. There was something I wanted them all to know. And so, at my brother's house, I told my family. Calm as I am now, in a different way, of course, I told them that my husband was dying, that it was only a matter of two months, perhaps less. I can only say it helped me so much to be with them at that moment.

And then things went on. Once again we heard from our lawyer. After talking with Henry and the doctors, he had little hope to offer. The doctors didn't know for certain what it was, but they could see that Henry was going very fast. The autopsy showed a cancer of the lungs, near the throat. Yet, Henry had fever all the time, which is not usual with cancer, and that may have puzzled the doctors most. They suspected it was cancer, and so did we, but none of us could be sure. So of course we all held on to that small thread of hope.

Henry remained in the Ullevold Hospital for about a month. Finally, we managed to get him out and into a private hospital where he had been operated on for the removal of his gall bladder in 1938. There he was under the very best care, and we could now send him all sorts of things he asked for. One day he wanted fresh pears and we got them by plane from Sweden. We sent him the first strawberries from our greenhouse in Kristiansand, and the first flowers. At Kristiansand we have two beautiful magnolia trees that Henry was very fond of. The moment the first buds came out we sent them to him.

One day Henry's oldest daughter went to Sundför and asked if she might go to see her father. Sundför said "Yes," and she went. It was a mistake. Henry was so shaken that on the lawyer's next visit, he said, "I don't want to see anybody—anybody at all."

Because of his throat condition, Henry found it extremely difficult to talk. My stepdaughter told me it was terrible to see him. I am sure she regretted the visit as much as he did. I myself

154

The Later Manuscript

never thought of visiting him at all. I knew it would be hard on him, and hard on me too. But there was something more. I knew Henry, and I knew he would send for me if he wanted to see me. He never did. Without my knowledge, however, Bendixen asked Sundför if I might pay my husband a visit.

"Only with a police escort will she be allowed to see her husband," was Sundför's reply.

No such condition had been placed on my stepdaughter's visit.

Bendixen came to me with Sundför's answer.

"Will you please ask my husband if he wants that?"

I knew the answer would be no, which it was. Knowing me so well and knowing how well I knew him, Henry must have felt it would be better to keep that thirteenth of May as our last meeting. I know he wanted me to remember him the way he was the last day I saw him in the garden of our home at Kristiansand. And I felt that way myself. I wanted to remember my husband as he was then, in good health, at home, with me, still free. Those were the reasons we did not want to see each other. . . .

Again I went back to Kristiansand, and waited, and hoped for a miracle. Instead of a miracle, Sundför once more appeared as a threat.

To keep me in Norway he had been using the argument that I was needed to disentangle the combined finances of my husband and myself. Since there was never any charge against me, and he was gracious enough to admit it openly, I naturally protested when along with the property of Henry's sons Sundför also took custody of mine. The matter had come before the court in Kristiansand. That had been in July, 1945, and Sundför had to make the trip down from Oslo to present his case.

The moment he walked into the courtroom and spotted me he came over to introduce himself. As he put out his hand I did what I suppose was a very stupid thing: I deliberately placed both my hands behind my back and ignored his outstretched

THE FLAGSTAD MANUSCRIPT

hand. I couldn't help it. Not after what I had had to endure. Because of that insult in open court, I think Prosecutor Sundför became my enemy more than he ever was Henry's.

I can't otherwise understand his efforts to hold me in Norway. And now, in June, 1946, another court meeting was called. This time I had volunteered to testify in court, hoping that I would be able to get my passport. I submitted satisfactorily to a long and involved court questioning about the property matters. Sundför knew he couldn't keep me back this time. But, then, one of the court questioners brought up the old charges that had been made by Ambassador Morgenstierne. That was too much for me. I'm afraid I completely lost my head. I said the Norwegian Embassy in Washington had lied about me and my husband. I remember the silence that followed; yet nobody called me to order. That to me is significant. You see, in a Norwegian court it is forbidden to accuse anyone of lying, least of all members of a branch of the government.

Almost at once the Foreign Office cabled the Embassy about my accusations. Meanwhile my own lawyer was busy. Documents and affidavits were assembled, and this time the Embassy found itself on the defensive. When the answer finally came it was honest and straightforward. It had been taken for granted that I had invited the Nazi minister to my concert in Washington, but there was no real evidence. That had been the assumption because it seemed odd that the Germans should have granted me a visa so readily.

That was the last I heard of the old charges that had been made against me in America. Once they were asked to supply proof, the attitude was modified. But then, how can anyone furnish proof of something that never existed and never happened? It is all as simple, and as painful, and as petty, as that.

This, too, I wish to stress here: I have never been *cleared*. I have never liked that word, because it never applied to me. The implication was that there was something to clear. There was absolutely nothing to clear, as far as I was concerned. There

The Later Manuscript

was never a Flagstad case; the Norwegian government has itself declared that they never had anything against me personally. This is a vital point. I was never cleared of anything for the very good reason that I was never charged with anything by the authorities.

Accusations later brought to my attention were loosely and carelessly made and would never stand up in any court recognizing the ordinary standards of evidence. What had been offered as evidence of irregularity in my attitude toward my country and the war turned out to be pure distortion or the flimsiest hearsay. Not a shred of real proof of the newspaper and gossip charges that have been made was ever forthcoming.

Among the many who have come to hear me sing there may have been some who, in their hearts, looked upon me as a symbol of a certain political creed. I can give such people no comfort at all. I never shared *any* of the beliefs of our enemies of the last war. I want to remember the applause of the crowd for what it was—a testimonial of their faith in me as an artist and a decent human being.

That I was politically inactive when others were sacrificing their lives I am prepared, along with millions of others, to admit. That I was neutral in my feelings toward the horrible tragedy that overtook my county is the grossest falsehood, and for a woman who loves Norway as I do, the cruelest unkindness of all. Nor do I think it fair of anyone to hold it against me that to the very end I believed in the goodness and decency of the man I had married. . . .

Think of going into that court to confront Sundför—and my husband destined to die in less than a week!

I shall never forget the day. It was St. John's Eve, June 23rd—a time of festivity in Norway, when people stay up all night and build big fires. I was home, alone. Stake had called the day before to say there was no hope. I looked out of the window, and I remember how I gave a start. A sudden fog had come in, and

THE FLAGSTAD MANUSCRIPT

the whole garden looked white and ghostly. I called out to my housekeeper, "Look at that fog, how thick and white it is! I've never seen it like that at this time of year. Isn't it too bad, with all those people out there trying to enjoy themselves. It will spoil their fun."

It must have been about eleven o'clock. I went back to have a cup of tea, when the telephone rang. It was Stake, the ever faithful Stake who finally had got permission to see my husband —for the last two hours.... Stake was now talking to me.

"It's all over now."

For a few moments I could say nothing.

"Were you with him?"

"Yes."

"Was it easy?"

"It was very quiet. He was holding my hand and I had no idea he was dead."

The moment Stake hung up I telephoned our factory chauffeur and asked him to inform the manager. The chauffeur asked me if I wanted any company, and I said no. I looked out the window at that wall of fog once more, and trying not to think, I went to bed. The next day the flag in our garden at Kristiansand was lowered. As I prepared to leave for Oslo several workers from the factory came to express their sympathy and say good-by....

Henry died on a Sunday and was buried the following Thursday. One of the darkest moments of my life was when we went to take the body from the hospital. Stake, his wife, and their youngest son accompanied me. All three of them went in to see Henry in death. I didn't. I just couldn't, and I believe I kept faith with Henry by not doing so. When I look back on those few days I wonder at my calm. Fighting Sundför in court, knowing my husband was dying. Then Henry's death only five days later. Somehow everything that was happening found me steady. It was one more indication to me that I had changed into an-

The Later Manuscript

other person on that thirteenth day of May in our garden at Kristiansand. . . .

I scarcely cried when my husband died. Just a little, I suppose, but no more. I'm afraid my tears had all dried up inside. And I haven't cried very much since, not even in moments of the greatest exhaustion, when my mind and body craved nothing but rest from this ordeal of work.

The worst thing about losing a husband is that you are suddenly left without someone to lean on, someone who loves to take care of you, helps you to live and have confidence. Henry was all of that to me. I never did anything without first consulting him. Whatever advice he gave, I always followed it. The death of a husband is like having something fall away from under you. You don't quite know what to do; you stand alone, and, worst of all, you find you must learn all over again to make your own decisions. . . . Of course now that my loss is far behind me, I have grown more confident and independent. I decide things for myself, and rather enjoy it. Sometimes it frightens me to realize how changed, how self-sufficient, I have become.

I must point out here that while Bendixen was in general my lawyer as well as Henry's, he was not mine as long as there was any court action pending over what part of the property belonged to me and what part to my husband. You see, one of the reasons the situation was so tangled was that ever since we had married Henry and I had maintained separate property rights. So when I needed a lawyer to help me get my passport, I asked Bendixen to recommend one.

"Why not approach Anneus Schjoedt," he suggested.

That was the lawyer who had prosecuted Quisling—one of the most brilliant in Norway. I went to him and asked him to take my passport case, which, of course, had no connection whatsoever with the property matters then pending in court.

159

THE FLAGSTAD MANUSCRIPT

"My hands are so full right now," said Schjoedt, "but I'll see what I can do."

He very kindly offered to accompany me to the office of the head of the department in charge of such matters, and of course when we arrived our old friend Sundför was there. I wasn't at all surprised. Again he gave as his reason for holding up my passport that I was needed in Norway while an inventory was being made of the Johansen properties. But Prosecutor Schjoedt's presence was sufficient.

"She should have her passport," said Schjoedt, and that was that.

Sundför was completely taken aback. He went on insisting that it was dangerous to allow me to leave the country at that time. I was told he had even put out the theory that my husband had hidden money away in various parts of Europe. Perhaps he suspected it was my intention to gather up these secret hoards. I don't know, and I don't know whether he really believed it.

In spite of everything, I owe Prosecutor Sundför a debt of gratitude. Without intending it, he did me a good turn. Had he not been so determined to prevent me from leaving the country, I would not have been home when Henry died. For that one unwitting act of mercy, I can almost forgive him everything. I would have reproached myself the rest of my life if my husband had died while I was in another country.

My passport securely in my purse, I drove to Kristiansand, packed my things hurriedly and made ready to leave the country. When I left, the factory workers again came to bid me good-by. I remember it was quite stormy outside. There was snow everywhere, and sleet.

"Please come back," they said, as I got into the car with the chauffeur. "We all feel we must depend on you now."

None of us had the slightest notion how it was all going to work out. I had only one dread: that I might be stopped and delayed again. So my idea was to get out of Norway as quickly

The Later Manuscript

as possible. Naturally I couldn't take any money with me. No one was supposed to then. I could buy my railroad ticket to the border, but that was all. Sundför had even seen to it that my old travelers' checks were taken from me. All my money had been taken into the custody of the court. I had been living on an allowance from the claims department, and Sundför, true to form, had even protested the size of the allowance, suggesting that I sell my jewelry instead. Strangely enough, he never prevented me from taking my jewelry with me. Whether that was an oversight I'm not sure.

None of that really bothered me, however. It was only the thought of Sundför that troubled me. I didn't want him to dig up anything else to delay me. We drove to Oslo, and from there went on to the border. Waiting for me on the other side were my oldest stepson and his wife. Not until I was well across that border was I certain that Sundför wouldn't put another obstacle in my path. We drove on to Stockholm.

Chapter Sixteen

I SPENT three weeks in Stockholm in a hotel. That was in December of 1946. It was a relief to get away, I admit. I saw a good deal of my stepson and his family, which included three children, one of them a newborn baby. Toward the end of my three weeks' stay, as Christmas was drawing near, I prepared to leave for Switzerland. I had grown very fond of the oldest of my stepson's boys, a handsome little fellow of eleven, whose name was Henry, like my husband's.

"Would you like to go to Switzerland with me, Henry?" I asked him one day.

"Oh, I'd love it, Tante!" he cried.

I hadn't really expected him to say yes, but there it was.

"You wouldn't leave your parents and your new little sister, would you?"

"Oh, yes I would!"

"On Christmas Eve?"

His answer was still a very eager "Yes!"

"Well," I said, "if Daddy can get you a passport for Switzerland, off we go."

Daddy did, and off we went, little Henry and I. So I had a little boy on my hands for the first time in my life—and for fourteen days. We went to my favorite hotel, the Dolder Grand at Zürich, and there, while I tried to take care of him, I soon

The Later Manuscript

discovered that Henry managed very nicely by himself. He went skating alone and was pretty much the independent little fellow. I remember one day he came to me at the hotel and said, "You know, Tante, my mommy and daddy would be very angry with me if they knew something."

"Now what would that be?"

"Well, I'm not doing something I'm supposed to be doing."

"And what could that be?"

"You know, when we go down to eat in the restaurant...."

"Yes?"

"I'm supposed to pull out the chair for you."

"Well, that's very polite and gentlemanly."

"But the waiters never let me."

He looked so sad as he said that, in his neat little dark suit and black tie. So, the first chance I had I told the waiter to let him pull the chair out for me, and Henry was the perfect little gallant ever after. Then he would tell me the tallest stories, with such seriousness. "You know, Tante," he would begin solemnly, and the most unlikely tale would come from his little lips. "Oh, really!" I'd say, trying to look suitably awed. The next day he would come to me very meekly, and with a guilty air say, "It wasn't quite that way, Tante. I exaggerated a little."

I think he began to realize that I knew perfectly well he was fabricating the whole thing. Then one day he began to worry about how much it might be costing me to keep him there in Switzerland with me.

"Couldn't I get permission to work here?" he asked me.

"But why should you want to do that?"

"So I might help you pay for me."

"And what makes you think of doing that?"

"Well, then you wouldn't have to sing so many concerts."

Henry and I were on the same floor at the hotel, I in one room and he in another room across the corridor from me. Outside each door there were three lamps, one green, one red, and one white. A guest would push a button controlling the lights, and

163

THE FLAGSTAD MANUSCRIPT

a maid, a valet, or a waiter would soon appear. One day Henry came to me breathless with excitement.

"I've found out something!"

"I can tell you have," I said suspiciously.

"I've found the place where the waiters and maids and valets turn off those lights."

"Now, Henry, don't tell me you've—"

"I've turned them all off, Tante!"

"But why?"

"I didn't think all those nice people should be answering so many calls. They work too hard."

Finally the time came for Henry to leave. I put him on a plane and back he flew to Stockholm. I think toward the end he was longing just a little bit for his new baby sister.

It had been such a new and lovely experience for me, just what I needed after all the sadness in Norway. I had never dealt with boys before, having only had a daughter myself. The two weeks had been in the nature of a holiday for me. I was on my way to Cannes, you see, for the first concert of my return. I needed so much to relax somewhere away from home before I started to sing again. I did not want to think of what had happened or of what lay ahead—and Henry was the perfect tonic for me at that moment. The little fellow went back home, and I missed him terribly for a while. Then I had to leave for Cannes, and my career began all over again.

What was it like coming back to it? Well, I still had a voice, I found out soon enough. I sang at two orchestral concerts in Cannes, at the second of which Grace Moore was present. She had just been made an honorary citizen of Cannes and her loge at the little theater in the Casino, I remember, was decorated with flowers. I saw her as she entered it, gay and radiant. After the concert she asked me to supper, also in the Casino. The band played two numbers for us—"Depuis le jour" from Charpentier's *Louise,* that one for Miss Moore, and for me, Grieg's "Ich

164

The Later Manuscript

liebe dich." A week later this warm and friendly creature, so much in love with life, was dead in a plane crash in Denmark.

I often think of her with the fondest feelings. She was so very sweet to me at that lonely turning point in my career, and we had a good time together that glorious evening in Cannes. Yet, charming as the whole episode in Cannes was, I didn't have the real feeling of returning to music till a few days later, when I sang in Paris. That was in January, 1947.

On my arrival in Paris, I was told that only a week before, the French pianist Alfred Cortot had had to cancel an appearance with orchestra. I believe the unions protested because of his behavior during the occupation. So, Cortot gave a recital instead. I mention this because for me that was the first indication that anybody in the musical world was being barred in any sense. It never once occurred to me that it might happen to me too, whether in Paris or anywhere else. That anyone would want to demonstrate against me, for whatever reason, never crossed my mind. . . .

I gave two concerts in Paris, and the audiences were just lovely. Quite a lot of American soldiers were there, and I understand many American officials too. I must admit I was happy, very happy, to be close to my audience again with my voice. My own response to the singing? I always find it hard to answer that. You see, apart from being carried along with the audience, it has always been, to me, an ordinary business. Except for once in a long while, as in Gluck's *Alcestis*, there has never been anything especially exciting about it. It is difficult for me to set myself up as my own judge, to analyze my own reactions to myself as a public artist. But this much I know. I found again in Paris that it was just as natural for me to sing as it had ever been—just as natural and just as easy, maybe even easier. And I wish to say this about those concerts in France. There was never a suggestion of anything political at any time—not that I knew of, at any rate. The public was most gracious, and the reviews were beautiful. I was glad to be working again, and everybody

THE FLAGSTAD MANUSCRIPT

seemed to be with me. I had absolutely no reason to fear unpleasantness from any source; on the contrary.

I hadn't been very well known in France. Two *Tristans* at the Opéra in 1938, then a concert, and nothing more after that till January, 1947. So, it was gratifying to find the public so friendly and receptive. I have always found that stimulating— coming before a new public. The Parisians I found no different from the others in their response. Of course, they didn't shout "Liebestod! Liebestod!" all the time. That, I am afraid, is peculiar to America, where the cry is always "Wagner! Wagner!"

I had one curious experience during my Paris concerts that still amuses and puzzles me. It had to do with my conductor. My two concerts were scheduled for Saturday afternoon and Sunday evening, at the Champs Élysées Theatre. Friday morning was set aside for my rehearsal with orchestra, which made it really three full sessions in all. Well, I arrived from Cannes on Thursday and the following morning went to the rehearsal. The conductor hadn't arrived yet, so, along with the others, I waited. A half-hour went by, and still no conductor. I waited, the orchestra waited, and finally we were told that the conductor had been delayed somewhere and somehow. Would we report for rehearsal at eight the following morning? Now the trouble with that was that we were supposed to hold an "open" rehearsal, with audience, at ten, and then at three the concert. The following day we were to repeat the program, all of which made things rather congested. But no one uttered a word of protest. Everything went very smoothly and according to schedule at all three of the Saturday sessions, including the concert. Then came Sunday afternoon. I arrived early at the theater. As on the day before, the program was to start with the Prelude and Liebestod from *Tristan und Isolde,* with me as soloist. Well, I was sitting in the wings waiting for the concert to start, when the conductor came over. Very casually, without any preliminaries, he said to me, "I would like to conduct the Liebestod without you tonight."

166

The Later Manuscript

For a moment I didn't understand what he meant. Then it dawned on me why he had said that. He was fearful of overworking me and was considerately offering to excuse me from the Liebestod.

"He thinks I've done more than my share and wants to spare me this added burden," I said to myself. It was truly chivalrous of him.

Very touched by this gesture, I replied sweetly, "I don't mind singing the Liebestod, I don't mind at all."

He seemed taken aback.

"I'm sorry," he said, "you don't quite understand. I would *prefer* to do the Liebestod alone this time."

I saw now what he meant.

"All right," I said, shrugging my shoulders. He was the boss. I have tried never to argue with a conductor.

So I sat there in the wings, resigned to wait just that much longer for my time to appear on the stage. As you know, there is a bit of percussion, a kind of gentle tapping between the Prelude and the Liebestod, when they are done as a concert unit. At that point, in the stillness, I could hear the audience getting restless, wondering, I suppose, where I was. So my conductor went on with the Liebestod, and Isolde just sat there in the wings, her hands folded patiently in her lap. After it was over, I could hear a little bit of applause, rather questioning applause. Finally, I came out from my hiding place and sang something— if I recall it was a group of songs by Grieg, and that was followed by the intermission. And of course some newspapermen and other people came up to me with all sorts of questions.

"Why didn't you sing the Liebestod?"

"Did you come too late?"

"Were you suddenly taken ill?"

"Were you nervous?"

"No," I said, "I wasn't late, I wasn't sick, I wasn't nervous. I've been sitting here all the time."

"But why didn't you sing the Liebestod?"

THE FLAGSTAD MANUSCRIPT

"I would rather say nothing about it," I replied.

I said that in a way that couldn't possibly hurt anybody. The conductor never explained it, as far as I know, but I am sure he was pretty ashamed. He should have realized that what he did, for whatever reason he did it, would hurt him and not me. But, of course, I took the blame—and he let me. I allowed them to assume anything they wished, that perhaps I was covering up, that I had been late, after all, or sick, or nervous, anything they wanted to believe, anything but the truth. The curious thing is that the papers said I sang the Liebestod, as if there had been no change from the previous concert, and what was worse, no comments for him. So I'm afraid my conductor gained exactly nothing by his sudden inspiration to keep Isolde in the wings.

It must have been the very next day that I left for London for a concert in Albert Hall. I remember my schedule was very close and crowded and that I was finding myself increasingly eager to go on. The reception in London was even warmer. *And again not a single hint of anything political.* I was glad that my work took up so much of my time, glad not to have the leisure to think. I must confess that I was a little bit nervous about the traveling. It was then a great deal more difficult to get about in Europe than it is now. But I managed.

Then I went on to Italy, to La Scala in Milan, to sing *Tristan und Isolde* with Victor De Sabata as conductor. That was my first contact with the Italian public, and I must say I was in some ways disappointed. From the things I had heard, things all of us have heard, I expected the Italians to be far more demonstrative about me than anybody else. But nothing of the sort, at least not at La Scala. I never saw anything like it. As we say in the theater when people don't applaud, "They had gloves on." They crowded La Scala all right. And it wasn't their indifference to Wagner. Of that I'm certain. To tell the truth, I was somewhat prepared for their curious restraint, yet not completely. I had gone to see three operas after I arrived in Milan—*Hänsel und Gretel,* Mascagni's *L'Amico Fritz,* and *Lucia di Lammermoor.*

168

The Later Manuscript

I saw then what a La Scala audience was like. When the curtain came down and the claque started to applaud the crowd didn't follow at all. People just sat there, amid a faint ripple of hand clapping. The poor artists came before the curtain, and a bit more applause started up, but never anything approaching an ovation. Only the claque was busy. The audience was too sophisticated, I suppose. Of course, I went back to my hotel each time hoping it would be different with me and Wagner and *Tristan*. But it wasn't. The same stony restraint, the same idle hands. What made it worse was that we of the German wing at La Scala had no claque. I immediately said to the others when the curtain came down, "I can't go out. Nobody is applauding."

They replied, "That doesn't matter. You have to go out anyway."

I remember feeling very foolish as I stepped out before them. There was some polite applause, and that was all. I had never realized what a fortifying thing applause is to an artist. I had to be denied it to know how helpless and futile and unwanted one can feel without it. Perhaps we of the theater get used to it, like the air we breathe and the food we eat, and we come to take it for granted. I have always found it a beautiful thing, that sudden clamor of recognition after a performance.

I sang three *Tristans* at La Scala; I was scheduled to do four, but the rehearsals took up so much time that the fourth performance was dropped. The public was the same at all three performances, relaxed, sedate, and completely undemonstrative. That may be a tradition with La Scala audiences. I learned later it was not characteristic of the Italian public as a whole, not even of the Milanese public, for that matter. For when I returned to Milan a year or two later, to give a concert, I found them quite enthusiastic. So it must be only the La Scala audience.

After my three *Tristans* I sang an orchestral concert in Turin with Jonel Perlea as conductor. I felt immediately at home there. The response was quite cordial, and I had every reason to change my mind about the Italian public. After that I went

169

THE FLAGSTAD MANUSCRIPT

back to London for a second concert and a broadcast. This takes me up to March of 1947.

Then came America.

I wish to say at this point that when I left Norway the thing uppermost in my mind was to go to America to see my daughter and grandson. I applied for a quota visa in March, 1947. If I remember correctly, this was arranged for me in Paris. The American State Department checked on me and gave me a one hundred per cent clearance—my so-called "clean bill of health." How well I came to know that patronizing and humiliating phrase! It made me feel as if I had been thoroughly disinfected and permitted once more to mingle freely with my fellow men and women.

Chapter Seventeen

I ARRIVED in America on March 14, 1947, entering as a resident alien, and almost my first experience was a big press conference. That more than any other single experience made me abnormally suspicious of reporters. There was one gentleman who cross-examined me as if I were a criminal who had been smuggled into the country. Through him I had my first taste of what a third degree must be like. That was the closest I ever came to it, other than watching its workings in such American films as *Detective Story*. I had always been cautious and fearful of the press, and this conference seemed to justify all my past misgivings. I have never again been subjected to such a barrage of inconsiderate questioning.

I had learned that a certain part of the press is always trying to make a sensation out of something, create a story even where there isn't one. Such people can be very reckless with the facts. I can't tell you the number of times I have been misquoted, or, what is worse, when I have said something and not been quoted at all. When I was asked a question and defended myself, my answer was rarely printed. . . . I remember how I was met at the airport a few years ago.

"Why haven't you defended yourself?" one of the newspapermen asked me.

"I have, but nobody prints my defense."

171

THE FLAGSTAD MANUSCRIPT

"Say, that's interesting," he said. "We didn't know that."
But even that wasn't printed.

One would have supposed from that conference of March 15, 1947, that some of those reporters knew things that neither my government nor theirs had been able to uncover about me. It left me quite shaken.

But not for long. I went straight to my daughter in Bozeman, Montana. I had been longing to see her and my son-in-law Arthur for such a long time, but most of all, I suppose, I wanted to see my six-month-old grandson, Sigurd Hall Dusenberry, and it is Sigurd who has been my very life ever since. After all, that was the nicest thing that could happen to me at my time of life. When I think of the unkind words that have been spoken and written about me, I say to myself, "How can anybody hurt me, when something like this has happened to me?"

We had a wonderful summer together at White Fish Lake in Montana, where we lived in a little log cabin in the simplest way imaginable. And that was where I got to know my grandson, and stored up what extra reserve of stamina and strength I might need for whatever might come.

While still in Norway I had been receiving clippings from America that gave me a few strong hints of what might be in store for me. I believe it was sometime late in 1945 that the late Oscar Thompson wrote a lovely piece about me in the New York *Sun*, the same Oscar Thompson who had "discovered" me in Oslo and returned to America to write that he had heard a new Isolde he believed in.

This time Mr. Thompson wondered why, now that the war was over, America shouldn't have Kirsten Flagstad back. The article reached me in Norway, and I was very pleased. However, after that article appeared, Mr. Thompson received several letters of protest, among them one by Marcia Davenport which he printed. Miss Davenport answered Mr. Thompson by saying that after what the world had gone through Americans had no need of people like me. This, too, was sent to me, and I was hurt

172

Kirsten Flagstad and her husband on vacation (1938).

ANGUS MC BEAN.

Kundry in *Parsifal* (London, 1951).

The Later Manuscript

and shocked beyond words. You see, Miss Davenport had been one of my complete admirers, and her articles about me in a theater magazine were always warm and inspiring. Now, suddenly, I found her against me, and I realized that into many people's minds there had crept baseless and ill-considered suspicions of me.

But I still had no idea what it was or would be like. I suppose both Edwin and my manager were a good deal more worried about it than I was. Naturally they knew about the whole thing better than I did, and they did all they could to spare me and keep me in the dark as long as possible. I was on vacation still and my first bookings were at least two weeks off.

Finally, as the date drew nearer, I was told quite frankly what I might expect. Picket lines. My very first concert was in Boston April 6th and I knew at once what might lie ahead, how naïve and unrealistic I had been to minimize those early rumors. For the first time in my life plain-clothes men rode with me to a concert. I saw dozens of police around the stage entrance. This was all so strange, because there had been absolutely no hint of anything of the sort in London or Paris or anywhere else in Europe. Another shock awaited me inside the house. It was only half full, quite a come down for one who had till then enjoyed only sold-out houses in America. But it turned out a glorious evening. From those who did come to hear me I received a welcome that threw me completely off my balance.

And no pickets—not quite yet. When I did see them later on, I wasn't taken altogether by surprise.

The crucial and dreaded day of my New York concert at last arrived. I was to sing in Carnegie Hall. That was on April 20. Before the recital Edwin said to me, "Now remember one thing —remember how the reception in Boston affected you."

I had been on the verge of tears.

"Remember how wonderful those people were, how they

THE FLAGSTAD MANUSCRIPT

stood and cheered for several minutes before you started to sing. . . ."

I promised to remember.

Edwin went on. "Now don't you start to sing until you've composed yourself. This much I can promise you: New York is going to be even more enthusiastic than Boston."

I knew what Edwin meant. Carnegie Hall was always the warmest place in the world for me as an artist. That is my audience. I have always felt on speaking terms with them. They are my public family more than any other. I have no hesitation in saying that my happiest moments as a singer were spent in Carnegie Hall.

Without referring to them, Edwin of course was worried about how the pickets and the shouting, if there was any, would affect me. You see, I hadn't quite learned to worry, not as yet, about this unpleasantness. I was still pretty innocent, even in my expectations, I have to confess. I had thought: I am prepared for the picket lines; if there are any demonstrations, they will occur in New York, only there. What really saved me that night was this: I could depend on my Carnegie Hall audience. I thought of the people walking outside, and I knew the audience was thinking of them too. I am sure it made them more conscious of me, and kinder and more attentive than they would have been. The concert went off smoothly, in a beautiful atmosphere of welcome and friendship.

The newspapers were not too good the next day. They were nice and polite, but rather cool, and of course everyone brought in the political background. I never thought that had anything to do with my art. But I suppose they couldn't resist it the first time. But time after time, whenever I returned to Carnegie Hall, the public was never allowed to forget. Couldn't they leave that old business out after the first and second and third seasons? Not a chance. Even after my last Carnegie Hall recital, several of the papers carried the usual references to my husband's arrest. They seemed to be determined to hammer it into the brains of

The Later Manuscript

the people, for what purpose it has never been clear to me. That's why I do not like journalism, or at least some sides of it. I always had the feeling that some of them would have preferred me not to come back, and not on musical grounds. Later I had a suspicion these same people were waiting for something to happen, for some little thing to crack, for me to miss a note, and humiliate myself in public. They seemed to be waiting to pounce on me. It wasn't a pleasant feeling, I can assure you, this feeling of being under constant scrutiny. But it served only to make me more resolved than ever that nothing of the sort would happen. I had made up my mind to sing as I had never sung before. . . .

When I went home after my Carnegie Hall concert I was happy. The chief thing I carried back with me was the memory of the audience standing up for me. That was what mattered, and the fact that I was glad to be singing to them and they to be listening to me. Those parading outside didn't matter. My conscience was clear, as it had always been, and as it is now. I knew I had done nothing wrong, and those people marching and sloganeering should have known better than to act on suspicion and rumor. It is very possible that among those pickets or those inspiring them there were some who thought that because I was a woman, it would be easy to frighten me. I feel certain they were not prepared for the way I took it. They must have been surprised that I never gave any sign of giving up.

I will say this in all honesty and sincerity: if I had been guilty of any of the things I was charged with, guilty either in word or action, I would never have been able to face my public. I would have been the first to surrender to the demands of the pickets. I could not have sung with anything of that sort on my conscience. It would have all been a lie, my voice, my singing, my being welcomed back so beautifully by all those good people. Instead, everything I was accused of was a lie.

I have said already that I was not and never had been a Nazi. I was not and never had been sympathetic to any part of the

THE FLAGSTAD MANUSCRIPT

Nazi program. All my life I had been against the things the Nazis stood for. To uphold me in this there were my friends and business associates, both American and European, there was my country and my country's government.

I was touched to see that the public that always believed in me had not lost faith. That night at the hotel, as I gathered my thoughts, I felt that time would take care of the rest. I knew I was strong enough to endure whatever else awaited me. And now I am glad I waited patiently and silently for things to take care of themselves. While it wasn't always easy I found strength in the simple knowledge that I had done nothing wrong and therefore had nothing to fear. One thing, however, puzzled me, and to be perfectly frank, even irritated me at times. I would think of the countless others, in politics and the arts, who were far more legitimate targets than I was, and whose names never even came up. . . . But I did not say anything and I did nothing about the so-called case against Kirsten Flagstad—and I am glad. I just sang. More and more I was sure that my singing would be answer enough, that and time. I shall never forget the support and confidence I received at all times from Edwin McArthur. For a while he was the only one who said, "You're right—don't make a move."

Through it all, he agreed with me in the way I was taking it. Like myself, he realized that the moment you start to answer, you've put yourself on the defensive, and how sure can you be that your answer will not be garbled or removed from its context and made to sound arrogant or self-incriminating.

There were some people who out of well-meant indignation wrote letters to the newspapers defending me. I never at any time solicited a single letter. Had I known ahead of time I would have discouraged these good people from sending such letters. I am afraid many of those letters hurt me more than if they had never been sent. They often brought other letters in reply, and that kept the whole thing going. I never thought there was any cause for controversy, not that I could see. I was

The Later Manuscript

pained to see people taking sides, whether for me or against me. Both sides helped to make of me an issue that had nothing to do with my one and only public function in life—which was to sing. Only I could reply, and the best way I knew how was by singing.

But the war over me went on. I hoped that people would stop writing about these things, that if there were no more letters the whole issue would die from lack of anything to keep it alive. It was useless. So many of those well-wishing people who liked to see their letters in the newspapers—out of the very kindness of their hearts, succeeded only in doing me harm. I really believe that. It made it appear as if I wanted them to be fighting for me. That was the last thought in my mind. I remember how furious I was when a letter of mine to an American admirer was printed in a magazine without my permission. I know she had meant well, but it only added fuel to the matter. It was such things that kept the issue boiling. If people had just left me alone, the newspapers, I feel certain, would soon have dropped the whole thing as an old story. Instead it went on almost to my farewell appearance last spring.

Chapter Eighteen

TWO days after my Carnegie Hall return appearance I gave a concert in Philadelphia, and that was something. I find it physically painful to think of it and almost impossible now to talk about it. Edwin and I came down very early. This time we knew, almost to a certainty, that there would be trouble, perhaps serious trouble. I was told, for example, that a certain wealthy gentleman of Philadelphia was prepared to spend one hundred thousand dollars fighting me if I dared to come back. Both Edwin and Marks Levine had warned me, but I could not believe the whole story, and again the consciousness that I had done no wrong strengthened me against any unpleasantness. I had my voice and I knew I would have the audience with me. On our arrival in Philadelphia we went immediately to the Academy of Music, where the concert was to be held. On the advice of my friends, I stayed there all afternoon, waiting and wondering just what might happen. I remember Edwin came in at one point, looking pale and nervous.

"There's going to be real trouble, I'm afraid," he said.

It seems the box-office girl had received a suspicious request for a huge number of tickets—seats in various parts of the house. The girl marked down all the seat numbers, and the list was turned over to the police to help them act fast in case of trouble. Later George Engles, then my agent, went out into the lobby and

The Later Manuscript

managed to talk to some of these people who were demonstrating. Most of them were young college boys. According to the story they told him, they were being paid fifteen dollars, plus the free ticket, for attending the concert. How true this was I have no way of knowing, but whatever it was they were paid or promised, they were evidently determined to earn it. Meanwhile other demonstrators had collected outside the hall. They had obtained a car with a loud-speaker, and by the time the concert started there must have been several hundred people marching and picketing and shouting. The police were everywhere. Inside the house they had been gathering rather early. By the time I came out for my first number, there must have been fifteen of them scattered in all corners of the stage. I could understand why Edwin was getting more and more fidgety as concert time drew near.

Finally, just before we went out, he said to me, "The police have asked me to tell you that if anything happens in the house, you are to walk out."

"I'm not so sure I'll do that," I said. "I'm not a bit afraid. I've done nothing wrong, and I'm not going to let them win, whoever they are."

The first thing I noticed when I came out was that the house was not full; it was a good-sized audience, but not as large as it should have been. No sooner had I started than it began. I had never heard it before, and it struck me as so strange. I mean the booing. You see, in Europe they whistle when they disapprove of anything. Frankly it caught me completely off my guard. Well, there was the booing, with the very first note of the very first song, Beethoven's *Busslied*. That was on one side. On the other side I could hear the applause, friendly and encouraging. Then, just as suddenly as it had begun, the booing stopped—stopped till I had finished the song, when it broke out again, and along with it the applause to counteract it.

And that was how it went. During each of the songs that followed, they would be quiet while I sang, and then, at the last

THE FLAGSTAD MANUSCRIPT

note become fearfully noisy. Just as I began another song the noise would completely subside. I remember it was very silent in the few moments before I started Beethoven's *Wonne der Wehmut*. In that silence, I heard it distinctly; it came from the balcony, in two deliberate, spaced-out tones: "Na . . . . zi!"

Someone in the orchestra immediately shouted back, "I dare you to repeat that!"

And the two syllables again rang out in the balcony: "Na . . . . zi!"

The startling thing for me was the contrast between the absolute silence and the unexpected cry that broke it. It was a well-executed plan, if plan it was. Shouting and fighting now broke out in the audience. In no time at all the police moved down to where the trouble makers were, and threw them out. I understand many of the demonstrators demanded their money back as the police escorted them to the door. I was also told that a few of them were detained at the police station till the concert was over. Perhaps what most impressed me about their behavior was that after my first number they never interrupted me during a song. As an artist I found that rather flattering. Of course the more they booed between numbers, the more stubborn I got, and you know how stubborn a Norwegian can get. I walked back into the wings when I finished my first group, and a policeman standing there greeted me with these words, "You certainly got guts, lady!"

To which I replied, "Thank you, officer. It must be my Viking blood."

I am sure I was less nervous than I am now. I remember saying to myself, "Well, now it's come out in the open, where I can face it."

After the intermission, there were no more demonstrations. But there was still another novel experience in store for me before that concert was over. I don't recall which song it was that I was singing. I suddenly could smell something very odd. I couldn't imagine what it was. It was unlike anything I had

180

The Later Manuscript

smelt before, and I remember thinking it must be my imagination. It was only later that I was told I had been the target of a "stink bomb." But it hadn't bothered me in the least, perhaps only because I thought I was imagining things.

The moment the concert was over, the police became very serious and active again. Edwin and I had planned to return to New York by train. Before leaving the hall, one of the policeman said, "We'd better go and search the station before you leave."

A few moments later he was back.

"I think you'd better go back to New York by car," he said. "There's no telling what they might do if you go into a railroad car. They look kind of determined."

We took his advice and drove back to New York. I remember feeling very sorry for poor Edwin during the entire drive. He has always taken everything much more to heart than I ever did, and that night he was more shaken than I had ever known him to be. I, on the other hand, felt curiously exhilarated. It had finally happened, this thing we all feared. You see, it had not been so bad two days before in Carnegie Hall. What had then happened had happened outside the hall, and even that had been rather mild and orderly. Inside Carnegie Hall it had been warm and inspiring. Yet even in Philadelphia I knew the applause was stronger than the booing. I knew the friends outnumbered the others. It was good to have the opposition right there before you, doing their worst.

"After that," I said to myself as we drew into New York late at night, "I can face absolutely anything."

And it added to my strength and determination. I wanted more than ever to give my very best and to work as I had never worked before. That was to remain my only reply. Nothing like that Philadelphia episode ever happened again. That was the worst, and almost the last. There were still pickets at Carnegie Hall in the seasons to come, and I have even seen them myself when I entered the hall. But those wonderful audiences every-

181

THE FLAGSTAD MANUSCRIPT

where more than made up for everything. I have always felt that they were the only real judges that counted. Several other concerts followed the one in Philadelphia, and it was then that I began to notice that fewer and fewer people were coming to hear me. I suppose that after the demonstration in the Philadelphia Academy of Music, people were afraid of something. That too could easily have broken my spirit, but I didn't let it. I fought off any mood of discouragement.

"Let's not admit defeat," I said to myself. "Let's go on."

Yet, several times, I almost weakened, and thought, Why should I sing in America when I can sing in Europe where they have all treated me so nicely?

I imagine it was that old Norwegian stubbornness again. I just had to go on. I knew I must resist any temptation to quit. I was not going to give up till I had made up my mind to give up. I wasn't going to make anyone force me to quit. That was going to be my decision, and mine alone. Again and again I thought that through my singing and by myself they would see for themselves, all of them, that I couldn't possibly have done any of the things I was so loosely being accused of. I remember the way several people put it to me, in speaking and in writing:

"Only to hear you sing would acquit you of anything mean."

I thought it was very sweet of them to say that, especially since it was the very thing I was striving and hoping for. If it had been any other way, I am certain it would have shown in my singing. What strength I had as an artist came, I believe, from this confidence in myself as an honest and decent person. I have tried never to be false to myself either as a singer or as a woman. I wanted my music to speak for me; it could say so much more than any words of mine. And there was this too: no one could misquote my singing.

In the beginning, for a while, I felt terribly sorry for myself. till that feeling of being right and innocent picked me up. I found, too, that after what had happened in Norway, there wasn't much that could get me down. The more they did these

182

The Later Manuscript

things to me, the more hard-boiled I became. That is the word I was taught in America, and that is the word that comes to me now. I had never been that way before and would have ridiculed it if anyone had predicted I would. But I could feel the difference in me, and the only word for it was hard-boiled.

Chapter Nineteen

AS I LOOK back now, my feeling is that if the Metropolitan had asked me to sing a performance or two the first season of my return to America, I would never have had any trouble. But I wasn't asked, and why I wasn't asked has never been completely clear to me. The Metropolitan season was still on, and if they had wanted to they could very easily have worked me into one or two places on the remaining schedule. Remember, I had not come over to sing—that is important. I was entering the country as a resident alien primarily to see my family. The rest I was leaving to circumstance and my agent. A Metropolitan invitation would have simplified everything and prevented a great deal of heartache and misunderstanding. It will be recalled that Edward Johnson, in answering questions put to him by the press, made it clear that he didn't want me back. Now, that was a real blow, I must say. I was deeply hurt by that, and I am not ashamed to admit it. We had had the friendliest relations in earlier years, and his attitude was hard to understand.

I was also hurt by the fact that so few of my former colleagues communicated with me when I arrived in New York. The few who did will never know how much their hand of welcome strengthened my confidence. Many whom I hardly knew rose to my defense, and I shall always remember Geraldine Farrar for

184

The Later Manuscript

her quick and genuine friendliness. Still, it never quite healed the hurt done by the others who ignored me. They stayed away from me as if I were something unclean. Not even a telephone call from many who had been among my closest artistic colleagues for years!

In the meantime, my concert seasons grew better and better. Houses began to be full again, and then, later in 1948, I went back to Europe. I sang at Covent Garden and in Paris. I gave concerts all over Europe. I was in Italy again, and once more in Zürich. Of that period I treasure my season at Covent Garden most vividly of all. It was encouraging and gratifying in every way. I met many wonderful people, some of whom were to become very dear friends in the years to follow. Of these the closest have been Bernard Miles, the brilliant actor-director-writer for whom I sang Dido, and his lovely and artistically gifted wife. I found that in many matters I needed sympathy and advice, and someone to talk to freely at all times. It was this place that Mr. and Mrs. Miles have come to fill in my life. It is one of the many lovely things for which I shall always cherish England.

While in London, sometime in June, I received a letter from a gentleman representing an organization * that staged benefits for the relief of Jewish children who had been victimized by the war and the occupation. Many of these Jewish orphans were being taken care of in Europe through this organization.

"Would you contribute your services to a concert for this worthy cause?" this gentleman, whose name was A. Schusterman, asked me.

I wrote back asking Mr. Schusterman to come to see me at my hotel. When he arrived, the first question he asked me was whether I had made up my mind.

"Before I give you my answer," I said, "I must ask you a question."

Mr. Schusterman gave a polite nod.

* United Jewish Relief Appeal.

185

THE FLAGSTAD MANUSCRIPT

"Have you any idea what is being said about me in America, the rumors going around?"

Mr. Schusterman nodded again.

"That I am an enemy of your people?"

Once more he nodded.

"I know everything about you, Madame Flagstad," he said. "I must be quite frank with you—just as you are being frank with me. Before approaching you, we tried every way possible to find out whether these things were true."

I said nothing, but listened with great interest.

"We discovered that there was no truth at all to the rumors. In fact, we would like to help you as much as we can, both here and in America."

"Help me how, Mr. Schusterman?"

"By telling whoever is interested that we are certain you have done nothing wrong."

"That's very nice, Mr. Schusterman," I said. "I can't tell you how deeply that touches me."

I was terribly nervous, however. There was a silence for a few moments. Then, I said, "You realize, of course, what a dilemma this puts me in."

Mr. Schusterman seemed to be prepared for what was coming.

"If I say no to this, certain people in America will say that I don't want to help your cause. You know what that will be like."

Mr. Schusterman didn't answer me; there was no need. The whole picture was as complete in his mind as in mine.

"And if I say yes," I continued, "wouldn't that indicate to these people that I am trying to buy my way back through an act of charity?"

Mr. Schusterman again nodded agreement.

"I will say this, however," he said. "We will do our utmost to prevent anyone from interpreting it that way."

"Will that really help?"

Mr. Schusterman shrugged his shoulders, and said nothing.

186

The Later Manuscript

"I leave it up to you," I said, "whatever you decide for me I shall do."

He shook his head, and said, "It's your decision, Madame Flagstad, and yours alone. That's the one place where we can't help you."

"All right," I said, "I'll do it—and with the greatest of pleasure."

Mr. Schusterman's face broke into a happy smile.

"We thought you would," he said.

Then we discussed a possible date for the recital, and that wasn't easy. I had been singing a rather long and crowded schedule at Covent Garden. I was booked for an orchestral concert in the Harringay Arena on July 2nd, another in Northampton, and a broadcast, and I was planning to leave for South America on July 7th. I thought at first we should wait till I came back to England. You see, Mr. Schusterman had approached me so late in the season. But he insisted on having it before the season was finished. The one open date in all that congestion, the only date at all possible, was July 6th. The place was to be the Central Hall, London. There was another difficulty. It turned out that his organization was not allowed to announce the recital till after my concert in Harringay Arena. That meant only three days in which to advertise it, and one of those days was a Sunday. Again I suggested to Mr. Schusterman that we wait till the following season.

"No," he said, "we ought to have it now."

Well, we did, and it was a lovely little recital, though not too well attended. That was the first. Then, when I returned the next season, Mr. Schusterman came to ask me once more to appear for them, this time at an orchestral concert to be conducted by George Sebastian. I, of course, was happy to cooperate. I was then invited to a dinner sponsored by the organization, and that proved a fascinating experience. Some distinguished English rabbis were present, and it was the first time I had seen Jewish ritual garments worn in real life. My dear

THE FLAGSTAD MANUSCRIPT

friend Becky Hamilton was with me, and several Jewish Members of Parliament made speeches. I was quite flattered by the things that were said, and extremely absorbed by the easy and graceful observances of the orthodox. It was an impressive evening.

Mr. Schusterman told me that they had written to several influential people in America to urge them to do their utmost to correct any false impressions about me. They seemed to appreciate the information, for Mr. Schusterman showed me many of their replies. After several talks with him, I realized that they had indeed done quite a thorough job of investigation on me before they invited me to sing at their charity.

"I must confess," he said, "we had one or two protests against asking you at the beginning, but they were all silenced by the results of our investigation."

The following year, 1950, I appeared once again for the benefit of those needy Jewish children, again with orchestra, and in Albert Hall. It had become a very sweet and gratifying association, and I was happy that through my singing I could reach out, in some small way, to those helpless innocents.

Here I would like to express a few thoughts about religious and racial differences. Such differences have never existed for me. Those who have known me all these years will bear me out in that. It is more than possible that, being the stubborn person I am, I have a few prejudices—that is, about music and morals and people's personal behavior. But bias against a fellow human being because of his faith or national origin is a feeling alien and hateful to me.

In the early part of the nineteenth century my country had laws forbidding the entry of Jews. This aroused all progressive-minded Norwegians, and particularly a great poet of ours named Henrik Wergeland. This man fought bravely and tirelessly against the Jewish ban. Because of his efforts, he more than anyone else was responsible for finally having the ban lifted. Wergeland wrote a poem which I, like all Norwegian

188

The Later Manuscript

children, learned as a child in school. I think it is the most beautiful poem ever written in defense and sympathy of the Jews. It is called "Christmas Eve"; it is a reminder of how much we owe the Jews and how we are all one family, Jews and Christians together. I was so happy to see it reprinted not so long ago in our Norwegian newspaper in Brooklyn. On Wergeland's birthday Norwegian Jews go to his grave and offer flowers. . . .

We Norwegians have always been proud of that—proud of the way we have done away with false barriers between people and proud of the way we have been trained to look on any minority as the equal of our own group, or as no minority at all. I don't believe I was ever conscious of the Jews as a minority or a group apart. Nothing could have been more against my nature, my upbringing, my schooling, my country, or my faith, than a remark that I was supposed to have made in America to the friend of a friend of a friend. I mention this only because the alleged aspersion found its way into the American press. The shame of it is that anyone at all should have believed me capable of such a feeling. This feeling would have implied a sense of superiority as a member of a majority group, a feeling I never had, even as a child. Sometimes I think it was the war and the evil forces behind it that spread the falsehood that there were differences among us.

Naturally, I had become a little self-conscious and that was why I had to be honest with Mr. Schusterman. I felt I had reason to wonder how my accusers would react to this gesture of benevolence. I would have done a good deal more in the way of benefits had it not been for the fear that my motives would be questioned. I knew that if my first concert in America had been a benefit—as was suggested to me—I would have been charged with trying to sneak back under the cloak of charity. I must say, however, that I never heard anything of the sort about those Jewish benefit concerts in London. If cynical comments were made by anyone anywhere, they were not brought to my attention.

Chapter Twenty

AFTER that first recital in the Central Hall I left for a rather long South American tour. I sang, either in opera or concert, in Buenos Aires, in Rio, in Montevideo, in Santiago, in Havana, in Puerto Rico. There were also two performances of *Tristan und Isolde* in Caracas. I don't know how true this is, but I was told that this was the very first opera they had ever had in Caracas, and of all operas, *Tristan und Isolde!* Probably an exaggeration! The response was quite cordial, and so was the response to my *Tristan und Isolde* in Havana. By November I was back in America, first in New Orleans, and then gradually back to New York and Carnegie Hall. The pickets were still there—but the interior of the house, as always, was stimulating and hospitable, which is what counted. Now followed the same old routine of concerts, concerts, concerts, traveling all the time, overnight stops in hotels, scarcely a moment to catch my breath. Then Europe again, and there too the same city-to-city routine. Nothing startling, nothing new—only work, and more work, and little time to think and take stock.

And during all this time there was still no word from the Metropolitan.

Finally, in July, 1949, I went for the first time in my life to Salzburg to sing in Beethoven's *Fidelio,* and I believe it was there that I received a cable from Marks Levine.

190

The Later Manuscript

WOULD YOU BE AVAILABLE TO SING THE BRÜNNHILDES AND KUNDRY NEXT YEAR AT THE METROPOLITAN AND ON TOUR IN BOSTON AND CLEVELAND?

I naturally assumed that the Metropolitan had asked Mr. Levine to cable this to me. Now, both Mr. Levine and I realized that I was already booked through that entire period. So that, actually, it was too late to ask me, and I had the feeling that the Metropolitan knew it was too late. This meant that the approach, if such it was, amounted to nothing more than a gesture. I cabled back the simple truth:

SORRY, NOT AVAILABLE.

That was all. No comments of any kind, just that.

Yet, somehow, with the usual embroideries, it all got into the newspapers—how, I'm not sure, perhaps from the European end this time. Mr. Johnson proceeded at once to deny having approached me at all. This of course also appeared in the papers, and so did my reply to the approach that wasn't supposed to have been made. It wasn't very pretty. But I was used to it by now. Then I began to receive furious letters and cables from friends and admirers. "How dare you say no to the Metropolitan? We have been backing you so strongly!"

I suppose they felt they just had to write to me to tell me it was my duty to come back ... for their sake. Some of them couldn't resist writing to the newspapers. And there it was once more, misunderstanding piling on misunderstanding, controversy all over again. As for the invitation, indirect as it was, I felt that if Mr. Johnson had really wanted me back he would have chosen a better time to ask me, when I wasn't already booked. Of course, he may only have been feeling out the ground.

Now for a confession. I was happy, so gloriously happy, when I received the cable from Marks. After I cabled back my reply,

THE FLAGSTAD MANUSCRIPT

I remember saying to myself with supreme satisfaction, "They've asked me to come back and I've said no!"

I can still feel the triumph of that moment.

I am a pretty proud person, and I sometimes let my pride stand in the way of my better judgment. But I believe I had always acted on the sound principle that in the end truth and right always win out. Time was taking care of the matter very nicely. I could afford to wait. I harbored no ill feeling against anyone, and I was now convinced that whatever ill feeling still lingered against me would vanish with time.

It was rather hard doing that *Fidelio* in Salzburg, to be singing in an opera about a wife's devotion to an imprisoned man, so soon after my own husband's tragedy. The others in the cast were aware of it, and I could sense their watching me and feeling for me. Their sympathy was warm—and silent. They said nothing at all. There was no need, really. They understood, and so did I. Yes, it was a hard thing to do, but I was glad to realize that I could do it at all. I discovered, after a while, that I was beyond the pain. But how close that role had become and how much I identified my devotion to Leonore's! There was this difference between us, however: Leonore got back her husband.

Then I went home. My first chance, in that crowded schedule of two and a half years, had at last come to return to Norway. Oh, I was happy! I had no intention of singing there, not then, certainly. Besides, it was in the middle of the summer. I was asked for interviews and I said no. Everything was smooth and tranquil. Nothing of any importance happened, except that the "case" was completed that summer, all except the verdict in the government's action against my husband's firms. I stayed mostly in Kristiansand, studying songs a good part of the time, and relishing the luxury of rest and isolation again.

Before me, in September, was the somewhat uneasy prospect of a season with the San Francisco Opera. There was still some uncertainty because of a little trouble that had started early

The Later Manuscript

in the spring when it was announced that I had been engaged to sing. While in Salzburg in July I had heard that a war veterans' group had protested against my engagement. The auditorium used by the San Francisco Opera is in a magnificent war memorial building. The organization that charters the hall had announced that they would rent the building to the opera company for the coming season only if the board changed their plans and eliminated me. To that the San Francisco Opera people immediately replied, "If we can't have Kirsten Flagstad, we won't have any opera season at all."

Which was quite a statement! It made me terribly happy to know that these people were standing up for me in no uncertain terms. At the request of the acting mayor of San Francisco, the American ambassador also cabled from Oslo that the "official Norwegian attitude," to quote the press, "was all favorable toward Kirsten Flagstad." A settlement was finally made while I was still in Norway, and, though I knew there might be some unpleasantness ahead for me, I tried not to worry, and went back to my songs and the peace and privacy of Kristiansand.

When at last I arrived in San Francisco in September I found everybody anxious and nervous. The opera people were particularly scared that something dreadful might happen, just what no one seemed to know. There was a certain tension, an expectancy in the air.

Frankly, I wasn't a bit frightened. There was only one possibility that had me worried for a while. It was that something in the mechanical setup of the performance might go wrong. That is, if there was going to be any protest, it might take the form of a clever piece of sabotage. Something, for example, might happen to the lights, so the performance couldn't continue. You see, everything was under thorough police surveillance. There was hardly a chance of disorder or demonstration in the house. The police were being doubly vigilant this time. If, after all, there was to be a demonstration, I felt I could handle it. I was, you might say, experienced. I had had my bap-

193

THE FLAGSTAD MANUSCRIPT

tism of fire; I knew I could take it. I just had this sneaky feeling that they might do something different this time. So I had this idea in my mind for a good part of the performance.

Nothing happened. The whole opera—*Tristan*—went very smoothly. No one bothered me at all. I should add here—that after my *Tristan* one of the San Francisco columnists said I was so scared I sang the entire first act with my eyes closed. Of course, I didn't. How would that have helped? I have always been happy in San Francisco. The company is an excellent one, and the performances have been of a very high order. The house itself is beautiful and an acoustical marvel, and the atmosphere has a reassuring quality all its own—cozy and welcoming and kindly, and the critics are kind too.

I believe that was the season I gave three concerts in Carnegie Hall, all of them sold out. When I came back to New York in December, Mr. Levine, tactful and thoughtful as ever, said this to me: "I know you don't want to talk about going back to the Metropolitan. . . ."

"But . . . ?" I prodded him.

"Rudolf Bing, the new manager, has expressed a desire to meet you."

"That's very kind of him," I said, pleased.

"If you have any idea of ever going back, Kirsten, I think you should see him."

I was silent for a few moments.

"I don't know," I said. "I can't make up my mind whether I want to go back or not. But I'd be very happy to meet Mr. Bing."

Well, after my Carnegie Hall recital, Mr. Bing came back to my apartment together with Marks and Edwin. I liked him at once. His whole attitude was that of a gentleman, and a man of decision. The way he presented the case showed supreme tact; it was straightforward and businesslike, and easy. He knew perfectly well what difficulty he was up against, and I knew too.

"Will you come back?"

194

The Later Manuscript

Of course my answer was yes.

"Will you do *Tristan, Fidelio,* and two Rings for us?" Mr. Bing asked.

"One will be sufficient, I think."

"Very well."

He then asked me to promise not to say a word about the contract till he had announced it to the press later that winter.

Not once did he even graze the subject of all the unpleasantness; he had probably been told there would be trouble; he had evidently weighed it all in his mind, and reached his own conclusion. We were all aware of everything that was involved, and we seemed to be silently agreed that it wasn't necessary to discuss it. I knew I was dealing with a man of courage and determination, and a man who had apparently never had the slightest doubt about me.

Shortly after that I sailed back to Europe, spending Christmas there and beginning my concert schedule again, in Paris this time, soon after the New Year. I appeared in Spain for the first time, and it was while in Barcelona that I had a call from London. It was a newspaperman, and almost his first words were, "Isn't it too bad about Helen Traubel?"

I was stunned for a moment, not imagining what had happened to the popular Metropolitan soprano, and perhaps fearing the worst.

"Why, what's the matter?"

"She's resigned from the Metropolitan."

Astonished and quite puzzled, I merely said, "Oh!"

"Haven't you read the newspapers this morning?"

"No. I don't read Spanish."

"Well," he went on, "the report is that she and Melchior have resigned from the Metropolitan."

"Melchior too?"

"That's what the papers say. By the way, what do you think of Traubel?"

195

THE FLAGSTAD MANUSCRIPT

"I think she's a very fine singer," I said, "and I don't understand any of this."

Then came the newspaper clippings of the reactions to Mr. Bing's announcement that he had invited me back to the Metropolitan, and some of them were painful reading.

"The whole thing has started again," I said sorrowfully to myself.

That was my unhappiest moment of all, when I realized that there was to be no peace for me. I had been deluding myself with the thought that it had all quieted down. I was sorry now that I had agreed to go back to the Metropolitan. I suddenly began to feel the strain of overwork. An intense depression about everything took hold of me. After being certain that nothing could ever hurt me again, I found myself taking it very much to heart.

What had evidently made matters worse was that just before Mr. Bing made his announcement about me, both Mr. Melchior and Miss Traubel were quoted as saying that they had not been asked to come back and were not coming back. Of course one paper went so far as to say that if they were not coming back to the Metropolitan, it was all because of me. You can well imagine my feelings, I who had nothing but the greatest admiration for both Mr. Melchior and Miss Traubel. It was all very dismal and painful. It hurt me and it saddened me.

I returned to America in the spring of 1950 for another tour. With Edwin conducting, I gave an orchestral concert in Carnegie Hall. That one was heavily picketed, I recall. I could hear them shouting in the street this time from my dressing room, not a very enviable experience. I read in one of the newspapers the following day that I had to be persuaded to go on the stage that night. Of course that wasn't so at all. I went out and I sang. I needed no one to urge me. I never have. Two of the columnists thought up another little scoop for themselves. They said that on account of what had happened in New York, Kirsten Flagstad had canceled her spring tour. That too

196

The Later Manuscript

was news to me. I suspect they thought it a good way of hurting my pocketbook, if nothing else. Of course, I didn't cancel my spring tour. Later I did call off two of my concerts, one in Montreal and the other in Ishpeming, Michigan, both of them because of a nasty attack of the flu. I was on my way back from California to Madison, Wisconsin, where I had planned to spend three days with my daughter Else. I had flown all day and part of the night. I remember I left right after one of my concerts in Canada. I hadn't made one connection in time, and finally arrived at Else's place in a daze of exhaustion. I went straight to bed, and the next day I knew something was wrong.

"I don't know what's the matter with me," I said to Else. "I don't feel well at all."

"Mother, I've never seen you look so awful! I'm frightened!"

So she took my temperature, saw that it was quite high, and immediately called the doctor, and that, I hope, explains my two cancellations, one of which I made up for the following season by opening my new tour in Ishpeming. I hate canceling things. A very long time ago I made it a principle of my work and my life never to call off anything once I had given my word to do it. After recovering, I left Else, Arthur and little Sigurd, and returned to New York. From there I went on to Europe.

That picketing outside Carnegie Hall was my last demonstration. Which surprised me, because I was certain that when I reappeared in America, the picketing would be even worse. But it had stopped. I was pleased and relieved. I felt pretty sure now that nothing bad would happen at my first Metropolitan performance, and nothing did. In spite of the precautions that were taken in the house, the police, the high expectancy of newsmen and photographers, I never for a moment felt that anything disagreeable would happen. The opera, of course, was *Tristan und Isolde*, the date January 22, 1951—almost ten years after that other *Tristan* of April 14, 1941, when I had promised to come back.

197

THE FLAGSTAD MANUSCRIPT

I remember how the applause broke out and continued as the curtain went up on the first act showing Isolde lying there on the couch. They must have thought I was nervous and that they were helping me, for they didn't seem to want to stop applauding. All I could think of as I lay on that couch was, "Why don't they stop?" I'm afraid this is going to sound calloused and cruel, but I wasn't at all touched. I kept thinking that there were still so many people in that house against me.

The truth of the matter is that I did not return to the Metropolitan with any happiness at all, in spite of Mr. Bing's kindness. My one thought was: this has got to be done. I must show them that I'm back where I should have been all the time, *and that I was asked to come back.* That was more important to me than anything else. Yes, it was a nice reception, very satisfying indeed—the critics even counted the nineteen curtain calls at the end. And naturally I have always liked to work. In fact, except when it exhausts me so much, as it has during these last months, I have always been happiest when working.

I wasn't pleased at being back for the sake of being back, not in the least. I was pleased only because of this feeling of triumph over my enemies. That is the way I feel they are being punished, by seeing that I still survive, and as far as I can tell, they must be "burning up" nowadays. And that, I am ashamed to say, is satisfaction enough for me. It was reason enough to return to the Metropolitan, to be on the top, where I had been before. I was again where I had always belonged, where it had been my pleasure and pride to be. Yet I was sad, really. I thought how cruelly unnecessary the whole business had been, and I could have wept.

I know that many people were worried about how I might sing again after such a long absence from the Metropolitan. I wasn't a bit worried. After all, I had been singing Wagner all along. That was no problem—returning to the Metropolitan as a singer. The tones came as easily as ever, if not more easily.

198

The Later Manuscript

There was absolutely nothing in the music that frightened me, but then nothing in the music ever did.

The only thing I ever dreaded in opera had nothing to do with singing. And this may sound funny. It used to give me quite a turn climbing up and down steep steps as if I were clambering over jagged rocks. Spear in hand, it is by no means an easy thing, particularly if you find yourself putting on weight. That is probably my only quarrel with Wagner. I must admit that the climbs have been easier at the Metropolitan than in London or Milan, and easiest and safest of all in Zürich. There the steps were plastic and for some reason they were very kind to my feet and my balance.

As I clambered up and down the rocky summits, I would reflect how nice it would be to have a repertory in which I stayed on level ground all the time. I used to think with envy of sopranos who sang operas like *La Traviata*, operas that didn't have dark staircases to climb and pointed weapons to carry.

In London the scenery was built of big black squares of stylized stone. I shall never forget one horrible moment in the last act of my first *Die Walküre* in Covent Garden. I was supposed to be lying asleep on this huge black block. Around it Wotan had just ordered the ring of fire to be thrown. I could hear him as he moved toward the steps to leave the stage. Suddenly there was this heavy thud, and I knew Wotan had missed his step and fallen off the rock the six feet to the stage below. The sound of his fall was so loud I leaped up. I was certain Wotan had injured himself badly. By what must have been a miracle, poor Wotan only hurt his little finger.

Tristan und Isolde, I admit, is a great deal easier to manage, as far as the floor technique is concerned. Most of it remains on one level. It is all quite safe and comfortable for Isolde, except when she shares the death couch with Tristan. That has always been something of a problem for me. It wasn't too difficult at the Metropolitan, because, you see, they always gave us a couch that was very wide. It was something else that worried me. The couch was covered with bearskins. Well, I always went out while the curtain was down and examined those bearskins in person. I had to satisfy myself that there would be no danger of sliding off. The inspection was quite elementary. I looked to see if the direction of the hairs in the fur was upward rather than downward. If such was the case, I knew there would be little danger of sliding off the couch.

In some opera houses, the couch offered only half this room. I would then have to collapse in some other place, and in some other and more awkward posture. With the opening of the Liebestod, I would try to get up gracefully and romantically, and that, you may well imagine, wasn't so simple after I had been lying in a difficult position for maybe a quarter of an hour. Everywhere I sang I made it a point to go out before the last act and examine the couch and all the other props. I wanted to be sure of where and on what I was going to collapse, and how I would be able to get back on my feet for the Liebestod. I have heard of singers with all sorts of superstitions. This was my only ritual, but I think a very practical one that spared me much embarrassment.

While I am on the subject of *Tristan und Isolde,* I should like to say that before I returned to the Metropolitan I sang my one hundred and fiftieth Isolde at Covent Garden, London. I was given a very beautiful reception that I shall long treasure in my memory. Since then I have raised the total to 182, and that, I believe, is enough Isoldes for one lifetime!

Chapter Twenty-one

BEFORE I speak of my farewell role at the Metropolitan, I must say something of another opera I have sung in English. The fact is that before I appeared as Alcestis at the Metropolitan in John Gutman's English version I had already sung Brünnhilde in an English *Walküre* at Covent Garden in 1948, and Purcell's *Dido and Aeneas* three years later. And that *Dido,* I think, is a charming little story. It began when my good friend Bernard Miles suggested that I sing Dido's Lament for a recording. I didn't know the aria at all, and in my innocence, I replied, "But isn't that for contralto?"

"It most definitely is not," said Bernard, who without being technically trained, is one of the most phenomenally musical persons I have ever met.

Well, I now know better, and of course I made the recording, and loved every note of that glorious music. Shortly after that I was invited to spend Christmas with Bernard and his family. That was in 1949. Before dinner he took me out on the grounds in back of his house, which had been renovated from an old school. And there he called my attention to a large and sprawling structure that he said had once been the school hall. It now looked like an abandoned barn. When he opened the door to show me around, I saw what must have been the discarded odds and ends of generations of tenants.

THE FLAGSTAD MANUSCRIPT

"I use it as a workshop," said Bernard, among whose hobbies are carpentry and construction of all kinds.

He did some puttering around while I watched; then he looked up again.

"Kirsten," he said, "believe it or not, this is going to be my own theater some day."

I refused to believe it. I knew Bernard Miles to be a practical joker, and I had learned to discount many of his announcements. But he was serious this time. He told me how the former school building had been converted into the house he and his family now occupied, how this old structure in the back yard had served as its auditorium, how the great singer Therese Tietjens had once visited the pupils of the school almost a century before in the very place where we were standing.

"Will you sing a few notes for me, Kirsten?" he said suddenly.

And without giving it a second thought, for Bernard was always asking me to do something of the sort, I let out a few notes.

"Hmm, not bad," he commented.

"Thank you," I said, "and just why did I have to do that?"

"This is why: I'd like you to sing here when I've made it into a theater. Would you?"

And I, of course, without thinking, said yes, just like that. And that was how I came to sing Dido in Purcell's beautiful opera, *Dido and Aeneas*.

I went off touring again, and Bernard, true to his word, worked on that ancient building till he turned it into a Shakespearean theater. I was in Italy, in March of the following year, when a large envelope arrived from London. It was from Bernard and it contained a contract the likes of which I had never read before and certainly never signed before. This was it:

ARTICLES OF AGREEMENT between KIRSTEN FLAGSTAD, soprano, hereinafter called "the Singer" and the Little Mermaid Company, hereinafter called "the Management."

202

The Later Manuscript

The Singer undertakes

1. To sing for twenty (20) performances the part of DIDO in the opera DIDO and AENEAS.

2. To assist in the production of the opera and to lend all such aid, advice, help and assistance as may be deemed necessary to the successful presentation thereof.

3. To use only her best quality voice, fully supported by the breath throughout each performance.

4. To sing all her notes in time and in tune but not to add any notes, grace notes, acciaccaturas, appoggiaturas, upper or lower mordents, shakes, trills, turns, titillations or other embellishments.

5. To let the Management or any part thereof look down her throat with a laryngoscope whenever they need encouragement.

6. To sing to the Management or any part thereof any or all of the songs of Schubert, Schumann, Beethoven, Händel, Bach and Grieg, as often as requested.

7. To be obedient, tractable, sweet-tempered and helpful in every possible way, and not to brag about the Vikings.

On their side the Management undertake

1. To treat the Singer in a manner worthy of her great name and fame, to look after her, to nourish, cherish, care for and make much of her. Also to hold her dear, to prize, treasure, cling to, adore, idolize and dote on her.

2. To appoint as her personal slaves their three youngest members, to wit Sarah, Biddy and John, who shall wait upon her hand, foot and finger.

3. To supply the Singer with all necessary scores, bars, notes and parts of notes, key signatures, leger lines, etc., as shall be deemed necessary for the adequate interpretation of her role.

4. To find her in board-lodging throughout the run of the opera.

5. To supply her with two pints of oatmeal stout *per diem,* at the following times and in the following quantities, viz. lunch one-half pint, dinner one-half pint, and one pint following each performance.

THE FLAGSTAD MANUSCRIPT

6. To give her plenty of little surprises, presents of flowers, fruit, fish and fresh foliage, to recite to her, to write letters and little poems to her; also to take every opportunity of making her laugh.

Given under all our hands and with all our hearts, this tenth day of February, one thousand nine hundred and fifty.

Bernard Miles
Josephine Ditson
Sarah Miles
Biddy Miles
John Miles

Sealed with a Kiss: ....

(Kirsten Flagstad)

Witnessed by:
Max Lorenz
Wilhelm Furtwängler

I was infinitely amused, as you may well suppose, and naturally quite touched. I did as requested. I signed it and sealed it with the lipstick mark of a kiss. Then I sent the contract back to Bernard Miles. And so it took shape, everything as planned. That old workshop and junk room in the back of Bernard's house was transformed into a lovely little theater holding 170 people, and I did as I had promised him at Christmas time. I sang for him, and in Purcell's *Dido and Aeneas*. The whole thing is almost indescribable. It was lovely, and sweet, and right. Bernard staged it, and Maggie Teyte came to sing Belinda for us. Geraint Jones, the leading organist and harpsichord player in England, conducted. The small orchestra, wearing period costumes and wigs, was seated on a dainty little balcony above us. Mr. Jones, of course, was up there with them, playing on a beautiful harpsichord, and as he played he directed the orchestra.

And do you know how we got our cues? This was Bernard's invention again; he invented everything, and when he didn't invent he revived and reconstructed with a miraculous sense of

ANGUS MC BEAN.

With Maggie Teyte, in *Dido and Aeneas* (London, 1951).

SEDGE LE BLANG.

Alcestis (Metropolitan, 1952).

The Later Manuscript

the period. We got our cues through mirrors! Since the conductor was above and behind us, we naturally couldn't see him, unless we happened to be facing his way, which meant turning our backs to the audience, and that, as a rule, just isn't done. So, there in the back of the theater Bernard Miles set up three mirrors through which everyone on the stage could see the conductor without craning his neck. Not that I needed them. I long ago discovered that I could sing without ever seeing the conductor. But it wasn't easy for the chorus. So we all looked into the mirrors and never missed a single cue.

I worked quite hard on the words and style of Purcell's opera. I found the rhythm rather difficult, and it took me some time to learn it and master it. But I loved it, all of it; it is impossible not to love it, the tenderness and nobility and beauty of it all. There were twenty performances, besides two fully attended dress rehearsals. The press was most gracious about it, praising every aspect of it, almost without reservation. I don't think either Purcell or his divine little opera ever got such a quantity of publicity. Later we made a recording of it. And now, when I go back to England in September, I shall do sixteen more Didos, and with them sixteen performances of a Bach cantata, in the same little theater—the Mermaid Theatre, which my amazing friend Bernard Miles constructed out of a rickety old storehouse that had once been a school hall in the back yard of his home.

I can think of no better or more logical introduction to Alcestis than Dido. Actually, my acquaintance with Gluck's opera antedated by several years my first meeting with Purcell's. It had all begun during the war in Kristiansand. I had returned from my first season in Zürich in 1942 and was working on some songs one day, when it suddenly occurred to me that it might be interesting to learn an opera again. I hadn't the slightest notion that I would ever do it in an opera house, whatever my choice might be. I wasn't even sure that I would ever sing opera again. I suppose it was the eternal student in me, or else I

205

THE FLAGSTAD MANUSCRIPT

wanted the challenge of something new, something different from what I had been singing. I browsed through many scores and my choice fell on Gluck's *Alceste*. The score I had was in French, so I set out to learn it in that language, which I knew after a fashion, but had never quite tackled in any serious way. And then Switzerland called for me again.

"Would you like to do something different this time?"

"That might be nice."

"Have you any suggestions?"

I turned it over in my mind and finally decided I would like to do either Handel's *Rodelinda,* which I had sung in Sweden in 1932, or *Alceste.*

"If it's the same with you," they said, "we'll take *Alceste.*"

I had already gone through the entire role in French, and now I got myself a German version and applied myself in real earnest to it. Nor was that all. In Zürich, they weren't altogether satisfied with the German text as it stood. So they kept making changes every day at rehearsal, making it better and better, but also giving me many new things to learn all the time. Everyone thought the production quite beautiful, and I realized it was a good role for my, shall I say, special talents. Some years later, the subject of a new role came up in a conversation with David Webster, director of Covent Garden.

"There is one opera I'd like to do for you," I said. "I feel it would suit me nicely, and besides it needs a beautiful chorus, just the sort of chorus you have here."

"Which opera is that?"

"Can't you guess?"

"*Alceste?*"

"That's it, and I've already sung it in Zürich. I would love doing it again, and in English this time. How about it?"

"I see only one way. If I could be sure to have you every year for five years, I'd be in a position to say yes and put it in the repertory for you. There's the budget, you know."

The Later Manuscript

"Then it's out of the question," I said. "I could only do it for one season. After that, I'm retiring from opera for good."

So there was no more thought of *Alceste* in London; not then anyway. Sometime later, when I had made up my mind to quit, I was asked to come back and do more Wagner.

"I'm sorry," I said. "No more Wagner. I've had quite enough, thank you."

"Well, if you won't do Wagner," Mr. Webster persisted, "how about Gluck—how about *Alceste*? It was your idea, you know."

"But you have your repertory problems, if you recall."

"I think we might arrange it. Shall we?"

"Of course," I said, and we left it at that. . . .

Now, Mr. Bing may have heard about it somehow or other, that I was ready to do *Alceste* for London. Just where he got the idea to tempt me back for another season with Gluck's opera, I don't know. But that was how it came about. It may have been a friendly hint from someone close to me; it may have been only a hunch, or a shrewd sense of fitness. I was so determined that my return season to the Metropolitan in 1951 would be my last and only season there. I had quite made up my mind to leave. I had so announced it, and I meant it, up to a certain luncheon. As far as the audience of my last *Tristan* was concerned—the audience that gave me a thrilling twenty-two minute ovation on that night of March 26, 1951—it was my farewell. I said so in my dressing room when the reporters asked me point-blank. And Mr. Bing, standing there with an enigmatic smile on his face, merely observed, "May I add that it is a lady's privilege to change her mind? We keep on hoping."

And of course the lady had already changed her mind and promised to say nothing about it.

It was my privilege, yes, but it was Mr. Bing's powers of persuasion that had finally done it. Again and again he urged me to come back to do more Wagner. All I said was, "No. I think I've had all I want."

Then, one day, at lunch, out of a clear sky he flung Gluck's

THE FLAGSTAD MANUSCRIPT

Alceste at me. He had been trying to persuade me to return for more Rings and more *Tristans,* for *Fidelio.* My last *Tristan* was approaching.

"No, no," I kept saying, "I'm not coming back—not for Wagner or anybody else."

"But suppose it were something else—something you especially like?"

"I'm sorry, you can't tempt me. I want to quit singing Wagner and everything else. Mr. Bing, I've been wanting to retire for so many years. Don't you think it's about time?"

He was very sympathetic, but far from discouraged. Suddenly, it came. "All right—how about *Alceste?*

He must have seen right away that he had the advantage over me. I hesitated, and in that moment of hesitation he had won.

"But I've told everybody I'm quitting...."

"I want you to decide here and now," he said.

It was too great a temptation, and Mr. Bing knew it. I asked for just a little time, and he was very sweet about it. I gave it very serious thought, and didn't make up my mind at once. There were so many complications. First, what would the press and the public think after I had emphatically announced my farewell to the Metropolitan? Then, it would upset all of Mr. Levine's plans for me. The coming season was solidly booked with concerts, and I would need time somewhere in-between for rehearsals and performances at the Metropolitan. For a while it looked like too much bother, too heavy a load to burden myself with in the year ahead. I consulted Mr. Levine, who was excited to hear that I wanted to do *Alceste.* So I said yes. Difficult as it was, the bookings were rearranged.

There was another reason for it, too—the fact that *Alceste* would be in English. You see, I had become just a little bit proud of my English, especially after the London critics complimented me so warmly on my diction as Dido. That was perhaps the hardest thing of all to resist. Then, always, there was

208

The Later Manuscript

the appealing story of a wife's readiness to die for her husband. For so many reasons Alcestis was the perfect role for me at this state of my life and career.

If I were to ask myself what more than anything else made me come back to the Metropolitan, not only the first time, but the second too, I would be tempted to answer "The personality of Rudolf Bing." The way he came to see me, his way of speaking, his grace and courtesy, and his quiet friendliness. I immediately said to myself, "I can trust this man to take care of everything."

I have not changed my mind about that. I liked him at once and I still do. It needed a man of supreme tact and persuasiveness to make me change my mind in the early spring of 1951. Particularly after I had once told the press I was singing at the Metropolitan for the last time. Mr. Bing had both these qualities and the consequence was—Alcestis.

There were one or two voices of warning, however, friends who knew how exhausted I was and perhaps dreaded the thought that something might go wrong. My voice might suddenly give out, or, even worse, my health. I laughed at their fears. I had never felt so confident before. So it wasn't long after that luncheon, no more than a few days, that I informed Mr. Bing I would sing *Alceste* for him. Five performances were later decided on, the first to be given on March 4, 1952.

I will admit this about *Alcestis,* as it was called in John Gutman's splendid English version: it has been hard work, much harder than I expected. I don't know why suddenly it should have become hard again. I usually learn easily. I imagine there were many good reasons why it was slow and arduous work, mastering this role. With the possible exception of Leonore it is probably the most difficult of my roles, and I am almost tempted to say the most satisfying, except that nothing comes above *Götterdämmerung* in the whole repertory—that, for me, is the highest point, and somewhere very close to it is Isolde. Then *Alcestis* was comparatively new—I had had only four perform-

THE FLAGSTAD MANUSCRIPT

ances in Zürich, and those in an entirely different version from the one we used at the Metropolitan. As for my other roles, I had been singing them hundreds of times. They had become as easy and natural and effortless as breathing. I suppose if Wagner had written more good operas I would have done those too, and not once, but repeatedly. Eva in *Die Meistersinger* was the one role I never sang at the Metropolitan, though I had done it in Sweden and Norway before I came to America. I was so eager to singer it, however, that one day I asked for it. They must have thought the role was too small for me, for their answer was, "We can't afford to have you sing that."

And now *Alcestis* interested me because it broke this pattern of singing Wagner over and over again. That was the real challenge, and perhaps the difficulty. I soon discovered that, while I had sung it before, it was practically a new role for me. I was learning it now in English, and I had already learned it in French and German; yet the curious thing is that none of it came back from my Zürich performances. It was to be expected that every word would be new to me; but that every note seemed new too, that was strange. It was just as if I had never sung the opera before. Whether it was due to the gathering exhaustion of my last few seasons, I don't know. When one or two of the critics wrote that I was making my Metropolitan farewell in a new role, they were wrong in one sense: I *had* sung it before. But they were right in the true sense. *Alcestis* was completely new to me when I sang it at the Metropolitan. I could draw on absolutely nothing from the past. I was starting from scratch.

Alcestis has given me a special satisfaction. I liked everything about the Metropolitan production, how it was planned and discussed, everybody's attitude toward it, the way it was worked out on the stage by Herbert Graf. There were those girls who followed me around the stage, gesturing to the changing mood of my lines. When I first saw them up in the ballet school, in their tights, I thought it all a little bit strange. Then I saw the whole thing at the dress rehearsal and I knew it was beautiful

The Later Manuscript

and expressive. They stood and walked about, lamenting in pantomime.

But, then, everything about the production satisfied me from the start. When I saw how Herbert Graf was staging it, how Alberto Erede was treating the music, I felt almost at once, "This is the way I have always dreamed of doing a role."

How I would have loved to be among the audience for just one performance—to be able to look at this beautiful production from out there, and to look at myself as Alcestis. I never had that feeling before, of wanting to see what I looked like in one of my roles. I know I have no right to say this myself, but I felt I must have looked striking, perhaps even beautiful. I was extremely happy about the whole thing. And that last performance of Tuesday night, April 1, 1952, my last performance of opera in America! I had no idea of what was going to happen, till Edwin called earlier in the day to say, "You must be prepared for something they are going to do for you at the opera house tonight. That's all I can say."

I hadn't the slightest suspicion what they were up to till the very end; to be exact, till I had taken my first curtain calls after the last act. It was then that I saw them assemble on the stage behind me, all the members of the cast, the chorus, the stage hands, the directors. In front of them I could see a table with something on it covered over with a large white tablecloth. Finally, there was George A. Sloan, the chairman of the Metropolitan Board of Directors. He said:

"We have here on the stage a group of your friends in the Metropolitan Opera and the Metropolitan Opera Guild. We are just a few of the countless thousands of music lovers in America who are deeply grateful for your glorious singing here at the Metropolitan Opera House.

"Tonight we are overwhelmed by the realization that we have seen you and heard you on this stage for the last time. . . ."

I could hear the cries of "No! No!" that came from the audience.

THE FLAGSTAD MANUSCRIPT

"From your first Sieglinde on February 2, 1935, until this evening's Alcestis, we of the Metropolitan have enjoyed a wealth of magnificent artistry from you that will never be forgotten."

The white tablecloth was then removed, and for the first time I saw this large and beautiful silver cup on a silver tray. Mr. Sloan raised the silver cup and read the inscription to me, a lovely tribute from the company and a list of the roles I had done at the Metropolitan, ending with Alcestis. I was so very happy at that moment, both happy and sad at the same time. But I wasn't sentimental about it at all. I had lost all that. I know it sounds strange, and it is strange even to me. In normal times, on such an occasion, I would have just felt awful. I didn't that night. It was my last performance at the Metropolitan. The audience was as wonderful as ever; and I was happy in my own way. But there was no nostalgia, and there was no weeping.

I'm told people looking at me through their opera glasses saw tears on my face. I suppose they did; but that was only my right eye tearing, and it was tearing from the make-up that got into it. I wasn't one bit tearful or worked up. This all sounds hard, I know, but it is true. I didn't speak, though I felt I was expected to say something. And it wasn't because I was choked up. I haven't felt like that for a long time. The truth is I had already said what I wanted to say as a good-by to my American public at my last recital in Carnegie Hall on February 1. They knew how I felt about them; they had known it at my last *Tristan und Isolde,* before I left for home in the spring of 1941. I had told them then that I was happy to be going home, but that I would be even happier when I returned to them. Well, I had returned to them, and I was satisfied, and they seemed to be too, and now it was time to go and there was nothing more to say.

But the company itself—I wish to say one thing more about that *Alcestis.* This was for me an entirely new company. I had known only the German, or Wagnerian wing before. The chorus was the same, but I had never had too much to do with the chorus in my other operas, except *Fidelio.* I never really knew

212

The Later Manuscript

the chorus till I sang *Alcestis,* and now they stood out there on the stage like old friends, applauding me as I tried to see what was going on behind me. *Alcestis* had brought us so closely together. It is that kind of opera. What beautiful and expressive singing they did in those five performances! And the soloists were mostly new people to me.

The stage hands, of course, I knew from away back; all of them, and it was good to see them there on the stage with me. I had never had the ballet before, and we too had become good friends through this magnificent opera. Of all the tributes I received for my Alcestis, the most touching of all was a telegram from the entire ballet. In it they expressed their pride in "having appeared on the same stage with me." And the ladies of the ballet sent me such lovely flowers, and such quantities of them! I shall never forget what an inspiration those girls were to me before that aria in the second act. Alcestis says to them, before she goes off to her death, "I must not see your tears."

I would walk down among these beautiful mourners, and they would look at me with their big sorrowful eyes and young and lovely faces, as if they pitied me more than anything in the world. That was when, if ever, I could get tears in my eyes, and I did so quite often, because they were so sweet and tender and convincing. That picture will always stay with me. I wish I could somehow convey how very much that device of Dr. Graf's helped me in the whole production. I didn't have to do very much, because they did it for me. It was such a rich and moving experience that I said to Dr. Graf, "I am so completely satisfied by this *Alcestis* that I don't care if I never sing it anywhere else."

To be perfectly frank, I did not think, at first, that either the critics or the public would accept me as Alcestis. I had reason to think this from past experience. Almost every time I had sung anything that hadn't Wagner's name on it, there would be fault to find. It might be a song, it might be Beethoven's *Fidelio.* The formula inevitably was: "She didn't warm up till...."

Oh, how often I read that! Will someone please tell me this:

213

THE FLAGSTAD MANUSCRIPT

why was I expected to shout from the very opening note? They evidently wanted to hear as big a noise as possible, and the sooner the better. Why couldn't I be allowed to sing something more restrained and tranquil for a change, and to sing it as I thought the composer wanted it sung? I was supposed to be afraid of letting go at all times.

"Well, where's the voice?" they seemed to be asking.

Sometimes, in *Fidelio,* that was said because I tried to sing the music as I understood the composer to mean it. I thought it vital in certain places to change the quality and intensity, to hold back. But these gentlemen knew better. It was caution, or fear, or bashfulness. "Where's the voice?"

Then came the big surprise. In *Alcestis* they all saw what I was doing. They accepted the fact that I knew what the style required. This time they all admired my restraint and control, and when I held back and gave a quiet phrase they weren't bothered by the whereabouts of my voice. I was terribly happy that we were all in agreement about *Alcestis*—I, the company, the public, and the critics. It has been a tremendous experience for me.

When I think of the many roles I would have liked to have done and didn't, I regret that I never sang more Mozart. I feel I could have sung the Countess and Donna Anna. I studied them, in German, but the chance somehow never came to sing them. I am sorry. Because I'm a classical girl, you know. Whatever Wagner may be, that other music gives a different satisfaction; the music of Gluck, for example, or Handel. It's the precise and orderly mind of these composers that I think appeals to me. I remember how I used to like to sing oratorios —the balanced style, the regular sections, everything in place. All of that appealed to my sense of tidiness.

Speaking of other roles I never did, I would have liked to have done both Elektra and the Marschallin in *Rosenkavalier.* I came very close to doing *Elektra.* While I was in Switzerland

The Later Manuscript

in 1942, they urged me to study it for them, and I went through the whole of it. I loved every note of it, and the challenge of the acting was strong too. But I finally refused, and the reason was the text. I found I couldn't sing many of the words, they seemed so coarse and indecent to me. They were just too much for a woman brought up the way I was. I cringe at the very memory of trying to sing them. I had a young man coaching me in Zürich, and I stammered and blushed more than I can tell you. It seemed perfectly horrible to me to be singing such thoughts in public. That was the reason, the only reason, I gave up *Elektra*. I knew I couldn't speak those words; it was impossible for me. Yet I loved the singing and the action so much, I remember I went so far as to try slurring over the bad words. It was no use. The very thought that the words were there was enough to turn my face red. I would have adored doing *Elektra*. But there you are.

And the Marschallin! That would have been a good role for me, I'm certain. The music lies so well in my voice, and I suppose I could act it. Then, it had something else in common with Alcestis and Rodelinda: it was a married role. I had decided that if I were to do any more operas, I would seek roles in which I did not have to be a young girl any longer. I wanted a role that would suit my age a little more plausibly. I don't think I'm betraying a confidence when I say that toward the end of our second season together, Mr. Bing asked me if I would be interested in doing *Der Rosenkavalier*. Having used Alcestis as bait to bring me back a second season, he shrewdly thought the Marschallin would tempt me back for a third. He knew only the appeal of a new role, and the role of a mature woman, would interest me. He never even suggested Wagner this time. My answer, of course, was no. And this time it was final.

I have been receiving letters lately from so many people, and not only friends, begging me not to give up singing. Which, of course, is very nice; nothing is more pleasing than to be wanted back just as much as ever, even when one has finally

THE FLAGSTAD MANUSCRIPT

quit. But some of these good people then go on and write, "Can I come to see you?" Now that hasn't been so easy, not in America. I should have wanted to see all of them; but didn't they realize that my last days would be so crowded? At the last minute they write in and ask for pictures. That, too, is flattering, yet how could I take care of that? I just didn't have time to do these things; it was out of the question, and I do hope all these kind persons will understand.

Now, there is one other thing I must make them understand quite emphatically. I gathered from their letters that several of them completely misunderstood why I quit. They assume it was because of what had happened to me in America. They remembered the bad things that had been written about me when I returned; they all knew about the picketing, the demonstration in Philadelphia, the episode in San Francisco, and the venom of the columnists. These were the reasons, they concluded, why they were losing me, and they were indignant. Grateful as I am for their sympathy, that just wasn't the case at all. I have been here in America five years since the war, so it can't possibly be because of those disagreeable things that I am leaving. If I had quit the second year of my return to America that would have been different. Everyone would have had a right to assume I had left because I couldn't take it any longer. But I did not quit then, and I did not quit the third or the fourth year, and I would never have quit under any circumstances until I was ready to quit. I know they mean well, these fans of mine, but they somehow never accept the correct reason. . . . I must assure them once and for all that I was not frightened away.

A very nice young man telephoned me while I was in Houston, Texas, for one of my last concerts in America. He was preparing a report about me for *Time* magazine, and there were just four questions he wanted to ask me. One of them was: "Why are you retiring?"

So many people suspect that there is another reason, the real one, behind the answer I usually give. I've given my reason so

216

The Later Manuscript

many times, that I think it is time to rest. Yet nobody seems to take me seriously. Well, I gave exactly the same answer to this charming reporter, and he apparently understood. I forget what he said, but I must have laughed, for he remarked, "Say, I wish I were there with you right now."

"Why is that?"

"You have such a hearty laugh."

Chapter Twenty-two

I HAVE had many crowded weeks in my life, but perhaps the most hectic and congested of them all was my last week in New York. I made three appearances with Bruno Walter and the New York Philharmonic Symphony in Carnegie Hall and sang an Alcestis at the Metropolitan. Those concerts were scheduled for Thursday night, March 20, the next afternoon, and the following Sunday afternoon, March 23, at which I made my very last appearance in Carnegie Hall. The program included the Wesendonck songs of Wagner and the Immolation Scene from *Götterdämmerung*. On Sunday, March 16, I arrived back in New York from a round of concerts. Awaiting me on Monday and Tuesday were two long recording sessions. At the first of these I recorded Schumann's long song cycle, *Frauenliebe und Leben* and six songs by Schubert. The following day I recorded eight American songs, reserving two more American songs and a group by Brahms for a later date. Wednesday night was taken up with my third performance of *Alcestis*. And of course, somewhere in-between, I was supposed to have my Philharmonic rehearsals.

The week was so frightfully jammed that I asked to be excused from the orchestral rehearsal at Carnegie Hall. After all, we knew the Immolation Scene, Bruno Walter, the Philharmonic, and I. So, the Philharmonic people said, "All right—we'll try to

218

The Later Manuscript

do without you." I gave a sigh of relief. But on Tuesday, the second day of my recording sessions, Dr. Walter, who was stopping at the same hotel, asked to come up to see me, and we went through the Wesendonck songs together, he at the piano, as it was to be on the Philharmonic program. From the very beginning we were in complete agreement on every detail of the Wesendonck songs, which, of course, was highly flattering to me.

"And, now, Madame Flagstad, if you don't mind," he said very sweetly, but firmly, "I think we should do the Immolation."

I hadn't the heart to protest. So I sang the entire scene, with Dr. Walter still at the piano, which he plays to perfection.

"Fine," he said, "now would you please come to the rehearsal Thursday morning."

"Oh, Dr. Walter," I pleaded, "I was told I didn't have to. I'm having such a trying week!"

"But, you see, Madame Flagstad, it would be good for the morale of the orchestra. . . ."

Well, Dr. Walter had to have his rehearsal, and that came the morning after my Wednesday night performance of *Alcestis,* and the morning of the Philharmonic concert.

It was not only one of the most strenuous weeks of my life, but I must now confess, one of the most panicky too. Because, you see, I woke up every single morning wondering whether I had any voice at all. What was the trouble with me? Simply that my voice was absolutely buried. I would wake up and find that I could barely speak. I had breakfast, and my voice would get just a little bit lighter. Then I did something that had become a daily routine. I would dig for that buried voice of mine, actually dig. I estimated that I brought it up one tone every half-hour. To loosen it faster, I would go into the bathroom and yell out as long and as loud as I could. I could sing quite freely in my hotel suite, but I believe my neighbors could hear me when I let go, with what feelings I dared not speculate. However, there hadn't been any complaints. But now it was

THE FLAGSTAD MANUSCRIPT

different. I hated so much to have anybody listening when my voice was in such bad shape. I didn't want to have them say they had heard Kirsten Flagstad screaming in her bathroom. I must have sounded like a sea lion. So what do you suppose I did? I turned on all the faucets of the sink and bathtub and made as much noise as I could to cover up all that yelling. I remember I kept assuring myself that no one could hear me. I'm almost positive they did. I was like the ostrich burying its head in the sand; I was trying to bury my voice in running water.

You see, there had been a cold, a rather nasty and lingering one that had started almost with the first rehearsal of *Alcestis*. And that week must have been the end of it. As I tell this, it isn't altogether gone yet. I can feel some of its aftereffects in my right ear even now. It had begun as a congestion behind the nose, and it must have finally moved to the area of the ear— the same ear I'd had trouble with in 1935. That's my own diagnosis. Ordinarily I would have gone to a doctor for treatment. But this time I was afraid. I had no way of telling how the treatment might affect my voice. There was a good chance the doctor would insist on my taking penicillin, or something like it, and I just couldn't risk what it might do to my voice. I might not be able to sing, and that would mean canceling a few, if not all, of these last performances of mine. The thought of being forced to do that was too dreadful. And then, where was the time to see a doctor? So, for several hours every morning, I had this feeling of panic. What if the voice closed up for good?

I had been coughing every day for weeks, and I shall never know quite how I went through my second performance of *Alcestis*. I was never so frightened about my voice as I was that night. I felt certain I would have to cough in the middle of an aria, or that my voice would freeze on me. Why and how it didn't I shall never understand. I don't believe I ever came so close to losing my grip on the stage as during that performance.

220

The Later Manuscript

I survived it, just as I survived the ordeal of the week that followed.

I find I have been saying a great deal about my voice. That is something I rarely do. I am often asked about it, of course; why it is what it is, how it does what it does. I'm afraid I can't be of much help there. The fact is, I don't know anything, really, about my voice. I have tried to tell what it was like in the beginning, small, thin, light; how I studied for so many years; how it grew. But why it behaves as it does, I have no idea. Sometimes I have the feeling that it is because of the solid groundwork of my early career. I have always had that firm base to stand on. Then, from training or instinct or whatever it was, I always seemed to know how to work everything out. But I can't tell you how I do it. My last teacher, Dr. Bratt, asked me, when I started to study with him, "Do you think you'll ever want to teach?"

And I said, "Never!"

"In that case, we can go faster."

That, I suppose, meant he wouldn't have to explain everything so that I could explain it later on to somebody else. There was no need to go into details, to give me pictures and diagrams of what was happening and why a tone came out the way it did, and just what was wrong when it didn't come out at all. I never asked and I never was interested in how it was done. Dr. Bratt showed me what to do, and I did it.

There *is* one thing I want very much to say about my voice. I never coddled it, or my throat, or myself. I was never careful about the weather, and I almost never worried about colds. In the coldest weather I always walk with an open fur coat. I never wore a scarf around my neck. To me a scarf is something pretty to look at on a table, the back of a chair, or around someone else's neck. What I mean is that I never spoiled myself, or my voice. I cannot say for sure, but it is quite possible that because I never took the usual precautions, my voice is stronger

221

THE FLAGSTAD MANUSCRIPT

and surer than it might have been after so many years of constant use. I do believe that by ignoring my voice I hardened it against any kind of punishment. I have been able to endure much more.

This may explain why, when my throat did finally tighten up on me from a cold, I was able to cope with it. If I had been in the habit of pampering myself, I could never have climbed over that congestion as I did. It was cruel, of course, that this should happen to me not only at the end of my career in America, but in music like that of *Alcestis*. It is much more difficult to sing Gluck with a cold than it is to sing Wagner. In Wagner you can somehow manage to bang through. And there is always that ocean of an orchestra to cover you up. A tiny little scratch couldn't possibly show. But where you have to phrase recitatives without support, where every note stands out naked and exposed, there you have reason to worry about that "tiny little scratch." I was worried in *Alcestis*, and I'm so relieved it went off as well as it did.

During the season of 1947–48, I was giving a recital in Zürich when something important dawned on me for the first time. The program was made up entirely of *Lieder*. I realized suddenly that I was singing to an audience that understood every German word of every German song on my program. That was the first time, really, that I found myself singing, as a concert artist, to a German-speaking audience. The significance of this was stimulating to me. I had already felt something of it whenever I sang English songs either in England or America. I had been so conscious of people understanding the words that I was twice as careful with my diction. Now nearly the whole program was in the language of the listeners. If I mispronounced a word everyone would notice it. In America or England, except for those who were native to the language or had spent a great deal of time in mastering it, audiences rarely knew the difference when I bungled a German word or phrase. But there in Zürich,

The Later Manuscript

for the first time, I felt completely exposed as an interpreter of German *Lieder*. That put me on my mettle as almost nothing had before. But the thrill of it for me was this: I found myself suddenly standing there and in the middle of a song realizing that the words themselves meant something to those who were listening. The effect of that realization was exciting and inspiring.

I remember saying to myself, "How wonderful this is. Anything I sing now, they will understand. If I color a word or a syllable because of its meaning, they will know why I am doing it. They can follow my interpretation, the mood. Now they can enjoy the song as a poem too."

That was a good thing for me at that moment, that sudden truth. I recalled the many times I had thought to myself, "What a pity they can't follow every word of this beautiful song! How much more they would get, and how much happier I would be to know that we understood one another completely!"

It has been the same with my Norwegian songs, those beautiful settings of beautiful poems by the great poets of my country. Often there would be synopses or explanations in the printed program; but it was never the same thing as knowing, from word to word and phrase to phrase, just what the poet, and the composer after him, had in mind. I always regretted that so much of our beloved Grieg was lost on my audience because of the barrier of language.

It was such a satisfying experience in Zürich to know, in a flash of awareness, that the poet and the audience spoke the same language, and that it was up to me to give those words everything the composer drew out of them. I had something of the same feeling later in England when I came to do *Dido and Aeneas,* and of course that was one of the greatest satisfactions of the *Alcestis* at the Metropolitan. It is very odd that I had to wait till the end of my career to make the discovery that it made a great difference to me when I knew the audience wasn't listening only to the music.

THE FLAGSTAD MANUSCRIPT

Speaking of songs, I'm afraid there is little I can say that might prove helpful to others who plan to go over the same ground I did. I have never really bothered to reduce singing to a method and a science, certainly not in any conscious way. I once told, over the BBC, how I would achieve complete vocal relaxation in my dressing room by a series of deep and satisfying yawns. I understand that came as a great shock to many who admired my Isolde and Brünnhilde; just as I know it was disillusioning to some people to learn that I frequently played solitaire while awaiting my cue backstage for the finale of *Tristan*. Such are the simple and prosaic facts about me.

I have been asked how I went about learning a new song. There I used a process that I found very effective early in my career, quite simple and far from mysterious. The very first thing I did was to play the song on the piano and sing it through, many, many times. Next, I would let the phrases filter through my mind till they haunted me day and night, the musical phrases, that is, with fragments of text. The time would come when I began to ask myself, "Now what was that word that went with those notes?" At that point I would sit down and copy the words from the sheet music into a little loose-leaf book that I always carried about with me. From there on the song was an easy thing to learn and master, once and for all. I would read through the poem several times. In-between readings I might find myself suddenly groping for the exact word. Out would come my loose-leaf book. When I no longer had to think of the text, when, I suppose, the words and the notes had become one thing in my mind, or wherever it is that a song stays, then I knew I had it. And once I had it, it was mine forever. I strongly recommend this method of copying down the words. I remember it was very helpful when I would try the song with my accompanist for the first time. If I tripped over a word, the notebook was there for immediate reference. . . .

I should add here that I never copied down the words of an opera. However, I always carried the scores with me—but not

224

The Later Manuscript

the complete scores, if you please! It was my old friend and associate Hermann Weigert who was kind enough to cut down the bulk of Wagner to my needs many years ago while I was attending opera in Vienna. I don't have to tell my Wagnerian friends that two or three of the Master's scores are much too 'weighty a load for one singer to carry around from country to country. Mr. Weigert very skillfully ripped apart each score, and pieced my role together in a neat and slender volume. Thus "slenderized" Wagner took up very little space in my luggage. Think of going about with an uncut *Siegfried* and *Tristan und Isolde!*

About my ability as an actress, that is something I must leave to the critics. They have varied in their judgment. A few have thought me quite static and unimpassioned. Others have found me satisfactory, among them Lawrence Gilman. I have only one brief remark to make on the subject. When I first came to the Metropolitan, some of the reviewers said that I did too little in the way of acting. That was only during my first season, however. The following year they reversed themselves completely. They now spoke of my minimum of acting as economy of gesture, and they said it would be a good thing if the others learned it from me. That pleased me tremendously at the time.

Chapter Twenty-three

NOW that I am about to leave America, I have been going over in my mind the operas and concerts and recordings still remaining to be done before I go into my long awaited retirement in Norway. I shall be counting the days till I have sung my last note in public. After each concert I shall say, "This is the last time here; this is one concert less. I am one step closer to home and peace and quiet." For those of you who may be interested, these are the things that must still be done in the year ahead, and this is how I shall be spending my time before I make my very last appearance on a public stage. You may consider it as a final page from my diary as a singer, written in advance. Let me see now:

April 15, 1952

I leave America for England.

April 18

Sheffield: recital.

April 23

In London last year I finally promised to talk over the BBC. The program is rather interesting, I must say. Which records would I bring with me if I were shipwrecked on a desert island? I said no ten times to the BBC people, but they insisted, "Please, please, won't you do it for us?" And I gave in. So far, I've chosen only one record for my desert island: Mendelssohn's *Midsum-*

The Later Manuscript

mer *Night's Dream* music, as conducted by Sir Thomas Beecham. I won't have any of my own records, if you don't mind!

April 24

London: Concert in Albert Hall, with Wilhelm Furtwängler conducting.

April 25 to May 5

Ten days of freedom—all of them in London.

May 6

Hamburg: Recital. A year ago, when my European agent, Mr. Horwitz, asked me about future bookings, I said, "There is one place I would like to sing before I retire, and that's Germany. I am a singer with a German repertory and the only singing I ever did in Germany was at the very beginning of my career, in Bayreuth, and that didn't amount to very much, a few small parts. I don't think that's sufficient for a Wagnerian soprano of my reputation."

"All right," said Horwitz, "I'll book you for Germany."

May 11

Berlin: *I shall sing there for the first time.*

May 11 to May 22

I'm not quite sure what's in store for me, maybe a little rest or even a trip home, maybe more concerts—or maybe just sightseeing, where I shall leave to the mood and fancy of the moment. Possibly a holiday in Switzerland.

May 23

Zürich: Concert. As usual, I'm very happy about that. I adore Zürich.

May 27

Milan: La Scala again, but a recital this time.

May 29

Rome: Broadcast—the Immolation Scene from *Götterdämmerung* with Furtwängler conducting. Furtwängler thought we should do the whole of *Tristan*. My answer was an immediate and emphatic no.

227

June 2

Rome: Broadcast again, a recital.

June 5

Paris: recital. For the first time I shall do an aria from Strauss's *Ariadne auf Naxos,*—Es gibt ein Reich. I am also working on an excerpt—quite legitimate, I think—from Strauss's *Elektra,* the long one beginning with the cry "Orest!" So, you see, I shall have my fling at *Elektra,* after all.

June 8

Helsinki: Soloist at the Sibelius Festival, where I am to sing six songs with orchestra, all of them new to me.

June 9

I fly back to London.

June 10

London: If all goes according to original plans, I begin ten days recording of *Tristan und Isolde.* Many years ago His Master's Voice made recordings of *Tristan, Die Walküre, Götterdämmerung,* and *Der Fliegende Holländer,* all from actual performances. They were never released, however, the reason being that none of us would O.K. them, that is in their entirety. I myself approved of fragments from *Der Fliegende Holländer,* but Fritz Reiner objected, so, as far as I know, nothing was ever issued. Few singers or conductors take kindly to releases of this kind, that is of "live" performances. They're never quite the same. For one thing the technical conditions and controls are so different. Then, we can't "retake" a faulty passage.

I've heard only just now and indirectly that the recording of *Tristan* in London may not come off after all. And do you know, I'd be happy if it didn't, just as happy as I am to know that I'm not going to sing *Alcestis* in London, after all. Now that's a bad sign, this sense of relief when something on my schedule is canceled for whatever reason. Now that I'm finished in America, I simply want to shout with joy when I'm told of a postponement or cancellation. I take this as further proof that I have had enough. Of course, I may still do that *Tristan* record-

The Later Manuscript

ing. At this distance I'm not at all certain either way. What surprised me was to find myself glad when I saw that there might be some doubt. Five years ago I would have grieved and fretted over a situation of that kind.

Now this is a sign of either laziness or fatigue, though I think, rather, of fatigue. I'm not tired of singing; it isn't that at all. It's just that I don't want to do any more of what I have been doing for so long. That moment of joy betrayed me to myself. It showed me more than anything else how right I was in making up my mind to stop, not all at once, but slowly and definitely. . . .

While I'm on the subject of *Tristan und Isolde,* there is one thing which I would love to see in print for the first time. It is a confession I have wanted to shout from every concert stage of America. In a few days, in Springfield, Massachusetts, before I finally leave America for England, I shall be singing my last Wagnerian aria with piano. No one will ever know what a great relief it will be doing that. I shall never forget the times I failed to put a Wagnerian aria on my program. At the very first opening for an encore, people in the audience would shout one word: "Liebestod!" That cry, I am sure, will haunt my sleep to the end of my life. Believe it or not, I have even had requests for the Immolation with piano. I think it is bad enough to do the Liebestod with piano, but the Immolation! Wagner would turn over in his grave! I've been using the same program everywhere this season, and as a parting concession I have put the Liebestod on all of them.

Only a few days ago I said to Edward Hart, who has been my accompanist of late on out-of-town engagements, "I started to count off my last American concerts ten concerts ago. 'Now there are only five,' I said to myself; 'soon there will be only two.' Now we've come down to one, and I will be extremely happy when that is over, and do you know why?"

Mr. Hart must have suspected, but he said nothing.

THE FLAGSTAD MANUSCRIPT

"Because I shall be saying good-by to the Liebestod with piano."

I would never have dreamed of doing that in Europe, singing Wagnerian arias with piano. In America they always expected it, even when it wasn't listed on the program. So what was I to do?

To come back to my schedule, I shall be busy recording *Tristan,* if it goes through, from June 10 to June 25.

June 26 to the middle of August

Freedom again, and home! Oh, it will be good to be back in Norway!

August 21

Lausanne, Switzerland: Concert with orchestra, Furtwängler conducting. On the program are several songs by Strauss, the inevitable Liebestod and the inescapable Immolation. Do you see what I mean?

August 31

London: *Dido and Aeneas* at Bernard Miles' Mermaid Theatre, the first of sixteen more performances, in-between which I shall be soloist in a Bach cantata, which one I don't know yet.

September 28

London: My last performance of *Dido and Aeneas* and *my very last performance of opera anywhere!* Flagstad's finale as an opera singer.

October, November, December

Europe: Up to Christmas of 1952 I shall be giving concerts in various parts of Europe. Then a Christmas vacation, where I'm not quite sure yet.

I am leaving 1953 as a year open for occasional concerts in Europe, including England—and of course Norway. I want first to take a good long rest in the early part of the year, then perhaps give a recital in Oslo. I have had so many requests to sing from all over Norway. Many of the larger cities have invited me to come and sing with their amateur orchestras, and to give

230

The Later Manuscript

recitals. I shall love doing that. Friends knowing of my 1953 plans have already been scolding me.

"If you plan to continue singing in Europe into next year," they say, "then why can't you come back to America for one more season?"

I believe I've given my reasons, but there is still another. Bookings in America have to be made so far ahead as a rule. It will be so much simpler in Europe to make arrangements on short notice. I might cable Mr. Horwitz from Norway, "I'll be glad to do a concert now and then, but first let me know what you have." Suppose I'm skiing at my country place. A letter might reach me there from Mr. Horwitz. "Would you care to sing at such and such a place on such and such a date?" I might say, "Yes," and I might say, "No." But it wouldn't have to be decided one year ahead. You see, I might suddenly get tired of doing nothing, that can happen, and I'm quite prepared for it. I could then write or cable my Paris agent to book a concert for me somewhere. All he ever needs is fourteen days to arrange it in. That, of course, is only for 1953, and the schedule is a loose and flexible one.

I have not quite decided yet, but I am almost positive that my very last public appearance will be on:

December 12, 1953

The place will be the National Theater of Oslo.

It was there that I made my debut just forty years before, on the same day of the month, and it is there that I think I should finish my career as a singer. That will be the end, definitely. I want my public life to end where it started, in the country I hold dear above all others, and among my beloved people.

Chapter Twenty-four

I SHALL have three places to enjoy my privacy when I go back to Norway to stay. The house in Kristiansand will be my regular home. About two and a half hours drive out of Kristiansand, away off the main road, I have my little cottage, surrounded by forests and lakes. I shall go there, as I have in the past, when I need absolute peace and solitude. During the war I spent a good deal of time there, all by myself for a week at a time, just to get rid of tension, and forget things. And in Oslo there will be an apartment waiting for me. I shall be there whenever there is a concert, an opera, a play, that I want to catch. I shall, of course, have my subscription to the Oslo Philharmonic. I mean to go to the theater much more than I ever have. Only lately have I begun to realize how very starved I am for the drama. There was never any time for it, really, not for any of these things. I want so much now to recover that contact, to go over lost ground, to make up for the years and years of traveling and concerts and rehearsing and operas. I never seemed to find the time to do anything between concerts. . . .

That is what I shall go back to, and that is what I shall come back to, when I am again in America. For I am eager to come back now as an ordinary visitor. I shall learn to know Broadway and its fascinating theaters; I shall go to the City Center for the beautiful ballets and operas and plays I have heard and read so

The Later Manuscript

much about. I shall at last go to Carnegie Hall as a ticket holder. And of course, I want to join the crowds that go to the Metropolitan. I have only one misgiving about that. If only I could be completely unknown to the audience, just one of them. I may be abnormal that way, but it bothers me to be recognized and accosted in public. I remember I went to *South Pacific* a year ago with Else and Arthur. During intermission they left their seats, and I sat there alone. Would you believe it, a young girl, meaning well—I'm sure they all mean well—came and sat down beside me and talked through the whole intermission?

"May I sit here beside you? I'm so happy to see you."

What could I do? That is almost the worst thing of all, people not leaving me alone. I've had it happen on the street time and again. Only the other day, on Fifth Avenue, where I had gone to shop, one woman came right up to me and began, "Oh, Madame Flagstad!"

There was a time when I would say, with a smile, "I'm sorry. You are wrong. My name is not Flagstad." I wasn't very happy about lying, however, and I don't believe I fooled anyone.

"I just had to tell you how glorious I thought you were the other night. . . ."

That makes me feel dreadfully embarrassed.

So, it shouldn't be hard to understand why I have seldom been to the Metropolitan as a listener. I can count the number of times on my fingers, and not all of my fingers by any means. I shall make up for that too when I return. As far as I can see now, I am definitely coming back to America in 1954, as a tourist. I plan to visit the friends for whom I have never had the time before. I am going to travel about the country, at my leisure, seeing the many beautiful things I've known about all my life but haven't yet had the time to see and enjoy. I've missed lots and lots of things in America because of my singing. I want to *visit* America the next time, and let it sink in. Sometimes, while I was on tour, I might be near one of the most glorious spots in

233

THE FLAGSTAD MANUSCRIPT

the world, a historic site, a landmark, a magnificent bit of nature. And I just couldn't go. I would arrive the morning of a concert and people would say, "Oh, you simply must see so and so!" But when, and how? I couldn't run around seeing people when I had a concert to sing or an opera to do. And so of course I missed it. But now I shall be like everybody else. There will be no concert or opera to stop me. And thank God for that!

People keep saying to me, "Think of what you're giving up." As if I were sacrificing something very dear. I'm not giving up anything at all, not in that sense. It is true I am retiring from singing, public singing, that is, but I'm not really *giving up* singing as such. How could I possibly? I shall probably sing a great deal more at home now, for my own pleasure and somebody else's, maybe only little Sigurd's, but it will suffice for me. This will begin when I have stopped giving concerts entirely. I shall then sit down and practice and sing at the piano, and accompany myself, which I love to do.

I do want people to understand I'm not *giving up* anything in the other sense. You see, I couldn't possibly think of it as sacrifice. I've had too much of it; I know this sounds dreadful, but it's been so—too much of the attention, the applause, the reviews. I suppose I've come to take it for granted. It isn't very nice for me to say it, but I really have had more than my share of that sort of thing, to be very frank. *And I will not miss it for one second.* There are others who love that contact with audiences, who need it as they do the air they breathe. They can't give it up because it is their very life. For me it has become meaningless.

I have lost little and surrendered nothing; on the contrary I have gained, and what I have gained most of all is my privacy. That to me is something priceless, to be placed above all things. I heard a beautiful voice on the radio the other day, while sitting here in my room, maybe the most beautiful voice I know. I had heard it more than ten years ago for the first time. I listened

234

The Later Manuscript

eagerly because it was saying that people should learn how to be alone; that if they could learn to live by themselves, and meditate, they could learn to do more with their time, and their lives. It spoke of artists, how they had to be left alone if they were to accomplish anything worth while. . . .

It was the voice of Queen Juliana of the Netherlands. I shall never forget her words; they said what I have always felt. If there was anything I wanted in my life more than anything else, it was just that, to be left alone. And that, as I've said before, I was never allowed to have for very long in America. Which is why it was so much more exhausting. I never minded the work. It was that people never learned to leave me alone in-between concerts and opera performances. Always there were letters, telephone calls, telegrams, requests for photographs. I just didn't have the time. And now I shall have it, the privacy and isolation I have always craved.

People have asked me again and again, "But how will you occupy your time; you who have had so much and done so much?"

I startle them with my reply, which is the simple and commonplace truth: "I am going to sit. I am just going to take a comfortable chair and sit. I shall do absolutely nothing at all."

"But you'll go mad! How long can you go on that way?

"Until I am tired of doing nothing. But until then I shall occupy my chair and enjoy the wonderful feeling of not being obliged to do anything."

I mean every word of it. Why should I decide what to do now? I don't know that I shall want to do anything whatsoever. I know only this: I am not going to think ahead. I am saying good-by to bookings and schedules and programs and seasons— and hotel reservations. In return I shall be free, free to go and come as I please, or to stay in my chair, in the peace and quiet of home, and think how marvelous it is to be alive. I can't wait for the luxury of that.

235

THE FLAGSTAD MANUSCRIPT

At the first intermission during my Saturday matinee of *Alcestis* at the Metropolitan, I caught a glimpse of my little grandson Sigurd standing down in front of the orchestra, clapping his tiny hands. It was so good seeing him there in his sailor suit with the white cord on the sleeves, which was the only way I could recognize him. Because of the blinding lights, I couldn't see his face, only his hands and those cords on his sleeves. I blew him a kiss.

Yes, Sigurd is the big thing in my life now; it is unbelievable what he has come to mean to me. I should never have thought it possible. Many years ago, while I was all wrapped up in my little daughter Else, my mother said to me one day, "Just wait till you have grandchildren. You'll love them even more."

I remember I cried out indignantly, "No! No! It's Else, only Else. Nobody can ever take her place!"

My mother was right. Little Sigurd now comes first in my life. Is he musical? That's hard to say, though he seems to want to be, maybe for the sake of his grandmother. This much I know: he can't sing a note in tune. I've tried to show him many times by asking him to sing the tone I play at the piano. He never finds it, but when I sing a tone he gradually finds it—so there is hope that he has a musical ear after all. One morning, in Madison, I came upon him by surprise, and listened. He was up in the high register, singing to himself. As I drew up to him, he stopped.

"Did you try?"

"Yes."

"And . . . ?"

"It was no good."

Would I make a singer out of little Sigurd, if I could? I have only one answer, and a very American one at that: over my dead body! Else thought she would like to have him become a pianist, though now she seems to be convinced he has the makings of an actor. I would like to see him a pianist, but for his own pleasure, and ours. No career. Not for my grandson. . . .

236

The Later Manuscript

I hope to have all three of them, Else, Arthur, and Sigurd, in Norway with me very soon—in Norway to stay. It has been a long journey and a lonely one. Having them with me, at my age, will be the crowning happiness of my life.

PART THREE: *The Reviewing Stand*

The Reviewing Stand

LIKE the autobiography, this supplement falls into two sections, the first preceding Mme. Flagstad's departure for Norway in April, 1941; the other following her return in March, 1947. The opening part is limited to the reactions of several New York critics to Mme. Flagstad's roles as she first performed them at the Metropolitan. It is exclusively an opera gallery. In those first few seasons a general pattern of opinion emerged from which there was little divergence in the years that followed.

In the second section the emphasis, inevitably, is on *Alcestis,* the only new addition to Mme. Flagstad's Metropolitan repertory and the closing role of her American career. After some hesitation, I thought it best to admit Dido to this gallery. Mme. Flagstad sang this role only in England, for which reason it did not fit into the consistent scheme of a New York reviewing stand. For the one exception I culled material from the British press. I also deemed it wise to include a few other writings in this section, among them reviews of one or two concerts. Some readers may well be startled by the changing fashions in musical criticism revealed by this lapse of a decade or more. Certainly few are writing today with the rapt intensity and gushing plenitude of the mid-thirties. For better or worse, a leaner rhythm and

THE FLAGSTAD MANUSCRIPT

more studious economy of word have replaced the leisurely amplitude of those years. There is the political picture too. Kirsten Flagstad came back to America in 1947 under very special circumstances. Newspaper reviews that followed her return could not very well ignore such circumstances. That, too, made a more flexible plan necessary for my second section. In any case, I have tried to confine the supplement to quotations from the critics. "The Reviewing Stand" is a critics' corner—only that and nothing more.

To appreciate fully the unique groundswell of praise that greeted Mme. Flagstad early in 1935, it is necessary to keep one fact in mind. Except to one or two globe-trotting critics and Wagnerian singers, Mme. Flagstad was totally unknown when she arrived here. Even as late as January 5, 1935, less than a month before her debut, Pitts Sanborn, who was usually tipped off long in advance about the Metropolitan's latest overseas acquisitions, carried this item in one of his Saturday columns: "Kirsten Flagstad, a Norwegian soprano, soon to be heard at the Metropolitan, is reported to have sung at Bayreuth. Will some benevolent statistician kindly tell when and what?" If Sanborn knew nothing about her, the general public knew even less. Which boat had brought her over and where she was lodging since her arrival, nobody seemed to know. Sanborn wrote:

Nor would she have been imported if, in the summer, Frida Leider had not unexpectedly decided to remain in Europe. Since Gertrude Kappel could not very well carry the whole burden of Wagner's heroic soprano parts the season through Anny Konetzni of the Vienna State Opera was the first choice for a successor to Mme. Leider. Mme. Konetzni's American debut occurred late in December as Brünnhilde in *Siegfried* and early in January she sang Venus in *Tannhäuser* and Ortrud in *Lohengrin*. In none of these parts was the impression she produced strong enough to warrant a long engagement. Her farewell to the Metropolitan took place on January 20th, when she sang Isolde for the first and only time here. And for the first and only time, her high notes had the power and

242

The Reviewing Stand

freedom proper to a full dramatic soprano. [Until a short time before, she had sung, the contralto repertory.]

The management now turned to Kirsten Flagstad. But still there was no attempt to build her up. At the matinee of February 2nd, virtually unheralded, she faced her first American audience, the management choosing to present her as Sieglinde in *Die Walküre*, the most important, let us recall, of the roles she had sung at Bayreuth. Her chief colleagues on the historic occasion were Mme. Kappel (Brünnhilde), Maria Olszewska (Fricka), Paul Althouse (Siegmund), Friedrich Schorr (Wotan), Emanuel List (Hunding), with Artur Bodanzky as conductor.

The performance, of course, was broadcast. During the first intermission the General Manager, Giulio Gatti-Casazza, was seated at a desk in his office when the telephone rang. It was Frances Alda, once a leading soprano of the company and formerly his wife, calling from her home in Great Neck, Long Island, where she had the radio turned on.

"Who was that singing Sieglinde?"

"*Perchè?*" asked the laconic Gatti-Casazza.

"*Perchè a una bellissima voce e canta molto bene.*"

"*Una certa Flagstad.*"

A certain Flagstad!

Sieglinde (*Die Walküre*)

The next day she was no longer *"una certa Flagstad."* In the Sunday *Herald Tribune* the late Lawrence Gilman wrote:

It is a pleasure to salute in Mme. Kirsten Flagstad ... an artist of surprising and delightful quality. Mme. Flagstad ... has come to us without benefit of ballyhoo.... Yesterday's audience was therefore unprepared for the disclosure that awaited it and to which they paid frequent tributes of enthusiastic recognition.

Mme. Flagstad is that *rara avis* in the Wagnerian woods—a singer with a voice, with looks, with youth.... I cannot swear that Mme. Flagstad is in her thirties, but the point is that she looks as if she were, and sings as if she were. The voice itself is both lovely and

THE FLAGSTAD MANUSCRIPT

puissant. In its deeper register it is movingly warm and rich and expressive, and yesterday it recalled to wistful Wagnerites the irrecoverable magic of Olive the Immortal (Olive Fremstad). The upper voice is powerful and true and does not harden under stress.

The singing that we heard yesterday is that of a musician with taste and brains and sensitivity, with poetic and dramatic insight. It was delightful, for example, to encounter a Sieglinde sufficiently imaginative to give their due effect to such significant details as the dream-like quality of tone and phrasing which should imbue the wonderful passage in which Sieglinde gropes for her memory of her brother's voice in childhood, and finds it in a recognition of her own clear tones as they echoed back to her from the evening woods —one of the most magical things in Wagner, and one that is often slighted.

Her acting is noteworthy for its restraint and poise. She does not indulge in those imbecile operatic gestures which Wagner detested —he called them "swimming exercises." Mme. Flagstad expresses volumes with a turn of the head or a lifting of the hand. She was at times a bit inflexible yesterday; but that may possibly have been due to nervousness.

She is solacing to the eye—comely and slim, and sweet of countenance. "I still need a Sieglinde," wrote Wagner despairingly to a friend while he was casting the "Ring" for Bayreuth sixty years ago. "That need," he added, "is a calamity—for she must be slender." Wagner knew his Germans. Yesterday was one of those comparatively rare occasions when the exigent Richard might have witnessed with happiness an embodiment of his Sieglinde. For this was a beautiful and illusive re-creation, poignant and sensitive throughout, and crowned in its greater moments with an authentic exaltation.

In the *Times* of the same Sunday, Mr. Olin Downes declared that no Sieglinde of the last ten years had made such an impression in New York "by her voice, stage business, her intelligence and dramatic sincerity, and by her evident knowledge of Wagner." He continued:

In her conception of the role she struck a note that was new to the Metropolitan stage of recent seasons, though not new to the

244

The Reviewing Stand

spirit of Wagner's creation. This was the note of compassionate interest and concern for the unknown stranger within the gates, who had staggered weakly into shelter from the storm weaponless, fleeing from his enemies. The crescendo of sympathy and emotion achieved as the first act mounted to its climax were the work of a musician and interpreter rich in all the resources of her art.

Thus the dramatic motivation of the part. Its inner essence was carried out in superb singing. The voice has the body, the color in the lower register, the brilliancy without stridency in the upper tones to cope with every demand of the Sieglinde role. In fact, the net results of this performance arouse keen anticipation of the enactment of the part of Isolde which Miss Flagstad will take on Wednesday evening. It seemed yesterday that the voice would be fully equal to the demands of Isolde and of Brünnhildes of the "Ring." This of course remains to be seen. The performance yesterday was the performance of an artist superbly gifted, physically a true figure of Wagnerian music drama, rarely eloquent and communicative in action and song.

It therefore appears that for once the Metropolitan has engaged a singer who is in her prime and not in the declining years that follow successes. . . . She is an exceptional soprano for Wagnerian roles. The second and third acts of "Walküre," though Sieglinde's appearance in the last act is very short, rounded and confirmed the earlier achievements. When the harassed pair of Volsungs came into view, fleeing the savage Hunding and his henchmen, the figure of Sieglinde, so plastic, so feminine, evoked pity, as did her broken utterances. In the last act the audience broke into applause as she left the stage. . . .

Isolde (*Tristan und Isolde*)

In the papers of Thursday, morning and evening, the reviewers poured out their praise of Flagstad's next role. Said Gilman (the *Herald Tribune*):

Last night's performance of "Tristan" at the Metropolitan was made unforgettable for its hearers by a transcendentally beautiful and moving impersonation of Isolde—an embodiment so sensitively

THE FLAGSTAD MANUSCRIPT

musical, so fine-grained in its imaginative and intellectual texture, so lofty in its pathos and simplicity, of so memorable a loveliness, that experienced opera-goers sought among their memories of legendary days to find its like.

They did not find it. For one of the characteristics of Mme. Kirsten Flagstad's Isolde is that it is wholly individual. This remarkable Norwegian artist, whose Sieglinde won such instant admiration in last Saturday's "Walküre," patterns after no model or tradition in her conception of Isolde. She has her own vision of the character. . . .

Mme. Flagstad is no whirlwind Isolde. She seems to have been impressed with the undeniable fact that Isolde must be, as Mr. George Moore once observed, "a woman that a man could be in love with—and that is not the impact and shriek of a gale from the southwest." And she reminds us of another fact, imperfectly realized: that Wagner's Irish princess is also an "Irische Maid"—that there is no reason implicit in Wagner's text or music why Isolde should be represented as an elderly and semaphoric Hausfrau in a red wig.

This Isolde is a young woman of royal dignity and grace, comely and girlish and grave, made desperate by the tragic passion that has enmeshed her. Afterward, she is an incarnation of poignant loveliness and ardor as the woman rapturously possessed and possessing; and finally she is the death-devoted and mystical celebrant, no longer of this earth, a creature of disembodied ecstasy.

This process of spiritual unfolding is exquisitely indicated by Mme. Flagstad, with a simplicity as subtle and restrained in method as it is irresistibly moving in effect. . . .

And always, throughout, Mme. Flagstad is the finely musical artist who knows the significance of the words she sings, and the shape and rhythm of the musical phrases that enclose them, and the quality of the tones they need for their conveyance.

Always the voice itself is pure and noble and expressive, of a beauty that is often ravishing to the ear, and a power and clarity that are equal to every demand that is made upon it by the music.

This is not a review of a performance of "Tristan und Isolde": it is a hurried note upon a new Isolde, one of the rarest, perhaps the rarest, of our time: an embodiment so deeply sensitive in its imaginative truth, of so exalted and enamoring a beauty, that the

246

The Reviewing Stand

function of the critic becomes, in its presence, a mere opportunity to exercise his highest privilege—what Swinburne called "the noble pleasure of praising."

In that same "noble pleasure" Mr. Downes (the *Times*) eagerly participated: "She sang the part gloriously, as it has not been sung here in many years, and almost immediately she captivated her audience by a beautiful stage presence, by youth, sincerity, and dramatic feeling conveyed equally by acting and by song. . . . The singer had her audience in her hand before she had been five minutes on the stage."

Henderson (the *Sun*) expressed his approval as follows:

Mme. Flagstad's Sieglinde proved that she had sufficient voice for Isolde, and it remained only to note how she approached this role which has been made everything from a raging demigoddess to a love-sick lady sometimes inclined to be peevish.

Mme. Flagstad was expected to make her first of all womanly, tender, and sympathetic, and in this she was not disappointing. The voice proved to be splendidly suited to such a version of Isolde. It rang out in plentiful power in the temperamental outbreaks of the princess and graded itself to lovely sensibility in the less agitated passages.

It was a delight to hear tones so excellently placed, phrasing so finished, and dynamics so perfectly adjusted. It is long since the music of Isolde has been so well sung at the Metropolitan. Wagner's lush melody was published in full, and there were moments, such as the description of the glance of the false Tantris, which had a depth of feeling quite beautiful.

Mr. Chotzinoff (the *Post*) found that:

Miss Flagstad met the histrionic test most adequately and the vocal superbly. . . . Not only did Miss Flagstad effortlessly scale the heights of her music, but she did so with no sacrifice of quality or of power. . . . It seemed indeed like an inexhaustible voice, one more than equal to the demands of the score for all gradations of power and for all the tints of the tonal palette. Equally remarkable was its unvarying fidelity to the pitch. . . .

THE FLAGSTAD MANUSCRIPT

This truly remarkable artist scored one of those successes last night that becomes legendary. And yet there was something about the great ovation she received which spoke not only of the gratitude of the audience for so talented and beautifully endowed a singer, but of its amazement and delight at the realization, even in part, of an operatic figure whose potentialities have, at least in this generation, never before been realized.

Five days later Mr. Chotzinoff returned to the charge:

When Miss Flagstad appears at the Metropolitan again the house will be as alive as an open meeting of Communists in Union Square. For that evening opera will cease to be a corpse. . . . Undeniably opera has fallen into a coma, and what it needs is the pulmotor of imaginative performers. If the gods would vouchsafe us a dozen exponents of music drama like Miss Flagstad, there would automatically be an end to the skepticism that is now the fashion.

Brünnhilde (*Die Walküre*)

Mme. Flagstad's Brünnhilde followed shortly. On February 15th she appeared in the part in the *Walküre* of the matinee *Ring* cycle, given without a cut. Gilman (the *Herald Tribune*) recorded the next day:

Mme. Kirsten Flagstad . . . whose Isolde of last week has been the musical talk of the town, accomplished yesterday another feat of another kind by singing Brünnhilde in "Die Walküre" for the first time anywhere—singing it with such poignant beauty and such varied expressiveness that one forgot to be astonished at the technical mastery of the performance and thought only of its fidelity to the musical and dramatic truth of Wagner's character.

There were occasional moments of tentativeness in her performance. It would have been astonishing if there had not been. But these things counted for nothing in the result, which was deeply and continually moving by reason of the harmonious unity of the projected image—the singular beauty and eloquence of the voice itself, the musicianly command of it as a vehicle of dramatic and poetical utterance, the histrionic intensity achieved by the simplest

248

The Reviewing Stand

means, and the loveliness and grace of person which focused these instrumentalities into an irresistible whole.

There were moments in the "Todesverkündigung" wherein the singer, unaffectedly youthful and simple though she is, rose to an astonishing height of Olympian serenity and majestic poise.... And later in the opera, when she pleaded with Wotan for the avoidance of her own appalling doom, she turned the heart to water through her realization, in action and in song, of the supreme pathos and nobility of Wagner's music.

According to Mr. Downes (the *Times*):

This was Mme. Flagstad's first Brünnhilde on any stage. Still more surprising, it was undertaken without even one orchestral rehearsal. ...The voice was no less remarkable than at the singer's earlier performances. There were the same freedom and solidity in its production, the same power, the same restraint and intelligence in its use, and, when need be, the fire, that were revelations of her singing when she scored her first success. ...

From her first entrance in the third act the soprano sang with a new assurance and an added splendor of voice. Brünnhilde's final appeal to Wotan was of an intensity and power, as well as a beauty of sound, to make altogether intelligible the result on Wotan's will. Other recent Brünnhildes have sounded the pathetic note quite as effectually as Mme. Flagstad. None has reached quite the peaks of exaltation she attained in moments of this scene.

To Henderson (the *Sun*):

...her impersonation was naturally not settled in all its details and it was evident that she had not had sufficient rehearsal with the conductor, Mr. Bodanzky. But she placed a good afternoon to her credit. Her voice is well suited to the music, lending itself equally well to the Valkyr cry, to the intimacies of the scene with Wotan in the second act, to the solemnity of the "Todesverkündigung," and to the tenderness of the beautiful pleading in the final scene.

Her clear enunciation added to the excellence of her delivery. This was a very musical Brünnhilde, and in moments it was eloquent. But that it was tentative in some places was unquestionable.... The outstanding features of the impersonation yesterday

THE FLAGSTAD MANUSCRIPT

were the vocal splendor, the appearance of youth, and the communication of the gentler emotions. The music has not been sung
with such beauty of tone and freshness of approach recently.

Brünnhilde (*Götterdämmerung*)

The matinee *Ring* cycle proceeded with an unabridged *Siegfried* on February 22nd, but Mme. Flagstad, who had been announced for Brünnhilde, remained out of the cast because of a
cold. Mme. Kappel replaced her. The next Flagstad Brünnhilde came on the 28th when *Götterdämmerung* took its place
in the matinee *Ring* cycle. Once more Mme. Flagstad was appearing in a role for the first time on any stage. But she had been
accorded a full orchestral rehearsal. Edward Ziegler, assistant
general manager, later testified that the entire staff was absolutely astounded by her performance. The press of the following day, for its part, "seethed and spouted in fresh geysers of
commemorative prose," in the acidulous words of Pitts Sanborn.

To Gilman (the *Herald Tribune*) it was the Metropolitan's

...amazing new soprano ... who ... aroused an audience of experienced and exacting Wagner-lovers to a pitch of enthusiasm
which brought back to many memories those fabulous days before
operatic singing went off the gold standard. ... Mme. Flagstad's
Brünnhilde ... yielded not only aesthetic pleasure of the deepest
sort, but a measure of incredulous delight. Knowing the character
of her Sieglinde, her Isolde, her "Walküre" Brünnhilde—those roles
in which she has lately been heard here and acclaimed: knowing
the specially fine-grained quality of those beautiful embodiments—
their delicate texture, their rarity, their peculiar sympathy and tenderness and warmly human loveliness—one could not but wonder
if the youthful and exquisite daughter of Wotan could possibly trans-
form herself into the towering Brünnhilde of "Götterdämmerung,"
with her immensity of anguished rage, and, at the distant end, her
sacrificial exaltation. ...

Mme. Flagstad is not equipped by nature to suggest in look or
in demeanor the sculpturing of heroic passions and superhuman

The Reviewing Stand

exaltations upon a human form. What she accomplished yesterday in this endeavor was effective in her own way. She set before us a Brünnhilde achieving tragic growth and exaltation by a process of spiritual intensification as secret and interior as it was poignantly indicative.

By the subtlest of changes in facial expression; by the aid of that eloquent repose and that reticent art of miming which she has mastered; above all, by the magicalizing beauty and intensity of her singing, she exposed Brünnhilde's spirit, sculptured astonishingly on the flesh. The outer image was lighted from within, became translucent and transformed. I can recall nothing more exact in its imaginative veracity than the attitude and gestures of this Brünnhilde as she sat among the falling shadows of her mountain top, kissing Siegfried's ring, awaiting the return of the hero who had unwittingly betrayed her. I remember nothing more piercing in its expressive and beautiful fidelity than the indescribable gesture—overwhelming in its compassionate tenderness and lofty grief—with which, at the tragedy's end, she removed that ring from the finger of the dead Siegfried who once had torn it from her own.

And always, bearing the tragedy upon its wings, was that extraordinary and overmastering voice, that moving loveliness and fervor of expressive song, so vitally creative and spontaneous and free. Hearing it, in actuality or in remembrance, one thinks of that other voice which Coleridge once described: "You might have fancied that it had a separate being of its own; that it was a living something, whose mode of existence was for the ear alone."

Mr. Downes (the *Times*) was no less overwhelmed:

Yesterday, as her (Mme. Flagstad's) Brünnhilde of "Götterdämmerung" developed, and grew to a climax of epic proportions and of the most moving tragedy, it seemed that the half of her capacities had yet to be told. . . . The results were of a nature to be remembered by everyone present, and of a quality to remind us of the feebleness of most contemporaneous musical effort, creative or interpretive as may be. Because for once a truly magnificent voice and a nature to feel profoundly and communicate with surpassing sincerity and vision the greatness of Wagner had materialized. The effect was to restore certain gigantic manifestations of art to their

THE FLAGSTAD MANUSCRIPT

proper proportions in the observer's consciousness, and these proportions, these rich and tremendous utterances made a good deal of our contemporaneous expressions appear fussy, petty, and pretentious.

In Mme. Flagstad's performance there are details to be further shaped and developed, and coordinated with other elements of the production—or those elements better coordinated with her. But here was the grandeur which cannot be taught or created by talking— this, with the elemental feeling, and splendor of voice, and large utterance of the early gods.

Mme. Flagstad was opening floodgates of song and emotion which had remained closed for some years. She is indeed blessed beyond words by her vocal organ and she has earned her success honorably in the fact that she uses it so magnificently. It is a trained instrument of almost endless resource, equal to a first act of "Götterdämmerung" with the Siegfried duet, and the tremendous drama of the second act, with the curse uttered on the spear-head, and the all-encompassing final scene.

In these scenes what was lacking in stage business and dramatic detail was provided by true and instinctive feeling and a spaciousness of mood, gesture, pronouncement which wonderfully conveyed the essence of music and text. The tone changed color for every mood, as a voice properly produced, in the case of a real artist, will naturally do. It was bright as the spear itself in the terrible pronouncement of vengeance and rage. It was dolorous, deep, and sombre when Brünnhilde marvelled at the horrible and inexplicable treachery of her hero—treachery against which all her knowledge and her lost powers of divination were vain. It had endless color, matchless virility and substance and impact. Phrase after phrase that can tear a voice to pieces was thrown off with tonal opulence and power.

The interpretation rose, as steadily as the music drama itself, to the moment when Brünnhilde stands revealed, the instrument for the final sacrifice, sybil and prophetess of the destruction of the gods.

No one who saw it will forget that entrance, the apostrophe to what had been and was to be; the tender homage to the fallen hero; the majesty of the gesture that commanded the preparation of the funeral pyre; the realization by her to whom at last everything was

252

The Reviewing Stand

revealed of the inevitable end, and the cleansing atonement that it was her destiny to proffer. *"Alles, alles weiss ich"* and *"Ruhe, ruhe du Gott!"*—the effect of the entire scene was unforgettable, bodeful, runic, and back of it the knowledge of the ultimate wisdom and renunciation.

Elisabeth (*Tannhäuser*) and Elsa (*Lohengrin*)

No new role entered Mme. Flagstad's repertory until April 17, when she portrayed Kundry in *Parsifal* in a post-season performance. Meanwhile, however, she had made further appearances in roles already discussed here and had supplemented them by adding Elisabeth in *Tannhäuser* (March 15) and Elsa in *Lohengrin* (March 18) to her Metropolitan list.

In the *Herald Tribune*, Gilman called her Elisabeth another of Mme. Flagstad's "extraordinary impersonations."

"Extraordinary" [he went on] is a conservative word for such embodiments as Mme. Flagstad has been offering to the incredulous operatic public of New York.... For there is no one in the current operatic theatre, so far as its occupants are known to well-travelled observers, who achieves quite what this Norwegian artist does.

Even if Mme. Flagstad were less richly gifted than she is—even if she had a less beautiful and searching voice, a less nobly gracious mask and personality, her remarkable art of revelation and projection would still distinguish her beyond her known colleagues of the lyric stage.

From the moment that she appeared last evening in the Hall of Song, joyous, virginal, irradiated, she was not only indissolubly and completely Elisabeth—as if the ardors and exaltations of Isolde and Brünnhilde had never been conceived—but she became the exquisite and sensitive instrument of Wagner's music and his drama, neither over-stressing nor under-stressing its inherent values, but simply realizing them to the last nuance and the last magnificence.

For Mme. Flagstad, like other artists of her rare and consolatory sort, is able, by some inexplicable chemistry of the imagination and the re-creative will, to precipitate artistic essences. Simply, magically, overwhelmingly, they come into being before our senses, complete

THE FLAGSTAD MANUSCRIPT

and unmistakable—Isolde's visionary passion, Brünnhilde's cosmic grief, Elisabeth's clairvoyant and heroic innocence—and hold us until the mystery is accomplished, and devoutness and integrity and genius have concluded their appointed task. . . .

As for *Lohengrin*, it was Mme. Flagstad's disclosure of Elsa, according to Gilman, that raised the performance

. . . to the plane of those occasional experiences which give a new validity to the world of the imagination and the life of the mind.

"The whole interest of *'Lohengrin'*," wrote Wagner in a famous essay, "consists in an inner process within the heart of Elsa, involving every secret of the soul." Mme. Flagstad made that spiritual process luminously clear and wonderfully eloquent . . . with the result that Elsa lived again in Wagner's music and his drama as she had not lived within the memory of the present generation.

By singing so flexibly expressive, so sensitive, so poignant, and so exalted that it stamped each phrase of Elsa's with the unmistakable impress of the music's truth: by the exercise of that power of imaginative identification which this unrivalled artist has brought to everyone of her impersonations, she made us realize why Wagner had found it possible to say that the "Lohengrin" drama as he restudied it in later years had touched him uniquely. "I cannot but hold it," he wrote Mathilde Wesendonck, "to be the most tragic poem of all"—and his "all," at that time, included "Tristan."

That tragic element centers, of course, in the character of Elsa. It is dormant and ineffectual in most embodiments of the part. Who of us has not suffered in the presence of the average Elsa of afflicting insipidity?

Mme. Flagstad restored the character to us . . . as Wagner had conceived it. She set the key for an embodiment of unforgettable reality and beauty and veraciousness at her first appearance, as she entered and stood before her accuser and judge, a figure of spellbound and visionary absorption, of grave and gentle loveliness. This was the clairvoyant, the mystical dreamer, of Wagner's poem and music, for whom the World of her inward illumination was far more authentic than the formidable reality of her surroundings. Her very first phrase, *"Mein armer Bruder!"*, as she uttered it abstractedly, to herself, was an inspired stroke of musical evocation;

The Reviewing Stand

in phrasing, in tone-color, in dynamic rectitude, it brought before us the essential Elsa, giving us in another dimension the figure upon whom we looked, with its delicately spiritualized image as of a wood-carving of the Middle Ages.

And later, as she stood on the balcony of the Kemenate in the coolness of the night and poured out her incredible happiness upon the quiet air, she made us aware that she had carried still further the searching and veracious expression of that inner process, from the beginning of the tragedy to its overmastering end she brought to life before us, charging each moment as it passed with the truth and beauty and intensity that were its own.

Mr. Downes (the *Times*) found the new Elsa

... beautifully and earnestly conceived.... She began the recital of the dream with a singular effect of intimacy and introspection. The climax when it came rang in her tones, a triumph of faith and a kindling pronouncement that heralded inevitably the appearance of the rescuing knight. This fine scale of values obtained all through the performance and gave the more effect to dramatic outbursts when the voice was sheer white flame and the woman and artist was revealed at her full height as a great interpreter.

It was Mr. Oscar Thompson, (later to become music critic of the *New York Sun*) who had already written in the *Times* of the new Elisabeth:

It had the now familiar splendor of voice in *"Dich teure Halle,"* and in moments of the scene with Tannhäuser leading up to her sigh of "Heinrich, Heinrich," was of rare poignance in its disclosure of the emotions with which Elisabeth was stirred at the return of the errant bard.

It was not in these lyric passages, however, nor in the smoothly and sensitively achieved "Prayer" of the final act that Mme. Flagstad contributed that which was truly memorable in this performance. The great finale of the Wartburg scene was her triumph. Though the ensemble has been better achieved in some of its particulars, the soprano's dominance of it was of thrilling pathos and power. There were moments as of a kind of transfiguration, not only in her

THE FLAGSTAD MANUSCRIPT

singing but her appearance. Her treatment of this scene stressed the virginal perhaps even more than the heroic. Her entrance between the swords was not more compelling to the eye than the picture of mute anguish she presented, her face hidden in her sleeve, her body slumped upon the throne before she flung herself among the raging men.

Of *Tannhäuser*, Henderson (the *Sun*) affirmed that

...each appearance of this much admired artist (Mme. Flagstad) deepens the conviction that the foundation of her success with the public is her beautiful singing. Her Elisabeth...was one of the most moving impersonations of the princess ever revealed on the local stage.

The impersonation had all Mme. Flagstad's best qualities, consistently fine, rich, and sustained tones, penetrating reading of every phrase and an eloquent version of every speech, plastic, reposeful, and significant action, and a remarkable range of emotional expression, so profound and touching in the tender pathos of the role as to lift the entire performance to unwonted heights. Her reproach of Tannhäuser in the duet and her thrilling defense of him in the finale of the second act should dwell long in the memory of everyone fortunate enough to hear them.

Mr. Chotzinoff (the *Post*) confessed to disappointment:

No artist can be expected to hit the bull's eye with every impersonation, and Miss Flagstad's average thus far has been very high. Perhaps Elizabeth is not for her or perhaps she has been singing too much. At any rate, her voice did not seem to be under as good control as it has been in the past....As an impersonation her Elizabeth lacked the warmth and the enveloping tenderness it should....These drawbacks, however, did not prevent Miss Flagstad from giving a creditable performance.

Kundry (*Parsifal*)

It was after the company's short tour following the close of the regular New York season that Mme. Flagstad returned to the

256

The Reviewing Stand

Metropolitan Opera House for three extra performances—one of *Tristan und Isolde* on April 10th and the two of *Parsifal* in Holy Week. Kundry in the Consecrational Festival Stage Play she had learned in the last few weeks. She set it before the public for the first time on April 17th and 19th to the usual obbligatos of praise.

Mr. Downes (the *Times*) led off the chorus on the 18th:

Mme. Flagstad took this, the most enigmatic of Wagnerian women's parts, for the first time on any stage and presented it with a distinction, an eloquence of gesture and song, and a conviction which would have implied long acquaintance with the role. . . . In the last decade in New York no Kundry has approached in significance and glory of song the interpretation of last night.

Mme. Flagstad did not attempt a new and unheard-of treatment of the character, or try to conceal and palliate her inexperience by any far-fetched devices. She followed Wagner's text and Wagner's directions implicitly, carrying them out in spirit and in letter. The fact that she sang the part with the same superb wealth of resource and ease of execution as she has sung the other big Wagnerian roles was one of the features of the occasion. Another was that she not only sang magnificently, but characterized by the color as well as the quality of the tone. In the first act the demoniac element was projected by tone-quality as well as gesture and action. No one will forget the hard and bright quality of the laconic rejoinder to Gurnemanz: *"Zu End' ihr Gram: seine Mutter ist todt"*—the mockery and bitterness in the voice, and then the dulling of the tone, the weariness and longing for rest: *"Nie thu' ich Gutes; nur Ruhe will ich."*

For sheer virtuosity, little could exceed the complete transformation from the weary-visaged hag of the first act to the sumptuous magic of the second. Now the song was lovely, sensuous in the extreme, eloquent with subtle inflections and shading, or brilliant with menace or defiance. How few Kundrys could thus allure with the sheer spell of the voice! It seemed that if the music had been ugly it would have become beautiful and a feast to the ear under such circumstances. And nothing can be substituted for this supreme vocal appeal, in opera.

Then there was the plasticity of the acting and the subtlety of

THE FLAGSTAD MANUSCRIPT

the conception, at one with the composer's. The wiles of the enchantress are given certain shadings by Wagner which would arrest the attention of a modern psychoanalyst. Here is the apotheosis of the Venus of "Tannhäuser," with new overtones and sophistications. Simple as Mme. Flagstad is always, unpretending in her directness and sincerity as an actress, she caught these overtones, and developed her second act to a wonderful climax.

Of course, many of her sisters of the operatic stage can envy her with reason for the voice and the vocal power which makes possible these achievements. But another great factor in the success of this Kundry needs emphasis, namely, that Mme. Flagstad has done every kind of a role in opera; has, in fact, acted in her native city of Oslo in something of the capacity of a stock actress who plays all parts. Her experience in many roles, her long years of good and careful cultivation of her voice, and supreme musicianship, enabled her to appear as Kundry last night with only the occasional suggestion that she was taking the part for the first instead of the tenth time. Add to this an uncommonly personable appearance, a Kundry credibly attractive and potent for good or evil.

Mr. Liebling (the *Journal-American*) remarked that

... Mme. Flagstad brought to bear all her tonal volume and richness, all her intelligent handling of the musical phrase, and her remarkable and consistent purity of intonation. As Kundry the enforced seductress and later as the moving penitent Mme. Flagstad sang with compelling verity and effect. Of especially poignant beauty was her delivery in the scene of humility and contrition, where she washes the feet of the compassionate Parsifal.

As an actress Mme. Flagstad again maintained her familiar straight-forward methods, avoiding rant and exaggeration of movement and gesture. She is no slave to traditions and has the courage to establish her own.

And then Mr. Liebling added a refreshing bit of wisdom:

Too much nonsense was written by earlier "Parsifal" commentators about the enigmatical character of Kundry, and her stage exponents felt constrained to attempt "psychological" instead of frank operatic impersonation. Study of the Kundry text reveals no

258

The Reviewing Stand

puzzling personage, and her manner and meanings are without esoteric implications in the printed words. They were spoken clearly and eloquently by Mme. Flagstad and registered Wagner's intentions convincingly. It is to be hoped that her example will suffice to lay the solemn bunk started by pioneer "Parsifal" lectures and so long believed.

Mr. Danton Walker (the *Daily News*) pointed out that Mme. Flagstad, since her American debut, had sung twenty performances of seven Wagnerian roles.

Her Kundry revealed little that was unexpected. The same splendid voice, fresher after a short rest. The same splendid musicianship. A Kundry at last, *Gott sei dank,* who still has her voice and face and figure all at once.

The role has one or two spots in it that lie rather too low for her range. And we are beginning to feel, alas, that the Norwegian diva is too temperamentally cold ever to show great passion or variety in her acting, since her Kundry is as nobly reticent as her Sieglinde and Isolde.

Also—a minor detail—we could quarrel with her choice of costume, since a pink nightrobe decorated with a harness of beads (under a scarlet cape!) is neither seductive nor becoming. She was a blonde enchantress, brunette as the penitent sinner, and the latter lady was the more enticing of the two.

Declared Henderson in the *Sun:*

Inevitably, the interest of the audience was directed largely to her (Mme. Flagstad's) creation. It has been unfortunate that the rapid expansion of the repertoire of this singularly gifted and accomplished artist has aroused so much excitement. She has become the star of all the evenings which her genius has illumined, and the operas themselves have been viewed as vehicles for her art. Happily there must be less of this next season, because there will not be many new worlds for her to conquer.

About Kundry's nature Henderson stuck to the older notion:

Kundry is not one character, but two. No logical dramatic development of the role is possible. The wild creature of the first act

THE FLAGSTAD MANUSCRIPT

can give no hint of the highly trained courtesan of the second. These are different persons and neither is theatrically illusional. That Mme. Flagstad would sing the music laudably was a foregone conclusion, and this of course she did. Her intonation, her phrasing, her unhesitating attack of every declamatory utterance and her sweeping dramatic style aroused constant admiration. But there was something more; her Kundry was astonishing in its completeness, its certainty, its apparently finished plan.

Mme. Flagstad will undoubtedly develop her impersonation, but last evening it seemed to be already developed.... It is evident that a sound musicianship is one of her most valuable possessions. She knows her scores. She was perfectly independent of the conductor last night; she made her entrances without looking at him. This certainly enabled her to throw herself with abandon and lyric eloquence into the part, and her second act was a triumph of dramatic singing. It was so intense, so rich in subtle nuance, and so splendid in the manner of its action and gesture as to lift the long hackneyed Kundry back to the level on which Wagner conceived her. She gave new vitality to the work in which she was instantaneously the dominating figure, and the audience was aroused to demonstrations of uncommon enthusiasm. It is something new to hear cheers after the second act of "Parsifal," but they were heard last evening.

On the 20th Gilman in the *Herald Tribune* wrote in partial summary:

Mme. Flagstad had never sung anywhere this baffling and perilous role, in which so many fine artists have come to grief. She had learned it here (it is said) in eighteen days. Yet she embodied it yesterday with a perfection of imaginative rectitude, a trans-illuminating beauty and intensity, that searched the heart of Wagner's music and his drama and left them, for sensitive observers, newly revealed and overwhelming....

Thus ends a musico-dramatic saga of personal achievement which would be difficult to match. In the dozen weeks since Mme. Flagstad arrived here for her Metropolitan debut she has learned, *de novo,* four of the greatest roles in the Wagnerian list—the three Brünnhildes and Kundry (one of them, the "Siegfried" Brünnhilde, she was prevented from singing because of illness). She has appeared

260

The Reviewing Stand

at the Metropolitan as Sieglinde, Isolde, Elizabeth, Elsa, the Brünnhilde of "Die Walküre," the Brünnhilde of "Götterdämmerung," and now as Kundry—the last three for the first time in her career.

In each of these formidable roles she has disclosed significances that had long been disregarded, implications that had been forgotten or undisclosed. Yet in nothing that she has done has she imposed upon Wagner's drama or his music anything that was not implicit in their texture. She has illuminated depths, extracted essences, intensified meanings. She has left each character that she embodied more veracious and moving and significant than it had been before. She has touched nothing that she has not exalted and enriched and deepened by her imaginative penetration, her ennobling and exquisite art, her consecrational devoutness as an artist.

She has restored an old tradition and created a new one. She has reminded us that consummate musicianship and the utmost beauty of delivered song are not alien to dramatic truth, but its deepest source and its most perfect instrument. She seems to have taken as her text the words of Wagner himself: "The music must be flawless, for then the chief thing is safe."

And she has taught us a new tradition and a new esthetic indulgence in physical exercise, but a more difficult and subtler thing: a process of inner sculpturing upon the outward form, a lighting and intensification from within.

Yesterday, in that third act of "Parsifal" which is so cruel a test for any actress, she stood for long moments motionless, in the rough garments of Kundry the penitent, grave and sad and inarticulate, looking backward through the ages and her many pasts. She made no gesture, no change of pose, she scarcely changed her head; yet in the pose itself, in the vision within the eyes, in the contour and plane and pallor of the beautiful profile, she gave us a poignant sense of that eternal moment in which the spirit rests in its pilgrimage that is outside of time—she gave us the nameless tragedy and grief and loneliness of Kundry, the woman of uncounted incarnations, the symbol of Nature, and of life itself.

Yet her gift as an actress is not only for this intensification of repose. At that moment when Kundry is summoned by Klingsor from the gulf of sleep and time and endlessly recurring death, her

THE FLAGSTAD MANUSCRIPT

tearing cry as she awakens to the realization of her endless task had all the anguish of re-birth.

Later, in the seduction scene, the exquisite pantomime of her enticements as she wove her blandishments about the tragically enlightened youth achieved a pattern of allurement that was all loveliness and flowing movement and flamelike grace. And here, too, she made us realize that Kundry the enchantress, as Wagner's music has inclosed her, was no smirking, simpering seductress, but a timeless image of insuperable beauty, a projection of that dreaming mind by which men live and die.

Afterward, standing before that redeemer who has come so late, whom, through endless ages, Kundry has awaited, she subdued us by the tragic intensity with which she recalled her mockery of the Saviour on Golgotha. In that moment whose pathos and sublimity rival the Bach of the Passions, this wonderful re-creator, in the agony and horror of her *"lachte,"* in the piteousness of *"da traf mich sein Blick,"* brought about us in their reality the sorrowful compassion of the music itself, its essence and its truth.

Leonore *(Fidelio)*

In the following two seasons Mme. Flagstad added three more roles to her New York repertory—Leonore in *Fidelio,* till the *Alcestis* of 1952 her only role in America not by Wagner; Senta in *Der Fliegende Holländer,* and Brünnhilde in *Siegfried.* Oddly enough, it was not Brünnhilde, as might have been expected, that came first, but Leonore. The occasion was the matinee on Saturday, March 7, 1936, when Mr. Gatti-Casazza revived Beethoven's sole opera after more than six years of Metropolitan disuse. Again the additional recitatives and "melodramas" composed by Artur Bodanzky for the Metropolitan revival of January 22, 1927, were used. "That production," wrote Sanborn, "though planned in honor of the centenary of Beethoven's death, dishonored the occasion to the extent of these supplementary incumbrances, which, however well intended, were a bore or a sacrilege, or both, in proportion to the seriousness with which you took them. In spite of disapproval'

262

The Reviewing Stand

emphatically expressed, they thus lasted into the Flagstad era as so much dead weight that clogged the progress of the opera and altered its character."

Again Gilman (the *Herald Tribune*) led the chorus of admiration:

Perhaps yesterday's demonstrative audience had been a bit anxious to learn whether Flagstad could triumph in any other role than a Wagnerian one. They learned that she can. For this proved to be a Leonore conceived in that great tradition of simplicity and subtlety and restraint and eloquent repose of style which Mme. Flagstad herself had established in her Metropolitan performances. There were no mechanical and semaphoric gesturings, no meaningless flinging up and flinging out of arms and fatuous stridings to and fro. There was instead the constant use of pose and movement and facial change to indicate essential things in the simplest and most concentrated way—as in that final moment of beautiful and effective pantomime in the last scene when she unshackled Florestan and touched with exquisite tenderness his tortured wrists.

Her singing of the music was at all points nobly beautiful, thrilling in its sweep of line and fervor in such heroic outbursts as the concluding allegro section of the great aria, where (despite a momentary lapse of memory) she took us to the heights of Leonore's fortitude and faith. At the other end of the gamut was her utterance of Leonore's poignant happiness as the irons fell from Florestan's wrists and he sank into her arms before the sunlit ramparts of the final scene.

Mr. Downes (the *Times*) added this:

Mme. Flagstad, attractively disguised as the youth and jailer's assistant, was inevitably the cynosure of eyes and ears. She sang cruelly difficult music, that asks almost the impossible of the singer, because of its prevailing instrumental character, which takes little account of the range or physical aptitudes of the voices, and the range of two full octaves, and the length of phrases which must seem to stretch to the ends of the earth for any but the greatest singers. She sang the music with a very high degree of technical

THE FLAGSTAD MANUSCRIPT

mastery, and, more than that, made it the vehicle of warm and womanly feeling.

There were other places which often pass by without anything in particular happening, where Mme. Flagstad found the revealing tone and accent. The part becomes her well, and she has in rare measure the qualities that it requires.

Other reviewers reported the occasion with more reserve. Mr. Liebling (the *American*) declared that attired as a youth Mme. Flagstad "hardly carried out visual illusion. She sang earnestly. Her voice could not show its best possibilities. She even seemed to fall short in power during her biggest number, the aria known as *'Abscheulicher.'* "

According to Henderson (the *Sun*):

The Leonore of the now famous soprano did not reach the dramatic level of those impersonations which so quickly clothed her in glory. It was sound, correct, beautifully sung in respect of suavity and tonal quality. It was full of tenderness; it was exquisitely womanly; it was poetic and imaginative. But the grand tragic note was missing. The heroic Leonore of tradition, the Leonore who confronted a would-be murderer with a better weapon than his own, the Leonore who proudly proclaimed her identity as the wife, risking all to save her husband, yielded her place in the tragedy to a very dignified, gentle, and sympathetic young woman, manifestly glad that she was not obliged to pull the trigger.

Technically the singing of the music was all admirable. Mme. Flagstad even negotiated with consummate skill the cruel ascending passage to B natural in the *"Abscheulicher,"* which Beethoven had to modify for the original Leonore, Frau Milder. The duet went well in the prison scene. But for once the artist who has so shaken the foundations of this metropolis seemed to be most of the time poised on the surface of her song, not plunged in its depths. That being the case, "Fidelio" could not strike fire in the few spots where flame should light the dramatic scene.

According to Sanborn (the *World-Telegram*) the performance

...was a decidedly uneven solemnity, and none of its elements more so than the Leonore of Mme. Flagstad. The Norwegian so-

264

The Reviewing Stand

prano had hardly seemed the obvious choice for the part, nor did she succeed in convincing one that a preconceived notion of that kind had been a mistake. Though she made a lovely picture in her disguise, her acting appeared to be chiefly of the when-in-doubt-don't sort, and though some of her singing was admirable technically and tonally, it was deficient in the throbbing warmth that is indispensable to a real Leonore.

Dramatic aloofness and vocal coolness are out of place in "Fidelio." On the other hand, the uncommonly fine quality of Mme. Flagstad's upper octave gave the usual pleasure, and her superior technic enabled her to execute clearly and fluently passages in which less accomplished vocalists come to grief.

Some of Leonore's music, however, lies rather low for her, and, strange as it may seem, she briefly forgot her part in the Allegro of "Abscheulicher!"

Senta (*Der Fliegende Holländer*)

Senta and the Siegfried Brünnhilde were added to the gallery in January of the year following. On the 7th the Norwegian soprano appeared as the Norwegian girl determined to save the Flying Dutchman's soul. The occasion was a special matinee for the benefit of the Florence Crittenton League, and the revived opera had not been given at the Metropolitan since the season of 1931-32, when Senta was embodied by Maria Jeritza.

Mr. Downes, in the *Times,* pronounced the performance

...an interpretation of historic eloquence, [owing] primarily to the presence in the cast of Kirsten Flagstad and Friedrich Schorr.... This writer never heard the ballade presented so movingly and with such quality of imagination. There was the woman of Wagner's imagining, whose soul hovers between two worlds whose fate is known to herself alone,...who waits, as one preordained, for the moment of her destiny.

The first call which ushers in the recital, that wild evocation associated with the thought of the accursed sea-wanderer, was sung, for once, as the composer intended: not as a whoop to the gallery, but softly, eerily in the opening phrases, almost in a disembodied

265

THE FLAGSTAD MANUSCRIPT

tone. Then commenced the tale of the ship with black masts and the blood-red sails which sweeps the ocean. . . . The initial G, written as a short "eighth" note, and as part of the beginning phrase, was properly, an indirect violation of the printed page isolated from its context. And it was as the lonely cry of the gull.

This was the wild preluding. Then came the change from the minor to the major tonality and the magnificently conceived contrast of the mood and of the sonority of the voice, with the *"piu lento"* passage—the music which clothes the words of Senta, that deal with her vision of the one way to the Dutchman's redemption. Word and tone, inflection and vocal mechanism in this lofty invocation were nobly one. The phrase, which is well known as the second theme of the Dutchman overture, can be sentimental, commonplace in the hands of the semi-competent. But this phrase mounted majestically, step by step, to a summit of intensity and devotion.

In the *Herald Tribune* Mr. Francis D. Perkins declared that it might be pushing enthusiasm too far to say that Mme. Flagstad's

. . . first (for New York) impersonation of a role of her own nationality is yet entirely on a par with her Isolde or her Brünnhilde, in which she has set a standard hard for anyone, even herself, to emulate. Yet it was a memorable impersonation, vivid and intent, delighting a listener's ears and strongly appealing to his imagination, a Senta, indeed, such as Wagner himself might have had in mind.

There were times, as in the ballad in the second act, when Mme. Flagstad's voice seemed not entirely oblivious of intensive concert and operatic activity but it soon exhibited its familiar strength and clarity and later it reached its familiar and unparalleled strength and clarity and concentrated expressiveness. The Norwegian soprano's essential musicianship was strikingly indicated in the duets of the second act, in an intensity of force and expressiveness reaching its culmination at the point where the music and the situation called for the climax. And her final proclamation, *"Hier steh' ich, treu dir bis zum Tod!"*, had an unforgettably stirring magnificence. The intensity of feeling which is a major characteristic of the role was reflected throughout with full conviction.

The Reviewing Stand

Mr. Winthrop Sargeant (the *American*) found Mme. Flagstad

...all that could be asked for as the dreamy-eyed daughter of the sailor Daland. Her "Johohae" at the beginning of the second act was intoned with rare sureness and poise, and the duet with the Dutchman in the same act brought forth as magnificent a flow of vocal resource as has ever been heard anywhere among the Metropolitan's current productions. She was, moreover, beautifully costumed and made a strikingly attractive figure from the visual standpoint.

Mr. Chotzinoff (the *Post*) maintained that

...Mme. Flagstad did not *appear* to be Senta. She *was* Senta. Not for a moment did she convey a sense of artifice. She was, as they say, born to be: the very instrument of the synthetic Dutchman's salvation. Her fixed gaze, her deadly, reposeful attitudes, her fantastic silences which held the audience spellbound, her lavish voice expressing the clear depths of a boundless peasant devotion, built up for one's eyes and ears the personification of an elemental force which there was no resisting. Because of her "The Flying Dutchman" was no longer only an eerie legend with dreaming sailors and phantom ships but the drama of a woman into whose being faith and devotion had entered like a dybbuk.

Mr. Thompson (the *Sun*) was no less impressed:

Mme. Flagstad has a new role in which she shines with a refulgence quite as brilliant, but more melting, than the splendid fire of her more heroic parts. She was the realization of Wagner's redeeming maiden. Her Senta had no tentative moment; she had absorbed the content of the opera before she offered her delineation for the examination of the public. Her impersonation was completely planned, firm in outline, employing few, but very significant, details, as all her portraits, do, and sung with plenitude of voice and authoritative comprehension of the music.

Her delivery of the ballad was perhaps the most dramatic the 'Metropolitan stage has known. With those broad, direct, and primitive strokes which characterize all the art of this admirable singer, she revealed the whole meaning of the spell placed upon Senta by

THE FLAGSTAD MANUSCRIPT

the legend of the weary wanderer of the seas and put the central pivot of the drama precisely where it belonged. Everything then fell into its proper place and Wagner's work went steadily and unwaveringly to its end. Not only did Mme. Flagstad vitalize the whole opera, but she brought to the detrimentally static action a picturesque element usually wanting. She looked like Senta; she was realistically the Norwegian maiden.

In the *World-Telegram,* Sanborn wrote:

Mme. Flagstad as Wagner's visionary and devoted heroine sang her part in the big duet of Act II with breadth and expressiveness, with rich and thrilling tone. In the earlier ballad her voice had sounded tired and somewhat shrill, and her mezza voce had been a bit shaky. Nor did I like the over-deliberate, over-declamatory, and fragmentary treatment of the piece.

Although the Norwegian soprano evidently took great pains with her impersonation of the Norwegian captain's daughter, the heroic maiden, a prey to a fixed idea, has been portrayed here more impressively.

No account of a new role assumed by Mme. Flagstad would be complete without Gilman's reaction. Though he did not attend her first Senta, he did her fourth.

Mme. Flagstad's appearance here as Senta ten weeks ago, he wrote, was her first assumption of it anywhere. She has now played it four times at the Metropolitan. Already she seems to have made it not only a natural extension of her own artistic personality, but an inevitable embodiment of Wagner's conception of the exalted and naive dreamer, the selfless, sacrificial woman of the mariner's anguished hope.

Wagner has insisted on Senta's fundamental naivete. In his article on the proper performance of "The Flying Dutchman," he remarks that "only in the heart of an utterly naive girl, a girl of the Norwegian north, could such an exalted monomania as Senta's take possession."

Unpleasant persons have said that Wagner's Senta was "hysterical." They are the same sort of persons who have said that Joan

268

The Reviewing Stand

of Arc was hysterical. But hysteria may·be an expression of the valorous and selfless as well as of the feeble and self-indulgent. Wagner himself, with one of his fine strokes of irony, calls Senta "morbid," inclosing the word within quotation marks. Possibly Senta would have been a poor hand at golf or tennis. One may doubt if she knew much about setting-up exercises—though it is not difficult to think of her plunging with zest, on sunny, windy days, into the "salt, unplumbed, estranging sea" that washed the rocky coast near Daland's home—that sea into which in fact she leaped, with tragic fortitude and epic faith, at the end of Wagner's great dramatic parable of sacrificial and heroic love.

The blend of poise and sensibility, vibrancy and resolution, strength and tenderness, pity and heroic faith which make this embodiment so rare, is conveyed to us by Mme. Flagstad from the first moment that we see her, sitting entranced, brooding, surrounded by the spinning maidens, but infinitely apart from them. We hear it in every tone of her voice as she sings the superb ballad out of which Wagner wrought this earliest of his true music—dramas; we hear it when Senta joins her voice with the Dutchman's in the rapturous duet with its high, ecstatic B's (sung with pealing splendor by Mme. Flagstad at yesterday's performance).

Cosima Wagner once described to Richard a certain portrait that had impressed her deeply as "an apotheosis of simplicity." There could be no apter phrase, I think, for Flagstad's Senta.

Brünnhilde (*Siegfried*)

The long awaited *Siegfried* Brünnhilde was at last revealed to New York on January 22, 1937. Gilman wrote of it in the *Herald Tribune:*

When Kirsten Flagstad sang her first "Siegfried" Brünnhilde last evening at the Metropolitan, she set before us one of the greatest of her numerous great achievements in the revelation of noble and heroic beauty. She sang the role more than a year ago in San Francisco, but her devoted New York public, oddly enough, was obliged to wait until last night to witness an impersonation which makes all possible comparisons seem futile and preposterous.

THE FLAGSTAD MANUSCRIPT

From the moment that she rose upon her couch and looked about her, raising her arms in greeting to the sun, the light, the day, accompanied by music whose resurrectional ecstasy takes away the breath, she was the visual and aural image of Wagner's tonal poetry. The beauty and fidelity of the presented image—the noble loveliness of the radiant face, the gestures of touching simplicity, dignity, naturalness, and grace, the pealing splendor and purity of the matchless voice—these were living symbols of the rapture and majesty and tenderness of Wagner's creative thought.

The use of the unique voice, the delivery of the musical phrases and the words, were deeply and ceaselessly expressive. When she sang *"Lang war mein Schlaf,"* the sadness that clouded momentarily the shining tones was like a passing memory of the Valkyr's tragic punishment. But the lofty and heroic splendor with which she shaped the contours of her Olympian greeting to the gods and to the morning earth were fretted with the golden fire of Wagner's mountain dawn.

This *Siegfried,* in the belief of Mr. Downes (the *Times*)

...reached one of the great climaxes of recent operatic history with Kirsten Flagstad's Brünnhilde, whose part in "Siegfried" she interpreted for the first time here. And in so doing she made operatic history. Mme. Flagstad sang with a glory and plenitude of tone that no other singer known to this generation in America can equal. And this was the expression of a concept which, for once, matched that of the composer-dramatist. . . .

In not one respect did Mme. Flagstad fail Wagner or disappoint her audience. We had not seen such a noble plastic. The grandeur of each gesture was the visualization of the moment and an emanation of the music. The observer was thus suitably prepared for the moment of the great invocation, glorified not only by grand movement and eloquent facial play, but also by the glorious sound of the great pealing voice. For once there was in this place the interpretive dimensions of the godlike. The scene developed with irresistible intensity but also with emotional reserve, and with a breadth that equalled the tremendous proportions of Wagner's thought.

And there was no demand of the music to which Mme. Flagstad

The Reviewing Stand

was not equal—physically, technically equal from the point of view of the most complete interpretation. There are those who find her Isolde to lack something of subtlety and sensuous coloring, wonderfully as it is sung. But she strikes profoundly the note of the heroic and virginal passion of Brünnhilde. It seems unlikely that the part has ever been more impressively presented in this city.

Henderson (the *Sun*) said:

Mme. Flagstad brought to the role of Brünnhilde a plenitude of opulent tone to meet the requirements of the long phrases of the awakening, and noteworthy musical sensitivity in the moulding of every phrase. Her *"Heil dir, Sonne, heil dir, Licht"* was nobly sung and she filled the duet with Siegfried with emotional eloquence. She was indeed a goddess no more, but a woman awakened by a kiss to the complete and yielding realization of womanhood.

In the *World-Telegram*, Sanborn agreed that inevitably the matter of paramount interest was the new Brünnhilde.

It is unnecessary to go into detail with regard to the difficulty of the "Siegfried" Brünnhilde—the exorbitant demands the music makes on the soprano's upper range, on her sustaining power, on her execution; the relentless histrionic exactions. This Brünnhilde has only a single scene, but that scene, unique in all drama, reaches the summit of inspiration of the entire "Ring."

Amid the distressing scenery employed for this section of the opera the sleeping Brünnhilde was awkwardly displayed. But after the trying moment of the actual awakening was past, the various greetings were managed impressively. Mme. Flagstad looked better than the average representative of the whilom goddess and, in particular, her Norse quality was the authentic thing for the part.

She attacked the first *"Heil dir"* boldly and delivered her phrases with breadth and conviction through the question to Siegfried. But strain was unmistakable in the vocal quality, which is not at all surprising in view of the singer's heroic labors this season. . . .

THE FLAGSTAD MANUSCRIPT

The *Siegfried* Brünnhilde completed the gallery of Mme. Flagstad's roles in America down to her departure for Norway in 1941. As we have seen, all were sung in German and all but one, Leonore in Beethoven's *Fidelio*, were characters in operas by Wagner. In the summer of 1935 word went out that in the course of the following season we might look for the Norwegian soprano as the heroine of a revival of Bellini's *Norma*. Later that project was quietly abandoned and the role transferred to Dusolina Giannini, the Italian-American soprano. Miss Giannini was expressly brought over from Europe, where she had made an enviable career in opera. Though a tentative date was set, February 26, 1936, the revival did not take place till February 20, 1937, when the Norma was not Miss Giannini but the Franco-Italian soprano Gina Cigna.

First American Postwar Appearance, Symphony Hall, Boston, April 6, 1947

On April 7th, the following comments by Virgil Thomson appeared in the *Herald Tribune:*

Kirsten Flagstad's first public appearance in the United States since her regretted (and regrettable) departure in 1941 took place yesterday afternoon at Symphony Hall in Boston. The house was full, and her reception was of the warmest.

Indeed, a more massive welcome could hardly be imagined. There was cheering, shouting, stamping of feet and such clapping of hands as only Boston's enthusiasm can produce. Nothing lacked for an ovation of the first category save possibly whistling, which is, after all, a New York, not a Boston habit. At no point was there an unfavorable demonstration of any kind.

Whether any such was merited from a patriotic point of view is not my privilege to judge. Miss Flagstad has been declared without taint of disloyalty by her own government, the Norwegian, notoriously the most severe in Europe toward collaborators. And I have no information which would cause me to question the justice of that

272

The Reviewing Stand

decision. So far as I am entitled to opine, this artist has been absent for six years on private business of a legitimate nature; and now she is back. She has gained about twenty pounds but looks well. And she is singing like an angel.

Her vocal powers are under better control than when she left. Repose of the singing voice has done her good. Perhaps one has forgotten how beautiful her singing always was. When she began her recital yesterday with Beethoven's "Busslied," the first thought that came to mind was that certainly since her departure none of us has heard anything comparable. Never in this writer's concert-going lifetime, as a matter of fact, has there been available any other vocal artistry of such sumptuous natural acoustics, such perfect technical control and such sound musicianship.

Miss Flagstad's is the dream voice of all time, and never has it seemed so lovely as yesterday. Neither have her interpretations seemed more vigorous, more rich in variety of vocal effect. She sang loud and she sang soft, very loud and very soft. She sang darkly and also with the brightest of tone color. She sang legato, staccato, portamento, and with that absolute equality of emphasis in wide skips that is the true bravura style of the dramatic soprano.

She sang a long program and lots of encores, showed no sign of fatigue. So far as a recital program permits, she showed us that she is as good as ever and probably better than when we last heard her. The highest note called for was an A, if I mistake not. That was long, full and glorious. So, indeed, was the whole recital.

First New York Postwar Appearance, Carnegie Hall, April 20, 1947

Olin Downes had this to say in the *Times* of April 21st:

Mme. Flagstad is still a great singer, though it is evident that with the years her voice has lost something of its original beauty, evenness, and power. Had the singer been judged by certain songs of her first group the estimate would be different, and lower than that. For in those songs the upper tones were poor, edged, and unsteady. Nor was there the infallible intonation of other days.

THE FLAGSTAD MANUSCRIPT

In her second group, which consisted of the cycle "Haugtussa" of Grieg and two encores of songs by the same composer, Mme. Flagstad was heard to much better advantage. Most of these songs lie in the lower part of the voice, which is emphatically the best part today. She sang them in Norwegian, presumably with the best of diction, with the musicianship which she always displays and with a folk simplicity.

Even so, there was not the freshness, ease, spontaneity of style which many who heard her sing this same cycle some seasons ago in Town Hall will remember. And sometimes there were vocal make-shifts. But the end of the group, and the following encores, representing the best singing of the afternoon, went far toward relieving a sense of monotony that the first part had engendered. By that time the voice was free, warm, steady and brilliant. The uppermost tones, which had previously been the most unsatisfactory, rang out with the old impact and controlled volume. A B flat came full and clear and the house went wild. ... These moments were the climax of the recital.

As Isolde in "Tristan und Isolde"
Civic Opera House, Chicago, November 16, 1947
(Benefit: Chicago Symphony Pension Fund)
First American Postwar Operatic Appearance

Claudia Cassidy wrote in the *Chicago Daily Tribune* next day:

Who says the great days of opera are gone? None who sat transfixed in the Civic Opera House yesterday and hovered between tears and cheers as the just tribute to the blazing incandescence of a magnificent "Tristan und Isolde" presented by Artur Rodzinski as his first and unforgettable contribution to the pension fund of the Chicago Symphony Orchestra, of which he is now the mesmeric leader.

But when, at the end of the opera, after a "Liebestod" that tore the heart to tatters Kirsten Flagstad stepped out unexpectedly to take her first bow alone, why then there was no question. Tears and cheers came out together in a half-choked roar that seemed to shake the huge house before it fell at her feet in tribute.

The Reviewing Stand

In that roar was the pent-up admiration, the trust, and the love the public has for this great singer, and in it, too, was the great sigh of relief that she has come back to us not just as good, but better, than ever. . . . Never before in my life had I heard such an Isolde, and I am rich in its memory should I be so luckless as never to hear it again.

Tristan und Isolde at War Memorial Opera House,
San Francisco, September 30, 1949

A review by Alfred Frankenstein, from the San Francisco *Chronicle* said:

No "Tristan" in local history seemed so intense, so totally absorbing, so completely overwhelming in its impact. The main reason for this, of course, was the return of Kirsten Flagstad after ten years' absence from the roster of the San Francisco Opera Company. Nothing has happened in that decade to dim Flagstad's luster as the supreme Wagnerian soprano of our time. Her figure is a trifle more Holbeinesque than it used to be. Her voice remains an instrument of incomparable golden glory supported by the most unfailing perfect ear in opera and by reserves of strength and power which belong in the realm of the fabulous.

There is, of course, more to it than that. One may speak, for instance, of the simplicity and refinement of Flagstad's acting. But when you have accounted for everything—beauty of tone, richness of phrase, tireless vitality, impeccable musicianship, splendor of presence—there remains a certain magic over and above the describable factors which is the product of their sum and the personality behind it all.

One result of this magic which I noted about the middle of the first act was a tightening and relaxation of my own larynx as Isolde poured forth her woes. Some people around me seemed to be singing unconsciously, and maybe I was, too. This is what the estheticians call "empathy," and it doesn't happen in an opera house unless something stupendous is going forth on the stage. . . .

For the rest, one was delightfully reminded of certain turns of phrase, gestures and mannerisms one had forgotten, including Flag-

275

THE FLAGSTAD MANUSCRIPT

stad's way of taking a curtain call as if she had wandered out more or less by accident and wasn't quite sure that this was the place where she belonged. The audience was violently, not to say insanely emphatic in reassuring her.

Metropolitan Opera, January 22, 1951
(Return to Metropolitan as Isolde.)
Olin Downes wrote next day:

It may be well to defer too precise an examination of Mme. Flagstad's voice at this time, for she must have been under a special nervous strain due to the particular circumstances of her return to the Metropolitan stage. Hers remains one of the great voices; she remains one of the great mistresses of the tonal art. Last night there was considerable shrillness of her upper tones, some false intonation, a tendency to parlando effects instead of straight singing at the end of certain phrases.

On the credit side, Mme. Flagstad was more careful and distinguished with her diction than ever before. In the middle and lower parts of her voice, particularly, she matched tone to text in a most eloquent manner. She used to be reproached by some of her critics for acting either "coldly" or not enough. Last night she acted more than ever before in our memory, and over-acted in places. And ever and anon the tones soared with the old ecstatic flight. It is true that her complete facility and effortless security in execution of former years appear now to be conditioned. Ten years will pass and no human voice remain immune to their passage. Even so, granted an occasion of less tension and growing ease upon the stage which she has not ornamented for a decade, these desiderata will probably be of small importance by the side of the singer's authority in her art.

Virgil Thomson in the *Herald-Tribune:*

Standing applause and lengthy cheers (19 curtain calls) were the reward of Kirsten Flagstad last night after the first act of Wagner's "Tristan und Isolde" at the Metropolitan Opera House. Absent from that stage for ten years, she has returned with her unique vocal powers intact and her dramatic projection more imperious, or so it

The Reviewing Stand

would seem, than ever. In a house that has long given the Wagner operas better, on the whole, than anything else, Miss Flagstad still set the place afire. Vocally vast and impeccable, and dramatically as convincing as this statuesque work allows, she held the attention absorbed and drew the gratitude of even so seasoned an anti-Wagnerian as this reporter.

Alcestis
Metropolitan Opera, March 4, 1952

Olin Downes wrote next day in the *Times* of this memorable event:

The revival of Gluck's "Alcestis," in English translation by John Gutman, last night at the Metropolitan Opera House was memorable, indeed unique, for the performance of the name part by Mme. Flagstad. She will appear in this role four more times this season. It is a role she has undertaken for the first time in her career for her last appearances. No artist could take a nobler farewell of the public.

It seems strange, indeed, that Mme. Flagstad has been so long in studying this part, for she seems to have been born for it. Her native dignity and simplicity in dramatic interpretation, her mastery not merely of the technique but of the finest principles of the vocal art qualify her especially for it. She sings it with a simplicity and an emotion that are unforgettable and in the finest classic style.

This style unites grandeur and nobility with great intensity of feeling. There is no bravura singing. There are no magnificent histrionics such as are offered by the Brünnhilde of Götterdämmerung," which Mme. Flagstad has interpreted so memorably. But this is a part that in range, in significance of every phrase, in the need of dramatic enunciation as well as vocal splendor, is one of the most demanding in the dramatic soprano's repertory.

And truth to tell, as Mme. Flagstad began last night, one was a trifle apprehensive. But the voice soon warmed, gained firmness and resonance and impact. The first great climax was the famous invocation of the gods of the Styx, and this was delivered with thrilling power and intensity, with the B flat in itself a drama!

THE FLAGSTAD MANUSCRIPT

Yet this was the lesser of two historical achievements of the evening. The second was the pathetic air at the end of the sécond act, as Alcestis bids farewell to life and friends and children to be with her Admetus, and prepares herself for the sacrifice, while all lament her going.... Mme. Flagstad sang with a beauty of sustained song, a profound pathos and a consummate art that no one who heard her can forget.

This also was notable: a character out of Greek mythology, a supplicant of the gods, a figure of fate, was singing. But never did the art of this singer seem more human in its communication. Mme. Flagstad made a singularly appealing and womanly figure to the eye and in her deportment, and her song fulfilled completely the impression. There was something in the combination of complete sincerity, simplicity and artistic finish that made the figure in the old court opera of Gluck's period the presence as well as the symbol of a very human being whose suffering we understood and knew.

Virgil Thomson in the *Herald Tribune* wrote:

Gluck's "Alcestis" in any language is a noble piece. As performed last night in the Metropolitan Opera House in a new English translation by John Gutman, it was no less so than is its custom. And the presence of Kirsten Flagstad, singing the lead, had sold out the house at a fifteen-dollar top for the benefit of the Production Fund of the Metropolitan Opera Guild....

The musical foreground, of course, as occupied by Miss Flagstad, was an ultimate in stylishness. No singer living could have sung Alcestis's arias with more sumptuous beauty of voice or a more impeccable respect for their classic line, their expressive rhetoric....

The evening belonged in glory to Miss Flagstad; and hers were the plaudits, the repeated recalls, the full gratitude. It is of no point at so late a date in this artist's career to analyze her vocal production, to describe the beauty of her vocal sound or the strength of her expressive power. She is unique among living vocal artists; and hearing her is a privilege, as remembering her will for all our lives be a pleasure. The privilege and pleasure were witnessed last night by demonstrations both out front, among the audience, and backstage, among her colleagues of the cast, unusual for length, for intensity, and for warmth.

278

The Reviewing Stand

From "ALCESTIS" TODAY—
(Article in Sunday *New York Times*, March 9, 1952.)

The revival in English of Gluck's "Alcestis" last week at the Metropolitan proved to be one of the most distinguished accomplishments of the season. The central reason was Kirsten Flagstad's Alcestis. The role is so remarkably hers, so characteristic of her own artistic personality and temperament, that one wonders why she waited so many years to undertake it.... Perhaps no other singer before the public today has in an equal measure the qualities demanded by Gluck's art....

She took remarkable care with her diction as well as her vocalization of the part. One imagines, in view of the noble and dramatic effect of her declamation, that if she had sung the part in Choctaw she would have delivered the text with equal significance, vocal mastery, and pathos and grandeur of style.

But there is something else that Miss Flagstad accomplished with this music. She could have done all that we have described and yet kept it, in a classic and objective way, aloof from us. We have heard Gluck sung with all due dignity and vocal care and musicianship before this and have never been so moved by it. For Mme. Flagstad, as no one we have ever heard, made this music live and breathe, made us feel the humanity and emotional reality of it. A woman stepped out of mythology onto the stage before our eyes, and losing no whit of dignity and queenliness, communicated emotions which were native to us and which we understood. The music lived and spoke the language of today....

Miss Flagstad accomplished a resurrection, we thought, with her Alcestis—not with every bit of it, because not all of the music is Gluck at his greatest. But in several places, perhaps the most remarkable of all being the great air at the end of the second act, she overwhelmed us, in an unforgettable revelation of that which is incomparable and immortal in Gluck himself.

Farewell Performance at Metropolitan Opera, April 1, 1952
Miles Kastendieck wrote in the *Journal-American*:

Kirsten Flagstad bid farewell to the American operatic stage last night. Appearing in one of her greatest roles, she sang the most

THE FLAGSTAD MANUSCRIPT

eloquent Alcestis of her five performances in this Gluck opera. That it was a singularly moving and thrilling experience makes her exit from the lyric theatre the more glorious.

Assuming the role at the end of her career was a feat in itself. To grow perceptibly in it during a month of appearances attests the greatness of her art as well as her artistry. Those who heard her last night will never forget the poignancy of the end of the second act or the anguish poured forth at the gates of Hell. This was magnificence of characterization as well as of opulent singing—an incredibly beautiful performance. . . .

At the end of the opera, after five minutes of an overwhelming ovation, the curtain rose again on the splendor of the final scene. With the company assembled George A. Sloan addressed Mme. Flagstad in tribute and gratitude. In presenting a silver cup and tray, he said:

. "We hope that this token will serve to remind you of those great days at the Metropolitan Opera House that will be recorded in opera annals as so much greater because of you."

Slowly the curtain fell. Its falling assigned her wonderful performances of Sieglinde, Isolde, Brünnhilde, Elsa, Elizabeth, Kundry, Fidelio, Senta and Alcestis to memory, one of the most cherished memories of the century in the world of music.

Dido (*Dido and Aeneas*)

Mermaid Theatre, London, September 10, 1951

It is a very real pleasure in this festival year to welcome the appearance of a new theatre, built with their own hands by a number of enthusiasts fired by the enterprise of Mr. and Mrs. Bernard Miles. The Mermaid Theatre has been designed as a portable Elizabethan "playing place." . . . It first opened its doors last evening for a performance of Purcell's opera *Dido and Aeneas*.

The Dido of Mme. Flagstad is a poignant and revealing achievement. Her physical presence and nobility of visual expression give moving tenderness to her portrayal of the Queen, whether in the simplicity of her first appearance, as the curtains part for the first scene, or in the tragic repose of her dying lament, while the familiar

The Reviewing Stand

dramatic fire enhances regality in her parting from Aeneas. In all Dido's music her magnificent vocal control, beauty of tone, and variety of expressive colour are of sovereign interpretive power.

the London *Times*, September 10, 1951

I have studiously avoided mentioning Mme. Flagstad, so that her colleagues' contributions might be appraised before consideration of the performance that was the *raison d'être* of the production, its primary attraction and its glory. I felt it symbolic of the whole enterprise that the prima donna, one of the great singers of our time, should be heard singing alto in an off-stage chorus.

When the curtains of the inner stage parted, we saw a dignified and supremely beautiful Dido seated on her throne, simply robed in blue that emphasized the nobility of her presence. When she reclined on Aeneas's red cloak in the Grove scene, when she dismissed him at the harbor, when she sank in death, she was still royal greatness. The tessitura of the music lies low, in just the register she wishes most to use from now on, and in just that part of the voice that would sound best in this theatre. Her sense of proportion and of style controlled the tone that she produced but there was no sign that she was sparing her voice, though we were never near being deafened by its full power—only flooded with its full beauty. Her phrasing of the melismata in "Ah, Belinda" was gentle affection, in "Hark how thunder" the mirror of fierce Nature; in the duet that follows "Thus on the fatal banks of Nile" the timbre was awesome and unrestrained, yet always queenly. Her control of breath and tone in "When I am laid in earth" was breath-takingly serene in its warm roundedness. To the English text she brought near-perfect pronunciation (an occcasional v slipped out instead of w, but she did not sound like a foreigner singing in English) and that appreciation of verbal colour that has shown us in the past the musical rightness of Wagner's un-poetic libretti. If her Brünnhilde was a cosmic interpretation, as Dido she revealed an intimate microcosm of operatic performance no less superb. The Brünnhilde of *Götterdämmerung* may have been the crown of her career. This was an exquisite diadem to set atop it.

William Mann, *Opera*, November 1951

ROLES SUNG BY KIRSTEN FLAGSTAD

Work	Role	Date	Performances
Tiefland (D'Albert)	Nuri	Dec. 12, 1913	20
Les Cloches de Corneville (Planquette)	Serpolette	1914	7
Helligaften (Schjelderup)	Engel	1915	8
Vaarnal (Schjelderup)	Emilie	1915	8
Der Evangelimann (Kienzl)	Marta	Jan. 16, 1919	6
Pagliacci (Leoncavallo)	Nedda	Mar. 23, 1919	13
Der Zigeunerbaron (Strauss)	Saffi	1919	10
Die Schone Galathee (Suppe)	Ganymed	Mar. 25, 1919	17
Die Nurnberger Puppe (Suppe)	Bertha	April 1, 1919	7
Abu Hassan (Weber)	Die Frau	April 1, 1919	5
La Belle Hélène (Offenbach)	Oreste	1919	8
Lustige Weiber von Windsor (Nicolai)	Anna	May 10, 1919	7
Die Zauberflote (Mozart)	Erste Dame	Jan. 18, 1921	6
Otello (Verdi)	Desdemona	Jan. 26, 1921	19
Un Ballo in Maschera (Verdi)	Amelia	Feb. 20, 1921	9
Das Hollisch Gold (Bittner)	Die Frau	April 17, 1921	3
La Fanciulla del West (Puccini)	Minnie	May 5, 1921	18
Orphée aux Enfers (Offenbach)	Euridice	1922	?
Boccaccio (Suppé)	Fiametta	1923	?
Carmen (Bizet)	Micaela	Nov. 22, 1924	47
Die Fledermaus (Strauss)	Rosalinde	1924	10
Les Brigands (Offenbach)	Fiorella	1925	?
Sjömandsbruden (Aspeshand)	Ragnhild	Dec. 12, 1925	4
Faust (Gounod)	Marguerite	Dec. 12, 1926	41
Orfeo ed Euridice (Gluck)	Euridice	July 6, 1927	11
Der Freischütz (Weber)	Agathe	Oct. 4, 1928	28
Saul og David (Nielsen)	Mikal	Nov. 29, 1928	15
Aida (Verdi)	Aida	March 7, 1929	27
La Bohème (Puccini)	Mimi	April 11, 1929	6
Tosca (Puccini)	Tosca	April 19, 1929	21
Lohengrin (Wagner)	Elsa	June 14, 1929	40
La Rondine (Puccini)	Magda	Oct. 4, 1929	7
L'Enfant Prodigue (Debussy)	Lia	Oct. 4, 1929	7
Die Meistersinger (Wagner)	Eva	Feb. 18, 1930	21
Jonny Spielt Auf (Krenek)	Anita	April 10, 1930	6
Schwanda der Dudelsackpfeifer (Weinberger)	Dorota	Dec. 3, 1931	14
Rodelinde (Handel)	Rodelinde	Feb. 16, 1932	7
Tristan und Isolde (Wagner)	Isolde	June 29, 1932	182
Die Walkure (Wagner)	Ortlinde	July 25, 1933	2
Gotterdammerung (Wagner)	Dritte Norne	July 28, 1933	2

Die Walküre (Wagner)	Sieglinde	May 24, 1934	14
Gotterdämmerung (Wagner)	Gutrune	July 6, 1934	3
Tannhäuser (Wagner)	Elisabeth	Oct. 5, 1934	35
Fidelio (Beethoven)	Leonore	Dec. 10, 1934	37
Die Walküre (Wagner)	Brünnhilde	Feb. 15, 1935	78
Götterdämmerung (Wagner)	Brünnhilde	Feb. 28, 1935	47
Parsifal (Wagner)	Kundry	April 17, 1935	39
Siegfried (Wagner)	Brünnhilde	Nov. 6, 1935	30
Der Fliegende Holländer (Wagner)	Senta	Jan. 7, 1937	11
Oberon (Weber)	Rezia	May 30, 1942	2
Alceste (Gluck)	Alcestis	May 29, 1943	8
Dido and Aeneas (Purcell)	Dido	Sept. 9, 1951	36

Note: Mme. Flagstad also sang in a number of modern operettas and musical comedies between 1919 and 1929, of which she recalls the following:

The Little Lark (1919)
Zigeunerliebe (1921)
Phi-Phi (1922)
The Lady in Ermine (1922)
The Cousin from Batavia (1922) (Denmark)
  (or, *The Girl from Holland*)
Die Bajadere (1922)
The Dollar Princess (1923)
The Queen of the Movies (1923)
Lucullus (1923)
Wenn Liebe Erwirbt (1923)
The Circus Princess (1925 or 1926)
Der Orloff (1925)
Gräfin Maritza (1928) (Finland)
Her Excellency (1928) (Finland)
La Teresina (1929) (Goteborg)

Mme. Flagstad appeared as soloist in the following oratorios and choral works:

Beethoven—Ninth Symphony
Beethoven—Missa Solemnis
Handel—*Joshua*
Handel—*Das Alexanderfest*
Handel—*Judas Maccabaeus*
Handel—*Solomon*
Handel—*The Messiah*
Haydn—*The Creation*
Mendelssohn—*St. Paul*
Bach—Various Cantatas
Rossini—Stabat Mater

Index

A

Academy of Music (Brooklyn), 76, 95

Academy of Music (Philadelphia), 178, 182

Adlon Hotel, 122, 123, 136, 138

Agathe, 35

Aïda, 11, 13, 23, 36, 37, 39, 41

Albert Hall (London), 168, 188, 227

Alcestis, 165, 201, 205, 206, 207, 208, 209, 210, 211, 212, 213, 214, 215, 218, 219, 220, 222, 223, 228, 236, 271, 277, 278, 279, 280

Alda, Frances, 243

Althouse, Paul, 73, 243

Amelia, 28

America, xii, xv, xix, 17, 18, 28, 35, 44, 62, 68, 71, 74, 80, 81, 82, 83, 84, 85, 89, 90, 91, 92, 93, 94, 115, 116, 118, 124, 134, 143, 156, 170, 171, 172, 173, 182, 184, 186, 190, 196, 197, 210, 216, 222, 226, 228, 229, 230, 231, 232, 233, 235, 242, 267, 272

Amico Fritz, L', 168

Andrea Chenier, 41

Antwerp, 49

Ariadne auf Naxos, 228

Arnesen, Conrad, 34

Ase, 16

Aspestrand, 30, 282

"Ave Maria" (Denza), 40

B

Bach, Johann S., 203, 205, 230, 283

Ballo in Maschera, Un, 28

Baltimore Symphony Orchestra, 115

Bajadere, Die, 32

Bayreuth, 54, 55, 56, 57, 58, 59, 61, 63, 67, 74, 227, 242, 243, 244

BBC, 224, 226

Beecham, Sir Thomas, 227

Beethoven, 5, 6, 10, 16, 29, 33, 61, 179, 180, 203, 213, 282, 283; see also *Fidelio*

Belgium, 49, 81

Belle Hélène, La, 26

Belinda, 204

Bellini, Vincenzo, 82, 83, 272

Bendixen, Trygve, 147, 159

Bergen, 23

Berlin, 31, 39, 58, 59, 117, 122, 123, 126, 136, 137, 138, 227

Bergljot (Björnson), 16

Bermuda, 105

Biering-Petersen, 28

Bing, Rudolf, 194, 196, 198, 207, 208, 209, 215

Binghamton (N. Y.), xiii

Bittner, 282

Bizet, A.C.L., 61, 282

Björnson, 16, 23

Bodanzky, Artur, 66, 67, 68, 70, 72, 73, 76, 81, 243

INDEX

Bohème, La, 37
Boseman (Montana), 172
Boston, xiii, 84, 173, 174, 191, 272, 273
Brahms, Johannes, 80, 84, 94, 135, 218
Bratt, Gillis, 20, 29, 22, 23, 24, 30, 37, 221
Brooklyn, 76, 94, 95, 96, 106, 189
Brünnhilde, xvi, 7, 31, 54, 57, 58, 63, 69, 70, 75, 76, 179, 191, 201, 224, 242, 243, 248, 249, 250, 251, 252, 253, 269, 270, 271, 272, 280
Brussels, 49, 59, 60, 74
Buenos Aires, 190
Buffalo (N. Y.), xiii
Busch, Fritz, 40

C

Cäcilie, (R. Strauss), 24
California, 97, 99, 197
Cannes, 164, 165, 166
Canada, 33
Caracas, ·190
Carmen, 6, 30, 31
Carnegie Hall, 84, 106, 107, 108, 173, 174, 175, 178, 180, 190, 194, 196, 212, 218, 233, 273, 274
Caruso, Enrico, 81
Cassidy, Claudia, 274, 275
Central Hall (London), 190
Champs Élysées Theatre, 166
Chaplin, Charlie, 86
Charpentier, 164
Cherubino, 13
Chimes of Normandy, 19
Christensen, Halfdan, 21
Chotzinoff, Samuel, 247, 248, 256, 267
Christiania, 3, 4, 5
"Christmas Eve" (Wergeland), 189
Cigna, Gina, 272
Cleveland, 92, 93, 94, 191
Cologne, 41
Copenhagen, 24, 25, 28, 36, 70, 71
Coppola, Piero, 23

Cortot, Alfred, 165
Countess (Figaro), 13, 214
Covent Garden, 185, 187, 199, 200, 201, 206
Creation, The, 51
Cross, Milton, 75
Crown Prince, 108
Crown Princess, 108
Chicago, 84, 98, 109, 274, 275
Chicago Daily Tribune, 274, 275
Chicago Opera House, 106, 274, 275

D

d'Albert, Eugen, 16, 282
Dalcroze School of Dancing, 22
Dalila, 14
Darbo, Erika, 31
Davenport, Marcia, 172, 173
Debussy, Claude, 48, 282
Delius, Elisabeth, 64, 66, 67, 68
Denmark, 24, 93, 165
Denza, 40
"Depuis le jour," 164
De Sabata, Victor, 168
Desdemona, 27
Dellera, Mr., 82, 83
Detroit, 78
"Dich theure Halle," 65, 66
Dido and Aeneas, 185, 201, 202, 203, 204, 205, 208, 223, 230, 241, 280, 281
Doerumsgaard, 152
Dolder Grand Hotel, 162
Don Carlos, 70
Don Giovanni, 14, 23
Donna Anna, 214
Downes, Olin, 244, 247, 249, 251, 252, 253, 255, 256, 257, 258, 263, 264, 265, 266, 270, 271, 273, 274, 276, 277, 278
A Dream (Grieg), 84
Dresden, 40
Dusenberry, Arthur, 91, 99, 197, 233, 237
Dusenberry, Sigurd Hall, 170, 172, 197, 233, 236, 237

INDEX

E

Edinburgh, 21
Elektra, 215, 228
Elisabeth, 7, 20, 66, 67, 76, 94, 253, 254,
  280
Elsa, 11, 12, 13, 40, 42, 253, 256, 280
Enfant Prodigue, L', 45
England, 4, 81, 205, 222, 223, 226, 229,
  230, 241
Engles, George, 178
Erede, Alberto, 211
Esberg, Mrs. Milton, 99
Europe, xvii, 35, 83, 84, 90, 92, 93, 94,
  112, 113, 179, 182, 185, 190, 195, 197,
  230, 231, 242
Eva, 48, 56, 210
Evangelimann, Der, 25

F

Fanciulla del West, 28
Farrar, Geraldine, 75
Faust, 13, 21, 23, 30
Festspielhaus (Bayreuth), 54, 56
Fidelio, 7, 62, 63, 66, 68, 69, 70, 190,
  192, 195, 208, 212, 213, 214, 262-265,
  280
Figaro, 23
Finland, 33, 228
Flagstad Family, 7, 8, 10, 18; see also
  Flagstad, Father; Flagstad, Mother;
  Hall; Dusenberry; Johansen
Flagstad, Father, 3, 4, 5, 6, 7, 8, 10, 11,
  12, 13, 14, 15, 18, 19, 21, 46, 110
Flagstad, Mother, 3, 4, 5, 6, 7, 8, 9, 10,
  11, 12, 13, 17, 18, 19, 21, 25, 26, 27,
  32, 46, 51, 58, 69, 110, 116, 127, 236
Fledermaus, Die, 30
Fliegende Hollander, Der, 12, 222, 265-
  268
Florence Crittendon League, 265
Forsell, John, 30
France, 105, 122, 165, 166
Frankenstein, Alfred, 275, 276

"Frauenliebe und Leben" (Schumann),
  218
Freischütz, Der, 32, 33, 34, 35, 39
Fremstad, Olive, 244
Fricka, 243
Furtwängler, Wilhelm, 204, 227, 230

G

Galathea, 26
Galli, Rosina; see Gatti-Casazza, Mrs. G.
Gatti-Casazza, Giulio, 63, 64, 66, 67, 72,
  81, 82, 243
Gatti-Casazza, Mrs. G., 66, 67
Germaine, 19
Germany, 19, 20, 38, 40, 49, 93, 105, 117,
  138, 227
Gianni Schicchi, 40
Gilman, Lawrence, 243, 245, 246, 248,
  249, 250, 251, 253, 254, 255, 260, 261,
  263, 264, 268, 269, 270
Giordano, 41
Götterdämmerung, 31, 56, 57, 63, 65, 67,
  73, 74, 76, 209, 218, 219, 227, 228, 229,
  230, 250-253
Gounod, 13, 21, 23, 30, 383
Graf, Herbert, 210, 211, 213
Goose Girl (Königskinder), 13
Grung, Grace, 23
Grieg, 15, 16, 23, 81, 84, 135, 164, 203,
  223, 274
Gutman, John, 201, 209, 277
Gulbransen, Ellen, 54, 55
Gutrune, 58, 61, 63, 74
Gluck, 165, 205, 206, 207, 214, 222, 277,
  278, 279, 282, 283
Göteborg, 32, 33, 34, 35, 36, 38, 40, 45,
  46, 48, 50, 51, 52, 62, 63, 68, 69, 70

H

Haakon, King, 17, 19, 81
Händel, 50, 135, 203, 206, 214, 282, 283
Hansel und Gretel, 168
Hall, Else-Marie, 26, 33, 48, 53, 70, 76,

287

INDEX

Hall *(cont.)*
83, 91, 92, 94, 97, 98, 99, 100, 110, 134, 164, 170, 172, 197, 233, 236, 237; see also Dusenberry, Arthur
Hall, Sigurd, 24, 25
Hamar 3, 4
Hamburg, 227
Hamilton, Mrs. Pierpont Morgan, 73, 188
Harringay Arena (London), 187
Hart, Edward, 229
"Haugtussa," 135, 274
Havana, 190
Haydn, 51, 283
Helsinki, 228
Henderson, W. J., 247, 249, 250, 256, 259, 260, 264, 271
Herold, Wilhelm, 17
Hislop, Joseph, 21
His Master's Voice, 228
Hitler, Adolf, 122
Hoffmann, Kammersänger, 137
"Ho-jo-to-ho" (Walküre), 65, 67
Hollywood, 99
"Holy Night" (Schjelderup), 19
Hoover, Herbert, xiv, 112, 113
Horwitz, Fréderic, 148, 150, 151, 227, 231
Houston (Texas), 216
Huguenots, Les, 70
Hunding, 60

I

Ibsen, 16, 23
"Ich liebe Dich" (Grieg), 84, 164, 165
Illingworth, Margaret, 106, 107, 108
"I Love You So," 29
Immolation Scene (*Götterdämmerung*), 63, 67, 218, 219, 227, 229, 230
Ishpeming (Mich.), 197
Isolde, 51, 52, 54, 55, 57, 63, 69, 82, 167, 172, 198, 200, 209, 224, 242, 245, 246, 247, 274, 275
Italy, 7, 41, 81, 168, 185, 202

J

Jacobsen, Ellen Schytte, 13, 18
Janssen, Herbert, 92
Janssen, Mrs. Herbert, 92
Japan, 102
"Ja Vi Elsker," 96
Javor, Maria, 27
Jeritza, Maria, 265
Johansen, Annie, 44, 48, 53, 102, 103, 104, 134
Johansen, Henry, xvi, 42, 43, 44, 49, 52, 53, 58, 97, 100, 102, 104, 110, 111, 112, 121, 127, 128, 129, 130, 131, 132, 142, 143, 144, 146, 147, 149, 150, 151, 152, 157, 192
Johansen, Henry, Jr., 162, 163, 164
Johansen, Mrs. Henry, 50
Johnny Spielt Auf, 48
Johnson, Edward, xv, 82, 83, 184, 191
Jones, Geraint, 204
Juliana, Queen, 235
Juliette, 30

K

Kahn, Otto, 46
Kappel, Gertrude, 73, 242, 243, 250, 280
Karlsbad, 49
Kastendieck, Miles, 279, 280
Kienzl, 24, 282
Kinokönigin, 32
Kipnis, Alexander, 57, 58, 63
Kittel, Professor, 55, 56, 58, 63
Kjelland, Olav, 15, 35
Klemperer, Otto, 39
Knudsen, William, 78, 79
Konetzni, Anni, 64, 70, 242
Königskinder, 13
Krenek, Ernst, 48, 282
Kristiansand, xv, 44, 49, 128, 129, 130, 131, 141, 145, 152, 158, 159, 192, 193, 205, 232
Kroll Opera (Berlin), 39
Kundry, 76, 77, 191, 253, 256-261
Kvartettforeningen, 6

288

INDEX

L

Lagerlöf, Selma, 23
Larsen, Sigurd, 126, 127
Larsen-Todsen, Nanny, 51
La Scala, 41, 168, 169, 227
Lausanne, 230
Leah (*Prodigal Son*), 48
Lehár, Franz, 7, 26
Leider, Frida, 64, 69, 242
Leoncavallo, 282
Leonore, 192, 209, 262-265
Levine, Marks, 97, 98, 100, 102, 107, 118, 127, 178, 190, 194, 208
"Liebestod" (*Tristan*), 55, 64, 67, 166, 167, 168, 200, 229, 230, 274
Liebling, A. J., 258, 259
Lieder, 8, 135, 222, 223
Lisbon, xvii, 119, 122, 129
List, Emanuel, 43
Little Lark, The (Lehár), 26
Lohengrin, 11, 12, 31, 40, 42, 43, 44, 46, 49, 76, 144, 242, 253-255
London, xv, 7, 44, 53, 168, 170, 187, 188, 199, 200, 207, 226, 227, 228, 230, 280, 281
Lorenz, Max, 136, 137, 138, 204
Lorenz, Mrs. Max, 138
Louise, 164
Lucia di Lammermoor, 168

M

McArthur, Edwin, 79, 80, 83, 96, 100, 104, 135, 173, 174, 176, 177, 178, 181, 194, 196, 211
McArthur, Mrs. Edwin, 80
Madama Butterfly, 21
Madison (Wisconsin), 197, 236
Madrid, 122
Majol, 28, 29
Malmö, 139
Mann, William, 281
Marguerite, 13
Márouf (Rabaud), 41
Marschallin (*Rosenkavalier*), 70, 214, 215
Marta (*Tiefland*), 13, 16, 17

Martha (*Der Evangelimann*), 13, 25
Mascagni, Pietro, 168
Meistersinger, Die, 48, 56, 210
Melchior, Lauritz, 31, 59, 92, 93, 94, 119, 196
Melchior, Mrs. Lauritz, 92
Mendelssohn, Felix M., 226, 283
Mephistopheles, 30
Mermaid Theatre, 203, 205, 230, 280, 281
Metropolitan Board of Directors, 211
Metropolitan Opera, xi, xv, 19, 38, 46, 47, 57, 60, 62, 63, 64, 68, 74, 75, 77, 81, 82, 84, 89, 98, 100, 102, 118, 119, 184, 190, 191, 194, 195, 196, 197, 198, 199, 200, 201, 207, 208, 209, 210, 211, 212, 218, 223, 225, 233, 236, 242, 244, 245, 248, 265, 276, 277, 278, 279, 280
Metropolitan Opera Guild, 211, 278
Micaela, 30, 35
Michigan, 197
Midsummer Night's Dream, 227
Mikal (*Saul and David*), 35, 36
Milan, xv, 41, 168, 169, 199, 227
Miles, Bernard, 185, 201, 202, 204, 205, 230
Miles, Mrs. Bernard, 185
Miles, Biddy, 203, 204
Miles, John, 203, 204
Miles, Sarah, 203, 204
Mimi, 13, 37
Montana, 99, 162, 172
Montevideo, 190
Montreal, 197
Moore, George, 246
Moore, Grace, 164
Morgenstierne, Ambassador, 95, 96, 115, 116, 117, 118, 156
Mozart, 23, 27, 214, 282
Munich, 40
Musical America, 48, 83

N

NBC, 78, 79, 104, 105, 106, 107, 108, 117
Nazis, 103, 116, 131, 175, 176, 180

INDEX

Nedda, 13, 24, 26
New Orleans, 190
New York, xi, 27, 46, 72, 78, 82, 85, 99, 173, 190, 194, 197, 218, 232, 241, 273
New York City Center, 232
New York Daily News, 259
New York Grand Central Palace, 82, 99
New York Herald Tribune, 96, 97, 98, 243, 245, 248, 250, 253, 260, 261, 263, 266, 269, 270, 272, 273, 276, 277, 278
New York Journal-American, 258, 259, 279, 280
New York Philharmonic Symphony, 218
New York Post, 247, 248, 267
New York Stadium, 98, 99
New York Sun, 48, 172, 247, 249, 250, 259, 260, 264, 267, 268, 271
New York Times, 244, 251, 252, 253, 273, 274, 276, 277, 278, 279
New York World's Fair, 355
New York World-Telegram, 264, 265, 268, 271
Nicolai, Otto, 282
Nielsen, Carl, 35, 36, 282
Nielsen, Ragna, 9
Ninth Symphony (Beethoven), 29, 61
Norena, Eidé, 19
Norma, 82, 83, 272
Northampton (Mass.), xiii
Northampton (England), 187
Northfield (Minn.), 97
North Dakota, 97
Norway, xiv, xvi, xvii, 3, 7, 12, 17, 24, 30, 41, 44, 46, 47, 49, 54, 55, 56, 69, 84, 85, 90, 91, 92, 93, 95, 96, 100, 102, 103, 105, 111, 113, 114, 115, 116, 117, 118, 119, 120, 121, 124, 125, 126, 134, 138, 139, 145, 156, 157, 160, 170, 172, 182, 192, 193, 210, 226, 230, 231, 232, 237, 241
Norway Musical Guild, 140
Norwegian Club (Brooklyn), 96
Norwegian Hospital (Brooklyn), 94, 95, 106
Norwegian National Opera, 34, 54

290

Norwegian Relief, 105, 106, 107, 108, 109, 115
Norwegian Wine Monopoly, 121, 129, 130
Nuri (*Tiefland*), 16, 17

O

Offenbach, Jacques, 7, 26, 282
Olszewska, Maria, 243
Opéra (Paris), L', 166
Operas, 281
Orestes, 26
Orloff, Der, 32
Orphée aux Enfers, 29
Ortrud, 242
Oslo, 3, 4, 5, 7, 9, 10, 15, 16, 20, 23, 24, 25, 26, 27, 28, 30, 31, 40, 42, 44, 46, 49, 51, 53, 57, 58, 60, 62, 74, 81, 114, 126, 128, 129, 130, 131, 138, 139, 141, 145, 152, 158, 161, 193, 230, 231, 232
Oslo Casino, 29, 30, 31
Oslo Central Theater, 5, 10
Oslo National Theater, 16, 17, 19, 21, 51, 231
Oslo Opéra Comique, 24, 25, 26, 27, 28, 29, 31, 52
Oslo University, 23
Otello, 27, 28

P

Pagliacci, 13, 24
Pamina, 13, 27
Panizza, Ettore, 82
Paris, xv, 3, 7, 53, 149, 150, 165, 166, 185, 195, 228, 230
Parsifal, 76, 77, 81, 253, 256-261
"Pathétique," 16
Pauly, Rose, 70
Peer Gynt, 16
Perkins, Francis D., 266
Perlea, Jonel, 169
Philadelphia, 62, 98, 178, 182, 216

INDEX

Planquette, Robert, 19, 282
Poland, 114
Portugal, 105, 120, 122, 129
Prague, 69, 70
Prodigal Son, 48
Puccini, 11, 28, 37, 40
Puerto Rico, 190
Purcell, Henry, 201, 202, 204, 205, 283

Q

Quisling, 121, 159
Quisling Party, 121, 128, 129, 130, 132, 134, 141, 145

R

Rabaud, Henri, 41
Red Cross concert, 150
Reiner, Fritz, 62
Rethberg, Elisabeth, 83
Richter, Carl, 23
Riedel, Karl, 61, 73
Ring (Wagner), 195, 208, 244, 245
Rio de Janeiro, 190
Rodelinda (Händel), 50, 51, 134, 206, 215
Rodzinski, Artur, 274
Roles, List of, 282
Rome, 227, 228
Rondine, La, 48
Rosenkavalier, Der, 41, 70, 214, 215
Rossini, 28, 283
Rovereto (Italy), 41
Russia, 102

S

Saint-Saëns, Camille, 6, 24
Salzburg, 190, 192, 193
Samson et Dalila, 6, 14, 24
San Antonio, 98
Sanborn, Pitts, xi, xii, 242, 264, 265, 268, 271

San Francisco, 84, 99, 102, 105, 192, 193, 216, 275
San Francisco Chronicle, 275, 276
San Francisco Opera, 192, 193, 275
Santa Barbara, 99
Santiago, 190
Sargeant, Winthrop, 267
Saul and David (Nielsen), 35
St. Moritz, 63, 64, 72, 81
St. Olaf's College (Northfield, Minn.), 97
Scarpia, 38
Schjelderup, 19, 282
Schjoedt, Anneus, 159, 160
Schmidt piano, 10
Schöne Galathee, Die, 25
Schorr, Friedrich, 77, 243, 265
Schubert, Franz, 8, 80, 94, 203
Schumann, Robert, 80, 203, 218
Schustermann, Mr., 185, 187, 188, 189
Schwanda, 50
Seaman's Bride, The, (Aspestrand), 30
Sebastian, George, 187
Senta, 13, 265-268, 280
Sheffield (England), 226
Sibelius, Jan, 22, 228
Siegfried, 31, 57, 59, 60, 73, 225, 242, 269-272
Sieglinde, xvi, 56, 58, 59, 60, 61, 66, 73, 74, 75, 212, 243, 244, 247, 280
Simon, Eric, 46, 62, 64, 66, 67, 68, 69, 70
Singer, Mr., 24, 28, 29
Slezak, Leo, 27, 28, 31
Sloan, George A., 211, 280
South America, 80, 187
South Dakota, 97
South Pacific, 233
Spain, 105, 122, 195
Springfield (Mass.), 229
"Spring Night" (Schjelderup), 19
SS. *Bergensfjord,* 92, 97
Staatsoper (Berlin), 58, 137
"Stabat Mater," 28
Stake, 142, 144, 146, 152, 157
Stang, Emil, 132
Stedink, Count von, 21, 23

291

INDEX

Stockholm, 20, 21, 22, 23, 24, 30, 36, 117,
134, 162, 164
Stockholm Opera, 24, 30
Storatheater, 33
Strauss, Johann, 5, 30, 282
Strauss, Richard, 23, 24, 41, 59, 61, 135,
228, 230
Sundför, Ingolf, 141, 147, 148, 151, 156,
158, 159, 160, 161
Suppé, von, 5, 25, 282
Susanna, 13
"Swan, The," (Grieg), 84
Sweden, 7, 19, 24, 32, 36, 37, 38, 41, 90,
123, 124, 134, 138, 206, 210, 214
Switzerland, 44, 63, 64, 133, 134, 135,
136, 149, 162, 163, 206, 227, 230
Symphony Hall (Boston), 272, 273
Szell, George, 69, 70

T

Tannhäuser, 20, 31, 60, 62, 68, 76, 92,
93, 242, 253-255, 256
Texas, 216
Teyte, Maggie, 204
Third Norn (Gotterdämmerung), 56
Thompson, Oscar, 48, 172, 267, 268
Thomson, Virgil, 272, 273, 276, 277, 278
Thorborg, Kerstin, 93
Tiefland, 16, 17, 31
Tietjen, Heinz, 55, 57, 58, 59
Tietjen, Therese, 202
Time Magazine, 216
Times (London), 282
Tirol, 38
"Todesverkündigung" (Walküre), 65, 66,
249
Tosca, La, 13, 37, 38, 44, 46
Town Hall (New York), 94, 95, 274
Tralleborg, 127
Traubel, Helen, 195, 196
Traviata, La, 13, 199
Trenton (N. J.), xiii
Tristan und Isolde, 49, 51, 52, 54, 55,
56, 57, 62, 65, 67, 70, 75, 76, 119, 166,
169, 190, 194, 195, 197, 199, 207, 208,

212, 224, 225, 227, 228, 245, 247, 257,
258, 263, 264, 270, 271, 274, 275, 276
Turin, 169

U

Ullevold Hospital, 152
United Jewish Relief Appeal, 185
United States State Department, 170
Ursin, Marlin, 8

V

"Valse Triste" (Sibelius), 22
Varberg (Sweden), 38
Venice, 41
Venus (Tannhäuser), 242
Verdi, 11, 27, 28, 282
Vernay, Alexander, 27
Vienna, 49, 51, 225, 242
Vienna State Opera, 242
Vikings, 180, 203
Violetta, 13

W

Wagner, Richard, 7, 11, 12, 31, 40, 41,
42, 48, 49, 51, 56, 58, 61, 77, 83, 94,
95, 115, 139, 166, 168, 169, 195, 198,
199, 207, 208, 210, 212, 213, 214, 215,
218, 225, 229, 243, 244, 245, 249, 272,
275, 282, 283
Wagner, Winifred, 54, 55, 56
Waldorf Astoria, 111
Walker, Danton, 259
Walküre, Die, 31, 56, 58, 59, 61, 73, 75,
76, 77, 199, 228, 243, 246, 248
Walter, Bruno, 218, 219
Washington (D. C.), xiii, 84, 98, 115,
116, 156
"Water Lily" (Grieg), 84
Weber, Karl Maria von, 33, 282, 283
Webster, David, 206

INDEX

Weigert, Hermann, 64, 66, 67, 72, 75, 77, 225
Weinberger, Jaromir, 50, 282
Wergeland, Henrick, 188, 189
Wesendonck, 218, 219
Westwang, Albert, 20
White Fish Lake (Mont.), 172
"Wiegenlied" (R. Strauss), 135
Willkie, Wendell, 98
Wisconsin, 197
Witherspoon, Herbert, 82
Wolf, Hugo, 23, 84
"Wonne der Wehmut" (Beethoven), 180

Wotan, 31, 77
Wymetal, 75

Z

Zauberflöte, 20, 23, 27
Zerlina, 13, 14
Ziegler, Edward, 47, 72, 82
Zigeunerbaron, 24
Zigeunerliebe, 26
Zirkusprinzessin, 32
Zurich, 133, 135, 138, 149, 185, 199, 205, 206, 210, 215, 223, 227

CPSIA information can be obtained at www.ICGtesting.com
Printed in the USA
LVOW112319220312

274289LV00002B/320/P